Dedication

This romp through four amazing years spent in North Africa
Is dedicated to Milly Langton, without whom it would never
have happened.

As the locals frequently said to us:
"Ma Soeur! Touch ma main!"

CW01499681

Contents

Part One: From England to Algeria

It was 1963. I had been working for three years on a small farm at Ascot in Berkshire. My daily duties were milking a small herd of Jersey cows, looking after horses at livery, teaching children to ride and farm work, you name it, I did it. The days were very full from before dawn until dusk. I loved the work and the farm, and I was very fond of my employers, but I *really* needed a change, I had no idea what I wanted to do, except that it must involve horses and animals.

A new horse was coming in, he was owned by a Miss Milly Langton and his name was, "C," he was a driving horse. That would be a change from the more usual hunters. "C" and his very smart carriage duly arrived; he was a lovely deep liver chestnut, like a well-polished conker. His owner, Milly, settled him in, and he soon became a familiar face looking out of his stable.

The farm was very close to Windsor Great Park and his owner was soon driving out 'C', in the Park daily. Special permits were required to use the Park and the farm was allowed to exercise the liveries within the Park. His owner, Milly, was the sister of Dolly Langton who already kept a horse at the farm. Dolly had often told me about Milly and her interesting life abroad.

Over the weeks, I got to know Milly; she was home from North Africa for three months. She told me that she worked for a British charity and worked with the poorest of people, trying to keep their animals fit and well so they could go on working. She worked with donkeys, mules and horses, plus the odd camel, goat, sheep, cows, dogs and cats! She had been working for 8 weeks in a liitle town called Reizane in Algeria. Before that she had been in Tunisia.

She explained that she wasn't a vet, but had picked up a lot of knowledge during the time she worked with horses and other animals. I found her stories so interesting!

I told her that I loved the veterinary side of looking after horses and was well up on illnesses and treatments. I think this is something you can't help but pick up over time.

Milly had travelled widely and spent time as a cook on a sheep farm in the Blue Mountain of Australia. I had her marked as a confirmed spinster, who didn't mind where she settled as long as she had enough to do to fill her days. She clearly loved to be in places off the beaten track. I liked her very much, and we chatted endlessly whenever it was possible. One day, she told me she was looking for someone to go back to North Africa to help her... and added, "Was I interested"? *Was I interested?*

Suddenly I knew what I wanted from life! She explained that I would have to meet the Organising Secretary of the Charity in London, and added a warning that he might think I was too young. (I was eighteen). The next couple of weeks were busy as usual, but my mind was mulling over everything she had said. I just knew that this was something I really wanted to have a crack at. Milly had spoken to the Organising Secretary of the charity, and he had said he would like to meet me. I was asked to make an appointment and it was to be the following Tuesday! With an air of great excitement I caught the train from Ascot Station up to London, then made my way across to Victoria, and, with Milly's directions, found the office.

It was an imposing old house, very close to Buckingham Palace. I rang the big brass bell, and was ushered into a large room where two ladies were feverishly typing. A door opened, and a very military gentleman stepped into the room. I could see him scrutinising me! I went into his office and he took his seat behind a huge desk and asked me to sit down.

I found, "The Major" very easy to talk to. I remember asking him almost as many questions as he'd asked me. He explained the work and the conditions that we would be working in. I asked about suitable shoes and clothes to work in, and details about Algeria as my knowledge was scant to say the least. He told me that I was very young for the post, but he added that he felt I was the right person and that if Milly had said I would cope, then I would! The job was mine.

He then discussed the salary! I had never thought about money, and had never had a *salary*... this really surprised me as I really thought that charity employees worked for the love of the cause! I was to be paid, and compared with agricultural wages; I was to be paid well. I was given a large blue soft covered book. It was written in French, and was a manual of everyday veterinary work. He explained that he visited the overseas centres once, sometimes twice each year, and that we would communicate by weekly letters, as there was no telephone at the centre we would be working in.

The Major asked if my parents were happy for me to go to, his words, "Such an unstable country". I hadn't told them! But I assured him they were happy as long as I was. On the way home I started to read the manual. I found my school French very good and was able to fully understand the text. I was very excited at the prospect of going abroad! As soon as I got back to the farm I told Milly I had the job, then I told my employers that I would be leaving; they were very understanding, and somehow not at all surprised. I asked for two days leave to go home to Hampshire to see my parents.

Mum and Dad looked up Algeria in the old atlas as soon as I told them where I was to work. Dad added that there had been a lot of trouble there in recent times, and that most of the French had left the country in great haste. They questioned me about the job, and, bless them, told me to, 'Go for my dreams'. Later that evening, I heard Arab music in the hallway and Mum was processing down the stairs to the strains of, "The Sheikh of Arabi", dressed like a belly dancer! That was so typical of her. It was only years later that my sister told me how very worried they had been until I wrote home to tell them I was safe!

I had one month in which to finish my job at the farm; buy suitable clothes to wear for working in the heat and to say 'goodbyes' to friends and family. I would be gone for a year, then home on two month's leave during the very hot months. That month was a whirlwind of action, and passed so quickly. Milly and I had loads of 'extras' to take with us. Scissors and forceps, needles and sutures, bandages, antiseptic creams and packets of dark green worming powders! She said we would have to say it was expensive talc if asked at the airport! Milly's case also contained various packets and tubes, but also a full farriers kit.

September saw us at Heathrow. We checked in our bulging suitcases, no problems with the worm powders, and eventually boarded a plane to Paris. Once there, we had a short wait to take an Air France flight to Oran in Algeria. I had never flown and loved every minute of the flight. Three hours after leaving Paris we arrived at Oran. I was *so* excited!

As the aircraft door opened, there was a rush of hot air, like that of an oven door opening! It was hugely hot down on the tarmac and we walked on towards the buildings. Immigration was very quick, and we were ushered onwards to the baggage collection. I searched in vain for my huge case. It was missing! Seeing my consternation, a steward took me to a desk and, in rapid French, explained that the case was lost, but there was a spare unclaimed suitcase, would I like it? NO! I wanted mine. The other case had a label on with 'SOPHIE JONES. PHILADELPHIA', written on it. Poor Sophie, I hoped she hadn't got my case! I was quite sure she wouldn't want the piles of frumpy cotton clothes and worm powders it contained!

My school French, whilst fine with the written word, was sadly lacking when it came to conversing with a person talking nineteen to the dozen! However, they assured me that my case would be on the next flight... tomorrow! Luckily we had already planned to stay the night in Oran and travel on in the cool of the late afternoon the following day. Hopefully with the missing case.

We took a taxi to the hotel. As we sped through the streets, Oran struck me as a once very beautiful place that was rapidly going downhill. The hotel, next to the railway station was rather dingy, but we had a room, a bed each and a washbasin. The'loo' was down the corridor.

I had never seen such an unsavoury looking loo in all my life; it was two bricks set about 1ft apart, with a hole between the bricks. I gathered you squatted and aimed down the hole! There was also a bucket filled with water... I surmised that you then tipped this down the hole?

There was no hot water, but we had a good wash and clambered, thankfully into bed. As I was doing so, Milly shouted, "STOP! She had spotted a Bed Bug. I had never seen one before, it was brown and about the same size as a very small apple pip. Milly simply opened a package she had in her suitcase and sprinkled some foul smelling powder all over the bed! I didn't sleep much. The adventure had begun. It was very hot in the room and I just laid on the bed, my mind was whizzing with thoughts.

I woke very early the next morning to the sounds of the Muezzins calling people to prayer at the Mosques; it was a haunting sound that I was to hear five times every day for the next year.   I looked out of the window very early and already the streets were bustling. Women, fully covered in white robes bustling about with baskets of vegetables; men standing around smoking and talking, and children walking along with trays of flat bread to the local bread ovens. Cars and lorries hooting and many, many bicycles. It was 4.00am and already felt very hot, Algeria was awake!

Without my suitcase I had no clean clothes, and had to don the thick suit that I'd travelled in. I hoped against hope that my suitcase would arrive as promised.

Breakfast was fresh French bread, apricot jam and very strong coffee and after that we went out for a walk in the city of Oran. It had once been a very wealthy place with a thriving port. Shops were boarded up in many places. Those that were open sold a mixture of cheap clothes and pots and pans. I was amazed at the different smells as we walked along, the air was spicy, with other odd scents I had never experienced.

I realised we were being followed. Milly said, just ignore him, he's a 'Slick Dick', (Milly had a name for everything)! I got used to the fact that wherever we went we were followed, mostly by men who thought they might be onto a good thing. If only they had realised that they had picked the two women who were only thinking about horses and donkeys! The other band of followers were children. Grubby little people who shouted, "Madame, Madame", but ran if you turned around to face them.

Milly pointed out the bank that was the one we would be using, it was a branch of 'Barclays International', she added that they spoke excellent english, so the banking side of things was easy.

When we returned to the hotel my suitcase was waiting! Three hearty cheers for Air France. I was able to pack away my winter weight suit and change into a cotton dress. Bliss.

At 4.00pm we boarded the train that would take us on to Relizane where we were to live and work. The train journey was about three hours and we passed many farms that had obviously been well tended at some time. Then, in complete contrast there would be a mule walking in circles tied to a central pole drawing water from a well. It was as if I was in a far-gone, almost biblical age. I loved it. Milly pointed out various landmarks as we passed them. The train stopped once at a little town on the coast called, 'Mostaganem'. After that we left the coast and travelled through farm land, in the distance was a range of high hills.

We drew into Relizane on time and clambered off the train with our huge bags. All of a sudden, a uniformed person came running towards us, waving his arms and shouting! I was rather taken aback, but he threw himself at Milly and kissed her on both cheeks! "Oh! Madame, welcome home". (In French) as Milly was still having her hand pumped up and down, she explained who I was, and to me, that she had treated his dog for worms! He screamed for a porter, and we were ushered along the platform and out to a waiting battered taxi. The same thing happened. This time it transpired that the taxi driver had a donkey that Milly had treated! We were driven through the little town, the streets bustling with donkeys, some ridden, some pulling loaded carts, plus horses trotting along at break neck speed; their owners yelling, "Ba'alek' to clear the way! The taxi driver delivered us outside the shabby brown solid metal gate of the house. No charge was made, and he left after much hand shaking!

There we were, outside 1. Rue Rouina, on a dirt road, with no key! However, Milly popped across to the little open fronted shop, lit by a parraffin lamp, and got the key that had been given to Mohammed the owner for safekeeping. The gate, opened into a small triangular garden, surrounded by high walls. In the gloom of the evening, it was difficult to see everything, but in the centre of the garden was a large tree. There was a wonderful, heavy scent on the air. A path led to a heavy wooden door, Milly unlocked it, we walked in, and she promptly locked and barred it!

She went to a box on the wall and flicked a switch... we had lights!

We were in a small room, the walls were peeling, the whitewash coming off in chunks, and it was completely empty with two closed doors leading off it.

Milly unlocked the smaller of the two doors, and this was the kitchen. High ceilings, stone floors with a two-burner cooker on a shelf on one side. There was a large table and chairs. It was a dark room with no natural light. It smelt musty.

From the kitchen we went through into a small dimly lit passage. To the left was a sitting room; to the right was Milly's bedroom, and straight ahead was a small room, full of boxes. Off this room was a door that led into my bedroom. There were two windows, both heavily shuttered, a bed and a little cupboard. In the corner was a small odd looking wooden box... more of that later! There was a second door that led into the sitting room.

As the house had been shut up for nearly three months, it smelt fusty, and wherever there was a crack in the shutters, dust and gritty sand had blown in from the unmade road outside.

I got the little cooker working and made some tea whilst Milly popped out to the little shop opposite and came back with bread, butter, honey, Edam cheese, eggs and milk! We ate sandwiches and then Milly showed me the rest of the house. The other door off the room inside the back door led into a huge hall... apparently, this had been the schoolroom for the missionaries. Off one corner was a tiny room with a sink and a proper loo and a tin bath hanging on the wall. One cold tap!

The hall had tall double doors on one side; Milly drew back the huge bolt and opened one of the doors; outside was a small yard. There was a further door off the hall, this led into a small room, heavily barred and shuttered! At the end of Milly's room were French doors, again heavily barred, with full length shutters and bolts; these opened into a little area inside the wall surrounding the house, with a further room at the end of a dirt passage. This opened into a good-sized room, with a door into the street. I had never seen so many locks, keys, bolts or bars!

The next morning, I woke very early and already the street was noisy with voices and passing carts. I got up to find Milly making a pot of tea. Milly made tea at any opportunity! We sat in the kitchen whilst she discussed plans of what we would be doing. We had carte blanche to do whatever we wanted to the house. I am sure that having donkeys and horses in the empty rooms was never mentioned!

The house stood in a triangular plot, with a tarmaced road on one side, and dirt roads on the other two. It was a single story building with a pantile roof. The walls were painted dark cream, but were very faded and shabby; the wall was topped with tiles.

Inside the entire floor area was covered with black and white tiles. It was built to give maximum comfort in hot weather. The house was owned by American Missionaries who were based in Tlemcen, a town further along towards Algiers. They had left the house when the troubles began, and now rented it to us. The Major had told us that they might visit from time to time.

Milly's idea was to make the big hall into a strawed area where we could fit in up to eight donkeys, and maybe three horses; during the day the big doors could be opened to allow them to also use the little yard. We would need some double gates through the wall onto the dirt road to allow hay and straw to be delivered by carts when needed. The little room off the hall would make an ideal stable for any animal that needed to be on it's own for a while; and the room outside Milly's room, with the access straight from the street, would make an ideal isolation box! I guessed that Milly had been planning all this whilst on leave!

The first day was spent removing the sand and dust from the house and washing the dusty curtains; Milly pulled down all the net curtains and boiled them up in a tin bath, she had them earmarked for dressings! We went out into the street and were greeted by nearly everyone. Opposite the cottage was a little low house, and women came out of it and threw their arms around us both! They knew Milly already. They seemed genuinely excited to see us. They spoke only Arabic.

We went to Mohammed's tiny shop and purchased bottles of bright pink floor wash and other things we might need; there was a limited stock. The shop was about the size of half a car garage; with the front open to the street; a huge shutter was pulled down on the rare occasions the shop closed. There was a large, glass fronted, dirty fridge with unsavoury looking meat and butter, along with everything else that needed to be kept cool. The shelves were sparsely filled with everyday items. All the brands were new to me. We met Mohammed's brother, Misoom; he was a tall, rotund man, but like his brother, always very helpful.

We wandered down into the town, going first to buy straw and hay and food for the animals, from the one street where it was possible to buy such things. The corn sellers all worked from buildings with open fronts; we soon found out who gave the best service at the best price along with the best quality straw and grain. Milly took me into a large empty yard, surrounded on all sides by little shacks where people lived. She explained that this was one of several Fondouks in the town. They were used only on market days, Tuesdays and Thursdays, and would be used by the many people visiting the town as a 'donkey park'. For a small fee, they could fetter their animals to a long rope where they would stay until the owner returned. Fettering was widely used to stop animals wandering off; the two front legs would be tied together, using a rope device called a Hobble; once hobbled, the animal could only move very awkwardly, and they didn't usually bother. When hobbled to the rope in the fondouk, they couldn't move away at all. It was all very orderly; the guardian of the fondouk would direct the donkeys and they all stood in line... rather like cars in a car park!

At this stage of my time in the town, I had never seen one in operation, but I was to spend many hours working in them as time went on.

From there we went on down into the pretty part of the town where the French had clearly lived and enjoyed. It was, by now, shabby, but some of the former grandeur was still there. There were shops selling carpets and blankets, a couple of small cafes, where people sat drinking coffee. We found a reasonably good chemist' shop where we could buy anything we wanted; this included such things as Antibiotics and drugs that were only prescribed at home. They would be useful in some cases. The owner, who was a trained pharmacist, told us that he would help us whenever we needed advice on dosages.

In the main square there was a beautiful Catholic church, the Post Office, and... joy of joys! A little Spanish run patisserie! We went home laden with little boxes of goodies! The owner was very nice and she said she was very pleased to see more Europeans as, once the French had left, they were totally alone, apart from the nuns in the Convent and the owner of the little hotel. We walked home via the covered market that was open every day. We bought fresh vegetables and salad, plus some meat from one of the little stalls, it seemed to be the cleanest!

As we arrived home an old man with a donkey met us. The donkey was big, with a large abscess on its side where the pack had rubbed him. He asked if we could help him. Milly shooed him through the gate into the garden, and then, after much unlocking, into the little room just inside the back door.

We dumped the cakes and provisions in the kitchen, and Milly explained in a mixture of French, Arabic and English, and much hand waving, that the donkey would have to stay, as he was too sore to work. The old man agreed and went on his way.

We washed the donkey's side to remove all the debris, and found that the abscess was draining well, so we flushed it out with antiseptic, dressed it to stop the flies from getting onto the wound, and led the donkey into the large hall. We found a large saucepan and gave him water, making a mental note that we would need several buckets. Later in the day, a carter arrived with straw, hay and feed, so the donkey was given a bed and food. I doubt if he'd ever has it so good. He became, 'EE-Aaw', the first in our new in- patient book, we were in business!

I feel I must add some details of the people who lived around us, and of whom we saw so much. They were all Muslims and all wore the traditional dress. The Men wore Djellebahas, the heavy, one piece, full-length woven garment that went over whatever they wore underneath. On their heads they wore the white 'Tarbush' of Algeria; this was several yards of muslin wound around the head to make a sort of turban. The women never left their houses without covering up; in the case of the poorest, this was a white sheet, draped over the head, covering everything else. Only one eye was ever exposed... after a while I got to be a dab hand at recognising the smiling eye under the sheet! On our once monthly trip to Oran to the Bank, it was noticeable that the women there wore burkhas of different colours.

All the locals got to know us very quickly, and in no time all the carters and animals owners would greet us like long last friends. Usually, the greeting was in Arabic; but occasionally it would be in dreadful French, "Bonjour Messiuers-Dames". Often adding, again in French, "Touchez ma main". ('Touch my hand'); this involved much handshaking! Following the Arabic greeting always came a long speech asking if your family was well; your mother and father; and so on!

Every morning a small group of elderly men walked past, some on crutches and they used to sit on the corner of the road all day long, under the shelter of an overhanging roof. They played a board game all the time, I imagine for small amounts of money. They were always very friendly and greeted us each day with a cheerful smile and a wave, and the usual, 'Salaam Ale Ikhoum'.

The people in Relizane were generally very poor indeed, barely able to earn enough to support their families, but somehow they managed. Housing would be anything from a substantial house procured when the French occupants had fled, to a small shack made of hammered out oil drums... anything and everything would be incorporated to make sure it was stable and waterproof!

They lived very frugally. Most people owned a donkey with which to work, and my goodness, how they worked! That is the main reason we were there, to attempt to help the animals that were worked so hard just so that their owners and their family could eat. Donkeys were generally used with a backpack, onto which were slung large wicker panniers; these would be filled with anything from bricks and cement to vegetables or loaded right up with masses of vegetation, etc. Their lives were so hard and they often worked with dreadful sores under their packs, simply because they were the 'real' breadwinners for the family.

To my eyes, they were dreadfully thin for the most part, put this was the norm and I soon accepted it. Often the donkeys would be used to pull a cart, the carts would be loaded fully, and the donkeys sometimes fell under the strain. Horses were also used but for pulling larger carts, they too were often so overloaded they too fell in the street. The animals right out in the country were used for all the farm work, including drawing water from the wells and treading the straw after harvest... both of these jobs involved hours and hours of just walking around in a circle, in fierce sunshine and great heat, they were often harnessed to pull a heavy arm of machinery. Sadly, through necessity, one could often see a donkey harnessed up with a camel... imagine the height difference, and how that poor donkey had to work.

The animals were tough, but continuous use under extreme conditions often meant they were working whilst carrying injuries and sores from ill-fitting harness. Their lives were unbelievably tough, often with little food. The owners often had large families to feed; their work animals were low down the pecking order. Most of the animals were thin, certainly very thin in comparison with British animals.

In no time, word had spread that we were in Relizane, and that treatment was free. People came from miles around with their sick or injured animals. The old house was full to bursting with in-patients, and we were extremely busy. Our treatment book was filling up very quickly.

I was really enjoying the work. It was hot, often very dirty and smelly, and always very challenging. I picked up the basic Arabic quite quickly, and spoke dreadfully bad French with great fluency! Some of the carters spoke a 'bastardised' variety of French, combined with Arabic... I used to converse in as much Arabic as I could muster, then French and also English always accompanied by lots of hand waving!

The men used to teach me words, and would often test me to make sure I had remembered them. It was a strange language, but one that I had trouble grasping.

As time went by, my Arabic improved and I was able to hold a conversation. That is, as long as it concerned horse, mules, donkeys or cattle but anything more than that was a struggle; every day I learnt new words and slowly I was able to chat to anyone; it was probably dreadfully pronounced, but it worked. When I couldn't think of an Arabic word, I would throw in a French one!

The trouble was that many of the men would not speak directly to a woman, so someone else nearby would listen to me, and then relay my words to the owner of the animal... who had understood what I'd said in the first place! That could be quite frustrating on occasions.

We had a steady flow of regulars who would come along to make sure their animals has a 'top up' of the medicine that had brought about a cure, or to have the sores re-dressed. This was very heartening for us as it showed that people trusted us.

Occasionally things didn't work out, and there was nothing we could do for the animal. This posed a tricky problem to us, as we couldn't be seen to be shooting an animal. The men knew when the end was near, and we would persuade them to leave the animal with us. We would then administer a strong sedative, from which the animal never woke.

When the owner came back to see if we had cured the animal, we could simply say he had died. The owners would accept this as 'The Will of Allah'. Getting rid of the dead animal meant finding a carter to collect the body. There was never a problem with this. He would drive into the big yard, and we would, with the help of many others, heave the body unceremoniously onto the cart and off it would go. We never found out where the bodies went to, but I suspect the local dump!

We hated having to do this, but sometimes it was the only option; we would fight for the life of any animal, often taking it in turns to sit with it night after night, only to have it die... the owners would always look up to the skies and say, 'It's Allah's Will'!

Early one morning there was a lot of commotion out in the street, followed by loud banging at the door. Outside stood a man with a mule. The mule had a nasty wound on her hock, but she wouldn't let either of us look at it closely! The owner insisted that she stayed with us, and said he would bring her food every day.

We named her, "Sylvia Brown', and put her into the little room off the hall. We then had to attempt to catch her and dress the wound. The more we tried, the angrier she became! Her eyes were flashing, teeth bared and she was squealing, her tail whirring round like a propeller! Cunning was called for. We tried to use a rope threaded over a pole... that's how you would approach a wild pony; but that didn't work. She kicked several chunks out of the wall during this process. Whatever we tried was countered by Sylvia Brown's big bottom, kicking legs and that tail!

We left her to calm down, and went and sat in the kitchen with a cup of tea, and we went through various options, none of which seemed to be any good. Milly suddenly said, "Yes!" She had been looking at the bottle of washing up liquid. "That would work".

We emptied the contents of the plastic bottle into another, and she washed it out to remove all the soapy liquid. The bottle bore the brand name, 'OLA'. Milly filled it with a mixture of Carbolic Oil; very useful for treating wounds, and it kept the flies off as well.

We went back to Sylvia's little room, and opened the door. The rest of it was really simple. Sylvia took up position with her back end towards us, ready to let loose with her hind legs, and Milly squeezed the Ola bottle. The Carbolic Oil shot out and hit the wound and covered it well. Sylvia Brown was so taken aback at the speed of the event that she stopped all her protestations, albeit for a split second! We left her looking very indignant.

That evening, we were sitting down reading with the radio on and Milly suddenly said, "Hola! Woah La! Here comes the Ola!" We both roared with laughter. We repeated this ditty twice a day as we treated Sylvia. Her owner didn't come for several days. He eventually arrived with a cart loaded with freshly cut Alfalfa; there was enough for Sylvia and all the other patients. We told him that we couldn't catch her. He laughed and said he would teach us how to catch a mule.

He carried a small bamboo walking cane, and, with the handle, simply hooked it around the top of one of Sylvia's forelegs, just above the knee. She stood like a lamb. From then on, the rest of her stay was so simple. We would catch her, treat her, and she was better in no time! When she left, her owner brought more Alfalfa for the other animals, and a large basket of eggs for us. He walked away chuckling at the thought of us trying to catch Sylvia!

The little triangular garden was the only place that escaped being occupied by animals. The huge tree in the middle was a Mimosa and the scent was really wonderful in the cool of the evening. There were a couple of tiny flowerbeds, so we planted some seeds that soon grew and flowers brightened up the space. In the corner, where the end of the house met the wall, was a little paved area with a shade over it. We realised that the only way to get hot water was to attach a hosepipe to the outside tap; the hosepipe got hot, and we could shower with ease; that was such a luxury. We rigged up a partition just in case anyone should attempt to climb the wall to peep!

Patient number 10 was Winny. She was old, weary and dreadfully thin. Her wobbly legs were like matchsticks, her hooves were so long, they curled upwards, and her coat was sparse and almost white. She had come in because along the entire length of her back there was a deep sore. In places, so deep that it must have been just a tiny way above the backbone. The owner told us she was really too old to work, but he couldn't afford another. Dear old Winny was the sweetest little soul, we dressed her sores daily, trimmed her feet, and she soon put on a little weight.

We decided that she couldn't go back to work, so we gave the man a young donkey that Mohammed from the shop had bought for us, (using our money). We knew that if we went to buy a donkey the price would be at least double. Mohammed came back with a sturdy young donkey and it had cost us £3.00 each! We didn't want to set a precedent and give people the idea that we would buy up old animals; we would have been inundated with them. Using a sheet of headed paper, we wrote, in English, a contract that gave Winny's owner full rights to the new donkey on the condition he visited us once each month to check that all was well. The owner was more than happy to add his thumbprint to the letter and went off very happy. Dear old Winny stayed with us for a year and then, sadly died very peacefully one night. At least her last year was a happy one for her.

The idea of a 'Donkey Bank' had been mooted by Milly on several occasions, and the ease of buying a replacement for Winny seemed to give the impetus to put the idea into reality. We bough three donkeys, and these would be 'loaned' to the owners of animals that had to be kept in for any length of time; they would only go to the pooerst of the people to ensure that they could work and feed the family.

We drew up a contarct and asked Mohammed to find someone who would type it out, and make copies. He asked his sister and she made a splendid job of them.

Our three donkeys were rarely at home for long. They were always returned to us in splendid condition, well-fed and devoid of any sores. The men who had the use of them were eternally grateful for the loan. We did very well for eggs and vegetables whenever they were in town!

One morning, three men arrived with a lovely bay horse; the horse had a very messy wound on his fetlock, his leg badly swollen and he was very lame. We explained that it would be best if they could leave the horse with us. After much discussion, they agreed and "Redskin" became our 100th in-patient. We led him into the big hall and examined the wound. Once the blood and dust was washed off, it didn't look quite as bad as we had feared. There was a lot of swelling; he must have banged his leg somehow. We dressed the wound and applied a bandage to the wound as well as a pressure bandage to his foreleg. He was a perfect gentleman whilst all this went on. Most of the horses were stallions, and Redskin was no exception.

Every day the three men came to see the horse. The first day they marvelled at the sight of the dressings. The second day they brought Alfalfa and eggs for us; this happened every day. We ate omelettes, scrambled eggs and ended up having to give eggs to Mohammed to sell in his shop! Redskin was with us for nearly a month, we wouldn't let him go home until he was walking soundly again.

Every month, one of us would go to Oran to the bank to collect our salaries and also the money to run the refuge with. There Barclays International was there. So the banking part was simple and transacted in English. We took the train. I now felt very much at home with the countryside and the journey passed so many farms and villages, each one different in some way. There were old vineyards too; Algeria had produced very good wine. The train sopped in a little coastal town called, Mostaganem. It looked such a pretty place; again, it was looking rather shabby.

There was little to do in Oran, so it was a case of going to the Bank, having a quick coffee in one of the little cafés and taking the next train home.

It always seemed strange to have to, 'dress up' to go to Oran. Our normal garb was dusty sandals and something that washed well; I suppose it was important that we had to be smart on rare occasions! But apart from that trip, the BBC World Service, and our wonderful letters from home, we had no contact with the outside world.

One such occasion to dress up arose when we had a phone call via Mohammed's shop, that one of the missionaries was coming through, and that she needed a bed for one night! This threw us into slight panic mode! We had to clear out the 'spare room', that we now used as a dispensary cum storeroom. The many boxes of missionary pamphlets were still with us! We put them in the corner of the garden and covered them with an old door! We hastily put the bed up and found some clean sheets for it. What we could do nothing about was the fact that the place was full to bursting with animals! We simply made sure everything was clean and tidy and awaited her arrival.

Miss Bishop was arriving by train from Tlemcen en route to Oran: I walked to the station and would return with her by taxi. There was no mistaking her. She was very short and almost as round, her hair in a tight bun, with a little 'pork pie' hat perched on her head. There were four suitcases! In a loud American voice she greeted me, and the stationmaster was on hand to usher her and her bags along to the taxi I had waiting. The bags were loaded into the taxi; we set off towards the house. "I expect there have been some changes?" she asked.

"A few" I replied and chuckled. We chatted on the way home. She seemed very nice and jolly. I noticed her eyes darting in all directions as she took in the town that she had lived in for some months prior to the troubles.

The taxi driver insisted on carrying the cases into the house and then departed. Once again, he didn't charge us. We had tea in the sitting room and then said we would give Miss Bishop a tour of the place. Her name was Eileen, and she didn't seem at all phased by the sight of donkeys and horses resting in the big hall and in the outside yard. We showed her 'Sylvia Browns' room, (As it was always known); there was a cow in there at the time! And on to the isolation room that was housing three donkeys... none of which were contagious, we had simply run out of space to keep them.

Once the tour was over, we sat and chatted. It seemed that the missionaries had occupied the house for only four years. They then moved on to Tlemcen.

Eileen had been a teacher back in the States, but had felt she was needed elsewhere and volunteered to do missionary work; hence her time in Algeria. She said that they were not too favourably received by the Muslims! That wasn't at all surprising to us.
We had supper and sat late into the night chatting in the sitting room. Eileen asked if the organ was still in

the house? *Organ*? Then I twigged that it must be the mysterious wooden box in my bedroom. She said she would see if it still played. The box opened and there were many hinges and panels; she deftly assembled it into a small harmonium. For the next hour we were treated to a variety of wheezing and hissing as she pedalled furiously to get the thing full of air; then, and only then would the keyboard work! Eileen sat there; pushing the two pedals up and down and played, and sang missionary songs! We were treated to, 'Jesus wants me for a Sunbeam', as her final offering. The organ was then carefully folded down into its box. We all went to bed.

I woke with a great start! It was pitch dark. There was dreadful screaming coming from elsewhere in the house! I shot out of bed and grabbed a stick, (every room had one!) Milly shot out of her room at the same time, she also had a stick ready to floor intruders. I put the lights on and there, in the kitchen stood Eileen; hands on her head, screaming hysterically at one of the donkeys! It must have crept through the door when she went through to the loo in the dark and Eileen had stumbled into it and touched it's hairy body! Once she realised what had happened she quickly recovered her composure. I think it was some comfort to her that she was only stopping for one night with the two potty Englishwomen and the donkeys! We saw her off in the morning and told her to come whenever she felt like it. We never saw her again!

We began to visit outlying markets to treat donkeys that never came to Relizane. This meant either going by taxi (too expensive) or by bus. The bus was perfectly adequate. It would be full of people going to the markets, the roof of the bus had low rails on top;

that area would be loaded up with chickens and boxes of vegetables.

I used to enjoy the markets. Rows and rows of animals, all tethered to a rope that ran along the ground; they were in lines, rather like a car park. Our job was to walk along the rows, feeling under their backpacks for sores and, if a sore was found, treating it. The packs often used to rub the backbone and cause nasty sores. It was quite obvious that we would need to do something about the packs. We went singly to the markets; one of us would always be back at the house to deal with callers.

We obtained a large number of jute sacks, and would spend our evenings sitting in the big hall, stuffing them with straw, cutting out a long slit in the middle, then sewing them into 'shapes' so they would fit a donkeys back. The slits in the packs fitted over the backbone, relieving the pressure. When we had enough, we began to take them to the markets to swap then with ill-fitting packs. We did it in Relizane too. The owners were very pleased to receive a brand new pack, and the animals were greatly helped by being able to work without the pain of sores on the backbone.

Each time one of us went to the markets on the bus, we took took of the new packs; they would be slung up onto the roof of the bus. One of the markets was at a village called, 'Zagora,' which was up in the hills. It was a very busy day, as it seemed to be a very popular market. I loved to see the various things that went on during the day. There would be men who sat all day mending shoes and sandals; others who repaired the wheels of the carts; a 'doctor' who would mix up smelly potions for his hapless clients and the dentist... I use the term very loosely. He would sit on the ground, with the tools of his trade, and a great number of diseased teeth laid in front of him in the soil. If anyone had toothache, he would sit them down on a large rock and proceed to extract the tooth; often he would call on passers by to hold the person down to stop them wriggling and screaming! It was gruesome but had a certain fascination! He was kept busy all day.

One morning a van drew up outside and two men stepped out and knocked on the gate. One of them was no other than the Regional Veterinary Officer. He explained that word had reached him of two women from England who were doing veterinary work. We got a little worried! The other man was his assistant.

He explained that he was the only Veterinary surgeon in the entire region; he worked for the Government as an Inspector. His name was Ahmed, his assistant was called Ben Salem.

We showed him round. Luckily we had some interesting cases in and he was very impressed with our treatments and with the way the animals were looked after.

He invited us to lunch in the town, which, of course, we accepted!

We ate at one of the little cafes in the town square. Lunch was excellent; more so because, much to our surprise, we drank red wine. We had always thought that the town was 'dry'; but he had uttered something in rapid Arabic, and a fine wine was produced. After lunch we parted company and he promised to call in whenever he was in town; he also asked us to contact him in the event of any problems, or if we needed any special medicines. He was an extremely nice man and we felt very relieved that we had passed muster!

Later that day a man leading a grey mule arrived at the gate. The mule had an injured shoulder. We explained that if the owner could leave her with us, she would get better much quicker than if she carried on working. He was happy to do this.

We called the mule, 'Gertrude' and once her shoulder was dressed, she settled in very quickly. The next morning her owner arrived with a big bundle of Alfalfa for her and some eggs and a live chicken for us to eat!

The worst thing you can do to an animal you are meant to eat is to give it a name. We named the little white bantam, 'Trude', as she'd come with Gertrude. One morning, Milly had just given all the animals in the hall a nice new bed, and as she did it, Trude walked along behind, scraping it all up. Milly said, "That little bugger, Trude is not helping". I explained in her defence that she was supplying us with eggs daily; from that moment on the little white bantam was known as, "Buggertrude'! Gertrude was able to return to work after a few days; her owner was delighted and brought freshly cut alfalfa for all the inmates!

Winter was coming and it began to get chilly and damp. The house was built for hot weather and had tiles throughout; it was in need of some heating. The fire in the sitting room was brought into use; we had a cartload of wood delivered. This was quickly sawn or chopped into smaller chunks, and we were able to settle down in the evenings in front of a big roaring log fire. This made a huge difference. We also decided to get rid of all the boxes of the missionary pamphlets. We discovered that nearly all of them told the the parable of the 'Prodigal Son'... in English! We thought we could feed some onto the fire each evening and slowly get rid of them. Every evening would see us feeding the fire with 'Proddies', our irreverent name for the Prodigal Sons!

At the end of two weeks we had one last box to dispose of. That evening we began poking them on, and heaved a huge sigh of relief when the final ones caught fire.

A while later there was frantic banging on the gate. It was a very agitated Mohammed. "Madame! Vous etes en feu!"... He pointed up to the chimney and there were flames shooting out of it into the night sky! "I have called the fire brigade," he yelled; he was beside himself with worry!

Milly and I got all the animals out into the yard and closed the big doors of the hall, at least they would be safe if the matter got out of hand. The fire engine arrived, bell clanging.

The firemen were on a platform on the side of the tender. The fire chief climbed out of the cab, stood to attention and saluted us! Then he barked an order to the crew who lined up and saluted us. Then, a further order saw the hose lifted from the tender, and each man held a length under his arm, and followed the fire chief into the house at the double. Once in the sitting room, the fire chief ordered the nozzle of the hose to be pushed up the chimney; no sooner had this happened than the hose bucked and water shot up the chimney. As fast as it went up it poured back down; black, sooty and very smelly! It quickly pooled in the sitting room and ran under the door to my bedroom, then snaked across and into Milly's and then to the kitchen. After some time, the hose was pulled back down. The fire was out. We were flooded!

The chief ordered the men to pick up the hose, and they went out as they had come in. They were all lined up and saluted. We thanked them profusely and off they went.

The incident had caused a large crowd, some of which dispersed with the departure of the firemen; but there were a few who stayed. We declined their offers of help, and they soon dispersed. We thanked Mohammed for his swift action and went indoors to review the situation! It was pretty dire! Actions plans were drawn up over a cup of tea.

The plan to brush the water out through the back door seemed the most simple. First we brushed it out of my bedroom, and we put sacks down to stop it seeping back under the door. Then we did the same in Milly's room; then a major sweep through the kitchen and outside into the garden. By 2.00am we had it more or less under control. We stopped for tea, and whilst we were sitting in the damp, smelly kitchen, Milly came out with one of her gems. "We put on the 'Proddies' and gave then a poke, and the whole flipping chimney then went up in smoke!" We dissolved into laughter.

The sight that greeted us in the morning was grim. Black, sooty floors and everywhere the strong smell of smoke. We spent most of that day washing floors and curtains; stopping only to answer the door to patients. By the evening, all was restored and we relit the fire to dry the place out. We made sure it was wood only from then on!

The following day we received a visit from the Fire Chief. He was in his everyday clothes, and we didn't recognise him at first! He wanted to see if we were all right, and that the fire had been properly dealt with. We made him coffee. He stayed for some time. He was most bemused by the sight of all the animals. I think he went away convinced that we were both completely mad.

Christmas Day arrived and we had made every effort to try to make sure it was a 'special day'. We had kept presents sent by our families, and had bought a gift for each other. Lunch was chicken, roasted in a big pot along with the vegetables. My mother had sent a pudding. All in all, we had a feast. There was no wine though, as we had never tried to buy wine, even from the little café down in the town.

We had several callers and an assortment of animals to treat throughout the day.

Our Christmas tree looked lovely in the firelight in the evening... it was a branch of a pine tree, decorated with anything we could lay our hands on. We ate pot-roast chicken and vegetables, and the small Christmas pudding. There were some carols on BBC World Service.

January and February were particularly wet and chilly. But by the end of February the weather began to change, the days were sunny and warm again. We received our weekly letter from HQ in London, and it announced that The Major was going to visit us. He wanted to stay for three nights and accompany us during the days to see the work we were doing. He wanted a room booked in the Hotel, and also asked one of us to meet him at the station. We had ten days to smarten things up. We splashed some whitewash onto some of the walls, and tidied the garden. Otherwise we were ready, apart from booking the hotel.

We walked down to the town square together to the hotel. It was a large white building with green shutters. Three of the letters on the sign were missing, so it was the 'Hotel Ari-a-e'. We guessed it was the Ariane. We went inside and stood at the little reception desk for an age. A man appeared from behind the curtains. He was an elderly Frenchman. His delight in seeing two other Europeans was obvious. He told us that the Major would be well looked after, and that he organised everything personally. The hotel provided breakfast only, and evening meals only on certain days. Unfortunately none of them when the Major was due to be staying. We left the hotel after much hand shaking with the manager.

The days passed very quickly and suddenly it was the day of the Major's arrival! We gave the place an extra tidy and made sure everything was in order. He was due at mid-day. During the morning we had the usual array of callers, including one very sick horse on his last legs. We took him in, but as he walked through the door into the hall he went down onto his knees and collapsed in a heap in the doorway... Dead!

It was almost time for one of us to go to meet the Major! Milly had already said that I should meet him; in the meantime we had the dead body to dispose of!

Usually there was a carter driving by who would be only too pleased to be paid to remove the poor horse, but today there was not one to be seen. I flew down the road at a rate of knots to see if I could find one. Luckily, there was a carter with his horse trundling up the road towards me; I stopped him and asked if he could help us; he agreed immediately, and I hopped onto the cart and we drove up to the house. It took five men and a lot of pushing and pulling to get the horse out of the doorway, across the hall and onto the cart, but we did it.

We paid the carter and gave each man some cash for his efforts. The big doors were slammed shut, and we began to clear up all signs of the mess caused by dragging the dead horse across the straw covered floor! Milly was still clearing up when I left to collect the Major. I walked down to the station and spoke to our usual taxi man. I explained to him that the 'Boss' was arriving, and he said he would be ready.

The station master saw me waiting and I told him that the Major was due to arrive. As the train drew into the station, I watched the stationmaster looking at the carriages for the Major. He spotted him long before I did. He opened the carriage door, saluted the Major and we were escorted along the platform to the waiting taxi. The taxi driver stood to attention and he also saluted! He then opened the taxi door and ushered us into the back.

The Major had come by train from Oran having flown in early in the morning. He said he was a little tired. We dropped him at the hotel. I then walked home but the taxi stayed to drive him up to the house as soon as he had freshened up and settled into his room.

That gave us time to prepare lunch and lay the table. It seemed no time at all before the taxi arrived. The taxi driver declined any payment, but we insisted as this time he had surpassed himself. The Major also thanked him in Arabic... not the Algerian sort, but in classical Arabic. The driver was quite taken aback by this, and didn't appear to understand a word! After much saluting, he went off waving happily.

Before lunch we showed the Major around the house. He stopped at each animal and examined them; only the mules were given a wide berth! He was clearly impressed by the place. Lunch was a simple meal and we chatted endlessly. The Major was up to date with all the news from home and that alone was worth listening to.

We were still at the table two hours later when there was banging at the gate. We all went outside. It was one of the regulars who had just brought this donkey back to have its leg wound re-dressed. We explained to the owner that the Major was from England, and that he was in charge of everything. The owner launched into a long speech about how well we had cared for his donkey and him... and shook the Major's hand with gusto. By then there was a little crowd gathering, and they all wanted to shake hands with the Major!

We went back into the house and continued our conversation. It was teatime!

After supper I took the Major back to the Hotel. He said he's like to walk, so we set off down to the town square. Every donkey and horse owner we passed greeted us. The Major remarked that the people treated us like royalty. I agreed and added that it was also very humbling that these people, who had nothing, were so genuinely pleased we were there.

The next morning Milly went to collect the Major from the hotel. He said he wanted to accompany us on our daily rounds. As it was starting to get so hot in the middle of the day, we suggested he came at about 6.30am. He laughed and told us that it was normally gone 9.00am when he went to the office, but he agreed it might be better to work in the cooler part of the day. We didn't like to tell him that by 6.30am we had been at work for two hours!

He arrived at the house as I was dealing with a queue of donkeys and their owners outside the gate. None of them needed more than a new dressing, so I was quite quickly finished. We told the Major that the 'stables' had already been cleaned out, and that we were going to take him on a tour of the fondouks in the town. He thought it wise to leave his linen jacket at the house as it was starting to get hot. We asked him if he minded having coffee whilst we were out; that would save us having to return home and waste time. He seemed happy to go along with this, and we set off to do a tour of the fondouks, as it was market day.

This meant walking all around the town, stopping at every fondouk to check every animal. This was always hot and dusty work. We were both aware that the Major was flagging when we got to the third fondouk. We had four more to go. The sun was beating down. We asked if he'd like to stop for coffee? We went across the road to a little stall and sat down on the steps drinking strong, black coffee. The Major was clearly hot and tired; we suggested he either returned to the house or the hotel for a rest and to cool off; he said he would return to the house and wait.

We carried on and got the work done by lunchtime, stopped by at the market for some salad and some meat for the evening meal, and then went home. As we got to the house we saw an extraordinary sight! A queue of animals outside the door, and the Major chatting away to the owners in his impeccable Arabic; the trouble was that only a few of then got the gist of what he was saying, as the Arabic as spoken in Algeria was far removed from classical Arabic! He had also drawn the usual crowd of onlookers who added their thoughts as to what the Major was saying.

I think he was quite relieved to see us and get inside and flop in an armchair whilst we sorted out the various animals and their treatments. The Major had lunch with us, after which we just sat and chatted until 4.00pm when It was time to sort all the animals that were staying at the house with us. The Major said he would go back to the hotel after that, and asked us if we would join him for dinner. He said he would go on down into the town to see if he could find a suitable place to eat as the hotel didn't do dinners.

Milly and I showered under the hosepipe and changed into our 'Oran' clothes! We locked up and set off down to the hotel to collect the Major. He came down looking refreshed and had changed into a clean shirt and slacks, he wore a linen jacket and looked every bit the quintessential Englishman abroad.

We walked down to one of the little cafés just off the town square. The Major said he'd checked it out and felt it quite suitable for us to eat there. We did indeed have a good meal of chicken with couscous and vegetables. He asked for wine, but the owner said he had none. It was the same restaurant that the Vet had taken us to; we knew they certainly did have wine; but we said nothing!

The day for the Major's departure was upon us; we both went to the hotel and went with him to the station. He said how genuinely impressed he was with our work.

We waved him off as the train drew away from the station, heaving sighs of relief that we had passed our inspection.

Following the Major's visit we were able to get back to our normal routine, one of us doing the house and the in patients and callers, (and cooking), the other doing the markets outside the town or the fondouks in the town on market day, along with the shopping. We were flat to the boards for the entire days. We did try to snatch a short rest after lunch; in the hottest part of the day no one seemed to call until the afternoon was cooler. It was lovely just to flop and read a book, or fall sound asleep!

Early in May we received a visit from a Policeman, bearing the inevitable clipboard. He explained that he had been told to visit us, and that we were to present ourselves at the police station the following morning to see the Chief of Police. He was unable to give us any more details; I doubt if he knew anyway! We were quite concerned about this as we were quite sure that none of the authorities knew we were working in the country.

The next morning, we did early stables and dealt with the little queue of patients at the door. We then had breakfast, dug out our passports from the cupboard and set off to the police station.

The Chef of Police beamed at us and waved us into his office; he asked for coffee to be sent in. He introduced himself in excellent French and proceeded to tell us that he had once visited London and had seen the palace where the Queen lived. His name was Boumedienne. Coffee arrived and after pouring it he explained the reasons for us being summoned.

He said he had received reports that two English Ladies were working amongst the poorest people, and he simply wanted to meet us! He said that if we ever needed the help of the Police to just let him know.

Phew! What a relief! I think we both secretly thought we would be deported at the very least! He did suggest we registered the fact that we were in the town, we agreed at once and asked where we had to go to do that? He opened a drawer in his huge desk and pulled out a book and a rubber stamp - "Here Mesdames". We left after much hand shaking both clutching a paper that permitted us to be in the town. We walked home chuckling at the events of the morning. When we got home there was no queue, so we had a cup of tea before decided what we would do with the rest of the day. We thought a spot of gardening was in order and set about weeding and moving plants about until it was time for lunch.

We had bought a small electric oven as we were fed up only being able to cook on the gas rings. The Major was only too pleased for us to buy one and sent the money in the next bank payment. We were no able to bake and make pies - even roast a dinner on high days and holidays.

Milly had a little battery operated record player and a handful of records. If I came home to the sound of Strauss, I knew she was making pastry! Apparently the Strauss waltzes gave her hands just the lightness needed to make good pastry!

If we needed something rousing, we would play Brigadoon or Gilbert and Sullivan! We soon knew every word of the records. The only time we could add new ones would be when we went home on leave.

One evening, after a particularly hard day in which we had several really bad cases brought in, plus a death to deal with. We had eaten our meal when Milly suddenly said, "I have awfully itchy feet! I feel that my job here is done. You are more than capable of coping with the running of the place. I think I will go to work in Greece for a while". I was very surprised at this news.

Milly explained that there was another charity in Greece that did similar work, and she thought she would enjoy it, as they needed someone to start a new refuge. I could see that she was really serious about this. Over the next few days, Milly talked more and more about Greece, and finally wrote a letter to the Charity to see if the vacancy was still open.

About ten days later a letter arrived for Milly; it was the offer of a job, and the post would be for September. It was April. She then wrote to the Major, explaining that she felt the need to go to pastures new, and that I could run the place quite capably.

The Major replied that he was sorry she was going, and offered her a job whenever she needed one, and wished her well. He asked if she would be able to stay until our tour in Relizane was due to end in July. That would give them time to find a replacement to work in Relizane with me when I returned in October. I wondered who on earth they would find as no-one could possibly be another Milly? Milly replied that this would be in order.

We carried on as normal. One morning there was a knock on the gate and we both went out to see what was needed. There were two men holding a really handsome grey horse; he was a lovely animal, better than than any we had seen before. The men told us that he had injured his leg jumping up onto a lorry. There were no horseboxes in the country, so animals had to travel on ordinary topless lorries, and had to jump up onto them. Often the lorry would back into a dip; this made it easier for the horses to jump. This horse had taken all the skin off his hind leg, right down to the bone and was very sore and lame.

The men led him into the garden and into the room by the back door. We were then able to see his wound better. We explained he would have to stay with us until he was better. They asked how long this would take as the horse was going to France.

Intrigued, we asked why he was going to France? They told us that he was going, along with forty others for meat. We were horrified; as we had no idea the trade was going on. That explained why this horse was looking so well.

The men explained that they had a large 'fattening yard' on the other side of the town, and offered to take us to see it. We both said we would be interested and told them that we would be able to go once all the animals were settled. They agreed to return at 6.00pm and walk down with us. I asked how they got to France and one of the men said they went to Algiers by road, then by cargo boat to Marseille where they were killed. The men left him with us and we told them that it would be ages before he could travel; they shrugged their shoulders and said they would send the others on and that he could go at a later date. They left.

This horse was entered into the treatment book as 'Hiawatha'; it seemed to suit him. We dressed his leg and spent time looking at him. He was a stallion and had a huge crest; his long mane was so grey it was almost blue; we found a purple bead sewn into the mane. This was a symbol of Luck. He stood quietly while we went all over him, and then we led him into the hall and left him to settle in. He was a really lovely looking animal.

We were both quite appalled at the thought of this lovely horse going for meat, but our job was to make him better. But the thought of it all made us very downhearted.

We called the horse Hiawatha, and he turned out to be a real gentleman. His owners brought him fresh food every day - with the sole intention of keeping him big and strong. More weight = More money!

The two men arrived on time and walked with down the street were all the horse feed suppliers; they turned off down a little alleyway and entered the grounds of a once lovely mansion. The garden were very overgrown, and the house was shabby. This had clearly been the home of a wealthy French family.

Behind the house was a large covered barn, it was beautifully cool inside, with three of the sides open. Inside, in separate pens were about 60 horses. All of them had good feed and were looking well. These were the horses that were being fattened for meat. What a contrast between these and the working horses that we dealt with! It was another world.

The two men explained that the horses stayed with them until they were considered fat enough, and then transported to France, where they were killed for meat.

We walked back to the house by ourselves. Both of us were quite shaken!

We went in and looked at Watha. What a waste of a lovely horse!

Milly was quite clearly besotted with this lovely animal, and she announced that she would buy him! Needless to say, a very hard bargain was struck with the owner, but she announced with an enormous beam on her face that 'Watha' was hers. She added that she would have to find a way to get him to Greece! The former owners, who we had struck quite a friendship with, went off happy with the offer to help to get him to Greece when she needed him - at a price! We chuckled at this ridiculous prospect! The two men were so different. One was small and wore a short blue raincoat all the time, he was called, Benama Hedi, he spoke good French. The other was tall, dark with a large hooked nose and a very pock marked face; he wore the traditional garb and he reminded us of a wicked uncle in a Pantomime... that's what we called him, although his real name was Ben Aziz.

Shortly after Watha's arrival, a young and very skinny young cat visited us; he was white from head to tail and used to come every day for food. Over the weeks he became very friendly, especially to Milly, as she was a real cat lover. He began to sleep in the big hall with the horses, and slowly wormed his way into the rest of the house and ended up sleeping in Milly's bedroom. Milly named him, 'White Wath', and jokingly said that she now owned a 'Twin Tub Wathing Machine'! I think the stresses of the days meant that we occasionally came out with silly things and even did silly things!

One afternoon, I donned the old pith helmet that had been left by the missionaries. Then I put an old shirt on, upside down, and tied the 'waist' up with rope. I put my wellies on and picked up a hairless broom on my way out of the kitchen and into the hall. Milly was there, sorting out the hay; she looked at me and grinned from ear to ear. She hurried off and returned soon afterwards, wearing a sheet around her shoulders, and a plastic bucket on her head! We had a silly five minutes, both clambering aboard the two donkeys that were ready to go home, and having a little polo match!

The perplexed donkeys just stood their ground whilst we sat and roared with laughter.

I think that without the occasional moments like those, we would have eventually turned into very depressed people! Being able to laugh is a real gift, and fortunately we were both blessed with the ability to do it with style!

We were both very pleased that Watha's injured leg was healing well. He was able to walk soundly again. That posed a few problems, as, being a stallion he got bored and started looking for things to occupy him. One day he got into the little bathroom and caused havoc. Milly decreed that she would walk him out for an hour every evening to, 'Take the tickle out of his toes'.

We both used to walk with him, and discovered places in Relizane that we had never seen. We even found a little abandoned racecourse, no longer used as the French had gone, along with their horses. As usual a crowd of little children, and the occasional Slick Dick accompanied us; generally, they soon tired of walking and went home.

After a few weeks of walking, Milly took deliver of a parcel from England; it contained her saddle. It fitted Watha perfectly, so from then on she rode him out every evening when it was cooler.

We took in a large horse that had been bitten by a snake. He arrived with a hugely swollen leg and was cold and trembling. He was put into the isolation box and we found the site where he had been bitten; there were two fang holes. The horse was clearly in real trouble and we tried everything we could to make him more comfortable and to ease the pain and the fever.

That night, we took it in turns to be with him. He thrashed around, getting up and down all night. He was delirious and was crashing round alarmingly. The next morning he was no better, but the swelling of his leg was softer. We gave hime constant treatments and kept bathing his leg with hot and cold water. He was sweating profusely. He had cut his head where it had banged against the wall.

The same continued throughout the next day, but he seemed easier by late afternoon.

That night he was a little quieter, but we still stayed with him and all night worked on his leg. There was not so much thrashing about. His temperature was almost back to normal and the sweating had stopped.

On the third day, he ate a little bran mash; the first food he'd taken since being with us. He also drank copiously, as if he was now trying to rid his body of the toxins from the snake bite. We gave him a fresh deep bed, and from then on, he was calm and there was no more thashing about. The skin began to slough off where the fang marks had been, but he was well on the road to recovery. We kept him for well over two weeks, until the leg was normal and the wound had almost healed. His owner had visited daily and had been so worried.

This was the only snake bite we had seen and it was very nearly fatal. We never found out what sort of snake had bitten him. The owner told us that every year many farmers got bitten and died.

It was starting to get very hot during the day, and we were beginning to think of home. Before we could go on leave we had a million things to do. We made sure all the animals were well enough to be discharged. The Spanish lady at the cake shop said she would look after Pussy Watha. That was very sweet of her as there were no such things as catteries!

Watha was more of a problem, and Milly thought long and hard before seeking advice from his ex-owners. Finally, she decided, somewhat reluctantly to ask them to help.

We saw them down in the town and asked if they would come to the house. When they arrived they saw Watha and offered at once to buy him back! This put Milly off her idea, but there was no option but to ask for help.

She explained that we were going away for three months and asked if they knew where he could be stabled for that time. They understood perfectly, and said that he could stay at their yard, they asked for some money in advance. Milly agreed to that, but told them the rest would be paid when she got back, but only if Watha was in good order. There was much spitting on hands and hand shaking to seal the deal. We arranged for them to take him the day before we left. Needless to say, Milly was very worried that something would go horribly wrong, but there was no alternative.

I went to Oran and bought our tickets at the tiny Air France office, and then went to the bank to collect the final payment for the year. It all seemed very strange.

The day before we left, Milly walked Watha down to Wicked Uncle's yard and he was installed into a decent fenced area with a shelter. There was fresh water and food. Again Milly reinforced the need to take great care of Watha, and again, much hand shaking. She paid him half in advance, with the remainder on Watha's collection and told them that he MUST be well treated!

Later that day we both went down to the little cake shop with Pussy Watha in a basket, complaining loudly! He was welcomed into the loving arms of the lovely Spanish couple. I think Milly felt quite happy about leaving him. We went home and began to lock up everything. We sealed the inside of the windows with tape to try to stop the dust from blowing in from the street. All the shutters were double-checked. We were very late to bed!

The next morning we washed our bedding and hung it onto the line. It was dry in about an hour! We had breakfast and took our suitcases across to Mohammed's shop. We handed him the keys and he rang for a taxi to take us down to the station. He had tears in his eyes as we left. He knew that Milly was going to Greece and that I would return with another person.

At the little Air France office in Oran we were transferred onto an Air France bus that took us to the airport. We were soon up and flying across the Mediterranean, I had very mixed emotions. I was thrilled to be going home to see my family and friends, yet sad to leave the place where I felt so at home and so needed. But I would be back again in no time at all.

Part One: Photographs

A donkey passes by No 1 Rue Rouina, Relizane

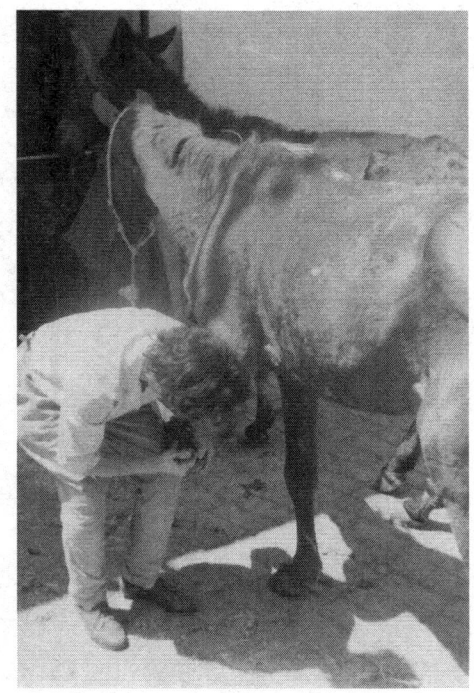

Milly putting the farrier tools to good use

Milly dressing the wounds of a baby donkey

Early morning in a local fondouk

Donkeys tethered in lines on market day

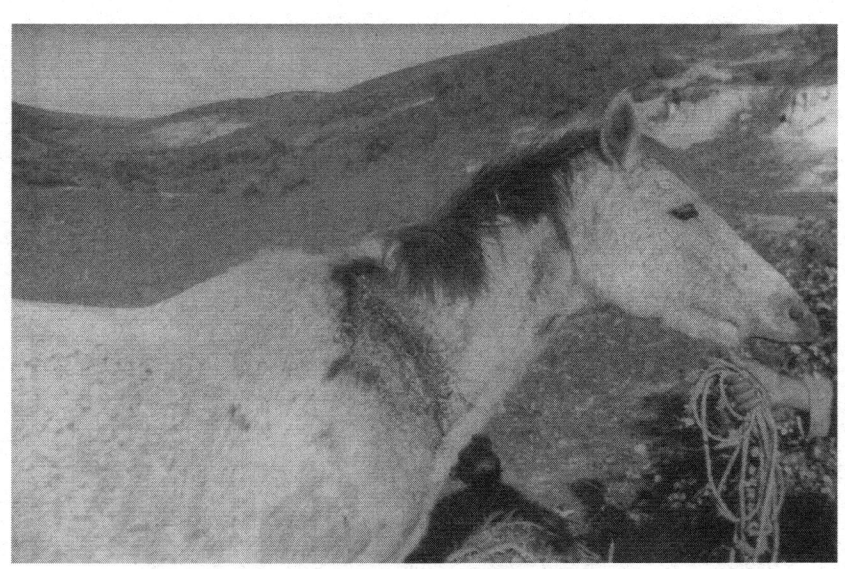

A horse with a 'Fistulous Wither'

Donkeys at a market in the hills

'Light Relief 1', silly moments when times were tough

'Light Relief 2', silly moments when times were tough

A very thin mare presented us with a bundle of joy

*An exhausted donkjey, the deep sores
visible all along her backbone*

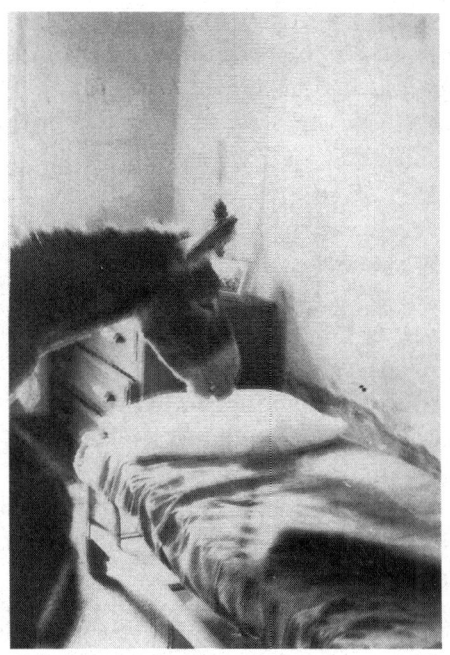

*The same donkey, much improved,
escaped into my bedroom*

Part Two: Algeria 1964-1965

After a glorious three months back on the farm at Ascot, I received a letter from London telling me that I should think hard about someone to work with when I returned to Relizane for another year. I had no ideas whatsoever, and relayed this information to the Major. He rang me to say that someone had approached him with a view to working for the Charity. He felt it might be a good idea for me to meet her to see if she might be suitable for the sort of work we did.   She was a little older than me.

After a couple of phone calls to make arrangements I was collected from the farm by the girl who was called 'Penny'.   She was returning home to Oxfordshire, and had asked me to go to stay for the weekend. She was on her way home from a horse show, and was driving a trailer containing two of her top winning New Forest ponies. Penny had bred them for several years and her stable was well known on the native pony show circuit.

Penny lived with her parents in a lovely old Manor House.   Her parents were so sweet, and listened avidly as I told them about the work and it's many highs and lows. They asked me if I felt that Penny would cope with it all, and I told them I felt she would be fine but added that I felt that she was leaving a lot of her very special life behind; her parents, her ponies and all they meant to her. Penny was adamant that she would be fine.

A few weeks later we were off. This time we were going via Morocco, where the Charity had a big refuge on the outskirts of Rabat, the Capital. I had to take some medicines to the refuge; then we would take the train to Algeria. The Major thought we might like to see the Rabat Refuge as it was one of the largest and more diversified in the animals it treated.

We flew to Gibraltar and crossed the short stretch of the Mediterranean by ferry, arriving at the bustling little port of Tangiers. During her life, Penny had travelled widely and had visited Tangiers before. We took a taxi to the station and then the train to Rabat; we were to be met there by the people who ran the refuge, the Hamers. The train followed the coast down to Rabat, but only a couple of times did we get a glimpse of the Ocean.

The Hamers were there to greet us, and drove us to our hotel where we were to stay for a two days. The hotel was rather shoddy place, on the corner of a street on a hill just off the main street. The concierge, Mohammed, showed us to the room. Adequate, but not at all what we had expected. It was very hot, dark and stuffy.

The Hamers collected us later in the evening and took us to the Refuge. It was right on the coast road, with a stunning view out across the Atlantic Ocean. There were no buildings beyond the refuge, just bare earth, and, in the distance, a large shanty - town. John Hamer blew the car horn at the large gates, which were opened by an imposing man in Djelleba and Tarbush; he smiled broadly at us. "This is M'Barek Ben Bouchaib", said John. "He is the guardian of the refuge, and my right hand man". M'Barek beamed again. He understood no English, but spoke French, (badly), and Arabic. I very quickly learnt that the

Arabic spoken in Morocco was a little different to that spoken in Algeria.

Penny's eyes were darting left and right as she took everything in! The Hamer's didn't live at the refuge; their house was seven miles further along the coast road at a little beach resort called, 'Temara'. There were lots of dogs at this refuge; John explained that some of them were boarded whilst their owners were away on holidays. He said there were a great many French people living in Morocco. There were two horses and two donkeys, all receiving treatment for sores.

The following morning we were collected early in the morning and taken to the refuge. We were greeted us like long lost friends by M'Barek; he was busy cooking up meat and rice for the dogs. We wandered around the animals whilst we waited for John to give M'Barek his orders for the day. In one of the stables we found another man, he was busy painting. He said, in Arabic, that he was Ali Dakhoudouki, and he helped to keep the place in one piece. Ali was very dark skinned, typical of the people of the very Southern, desert areas. He seemed a very nice, gentle, man.

We were whisked off to a daily market to do some treatments to the animals. The Market was held at a place called, ' Khemissett", about 30 miles from Rabat. I showed Penny how to work along the rows, lifting the packs on the animal's backs to check for sores. She seemed to cope very well. However, she was a little distressed that there was nowhere to wash the mess off her hands once we'd finished. I explained that in Relizane we always carried a disinfectant to wipe our hands with, as there were no washing facilities at all.

The day went quickly, and we found ourselves back at the hotel with time to shower and change before being picked up and taken out for a meal. We ate in one of the restaurants in Rabat. It all seemed so very different to what we had in Relizane! We bade the Hamers farewell when they dropped us back at the hotel, as we were taking the early morning train to Algeria.

I liked Rabat enormously; although we were only there for two short days, it had made a great impression on me. I think the proximity of the Ocean played a part in this! It was quite a small, modern city, with sprawling old suburbs. We really only saw the part where the hotel was situated and the drive to the refuge. I wished we could have had longer to look around the city and the surrounding area.

At the hotel, Mohammed the concierge had arranged a taxi to take us to the station. It was a short drive. The station was a very grand building situated in the main street. I got the tickets and we were ushered to our carriage, luckily we were the only ones in it, so it didn't get too hot.

The train stopped several times and people would be waiting on the platform with little stalls selling hard boiled eggs and bread and bottled drinks. It was a long journey and we would pass through customs at the border.

The train sped along, and I could see Penny was as bemused by the sights as I had been on my first visit to North Africa. These biblical scenes always fascinated me.

The train was going through to Algiers, so we were able to stay on it until we arrived at Relizane, which was a blessing. When we stopped at the border, we had to get off and were asked into an office; we were the only foreigners on the train. The Algerian Official looked at us and inspected our passports; he asked me where we were going, and for what purpose?

I explained in French what we were doing and when I told him we were going to Relizane, me for the second time, and Penny for the first, he beamed. "My brother lives there. His name is Boumedienne: he is the Chief of Police". I explained that I had met him when he had granted Milly and I work permits. He asked to see my permit. "This is great work that you do". He said. He stamped our passports and personally escorted us back to the train; shook us by the hand, saluted us, and asked us to greet his brother!

The train continued on its way. Algeria looked so much poorer than Morocco. I put this down to the fact there had been such troubles over the past few years.

We stopped at Oran and then Mostaganem, and very soon we were approaching Relizane. The Station Master met us at Relizane; this time, it was me that he flung his arms around; Penny looked on with alarm! He swept us along the platform and out to the taxi rank. Our usual driver was there, and he seemed very happy that I had returned, he drove us to the house, along familiar streets and we were dropped right at the gate. Penny waited whilst I collected the key from a delighted Mohammed. He told me that there had been many, many callers at the gate. I felt a little sad at this news as it meant that many sick animals had been neglected.

Penny took a long, hard look around the old house. I had warned her it was very basic, but she seemed taken aback at just how basic things were. We had only been back for a short time when the first knock came at the gate. It was one of the local carters. He had come to see us and said he would pass the word that we were back.

In the morning, we ate our breakfast and then walked down to collect Watha from the fattening yard. He looked magnificent; Wicked Uncle beamed as he walked him out of the pen. I thanked him and paid him the rest of the money that Milly had agreed for his safe return.

He walked straight back into the house as if he'd never been away.

As we walked back through the streets to the house, I could hear people asking who the new lady, (Penny) was, and being told that she was the new, 'Donkey Doctor', as we had become known. It was lovely to be welcomed back by so many of the carters and the people in the street. Penny was amazed at the way we were being greeted.

Within no time at all, the old house was full of animals, and life soon got into a swing. I was very pleased to see that Penny was really taking to the work. She got very frustrated that her French was not understood; I explained that she would very quickly pick up enough Arabic to get by with... and she did.

We resumed the normal day to day running of the place; and dealt with the many door callers; treating large numbers of animals each day. I also began the trips to the markets and the work at the Fondouks. Penny came with me at first until we both felt that she could cope by herself.

We quickly bought ourselves three new 'bank' donkeys, again we asked Mohammed to make the purchases for us. The donkeys were soon put to work helping the owners of sick donkeys that would stay with us for treatment.

Penny seemed to be coping well with the work, but she was inclined to get very anxious about certain things. She didn't like to be left alone in the house for too long, nor did she relish the thought of going off alone to treat an animal away from the town. Occasionally her frustrations would boil over and she would erupt! Things calmed down after a short while.

I found this quite hard to cope with. I have always been very happy to be alone, and working away from the house posed no worries to me. I really enjoyed going off in a battered old taxi, along with the owner of animal that was too sick to make it to the house.

This didn't happen very often, and the owners didn't always tell you the full story! One day, I went off in a taxi, the owner said his cow was in labour, only to find the animal owner's wife in labour and having problems! On that particular trip I was able to help, but I had absolutely no training to cover such things! The man told me that it was his wife; I wouldn't have gone to help.

Late one evening there was frantic knocking on the gate and a man that I'd seen in town before was there. He was very agitated as his cow was calving, and was having dreadful problems. He said he would find a taxi to take me, 'to the mountains'. The mountains meant anywhere in the distant hills. I got my kit together and he arrived in a taxi with two other men. I had seen them all before. Penny told me to be careful! Taxi's tended to be large and very old, tied up with bit of wire where needed. They cost little to hire, but if you could fill the taxi, it was very cheap indeed. The taxis tended to have no suspension, and few, if any proper seats! I sat in the front and the men piled into the back.

The taxi drove some miles out of town and then the road began to climb steadily. There was a lovely full moon. The hill was very steep, and we drove on for a considerable time when the taxi stopped. I was ushered out by the men to find that we were in the middle of no-where! The cow's owner went to the edge of the road where it fell away into a steep valley and he cupped his hands and shouted across the valley. He did this twice, when another shout came back at us. In the moonlight I could just make out a small building on the top of the steep hill across the valley. Words were exchanged, and I heard the cow's owner mention the word, "Mule".

There was a lot of shouting back and forth and suddenly I could just make out two men and a mule going down, from the building to the bottom of the valley. Then, eventually came up the steep slope towards us. Greetings were exchanged, and I was asked to get onto the mule! The cow's owner gave me a leg – up; we then set off back down the slope and up the other side! I was astride the mule on a blanket, and on the ascent I had my arms locked around her neck to stop me slipping off backwards! I had ridden many horses, but never a mule, but she was so sure footed that I felt quite at ease.

Finally we arrived and several women came out and greeted me. I was shown into a small building where there was a cow, clearly in some trouble.
I asked for some hot water and some soap... or oil, just incase they had no soap.

One of the women scuttled off and quickly returned with a bowl of hot water and some soap.

I soaped my arm and popped it into the back end of the cow. I could feel the calf and I could feel that one of its legs was in a very awkward position. It was some time before I was able to turn the calf into a position to get it out. All this took place to a series of gasps and lots of chatter from the men. I withdrew my arm and asked for a length of rope... the cow's owner went to a corner of the shed and came back with a piece of rope that was perfect for the job. The cow was very tired and I feared we might lose her... I hated to think how long she had been straining and trying to give birth, and what they had already done to her.

I put my arm in again and managed to place a loop of rope around her calf's front feet. I asked the owner to pull steadily on the rope and to stop at once if I told him to stop. He pulled, the cow bellowed and strained and I felt the calf move; we repeated this, keeping tension on the rope, and slowly, slowly, the calf was pulled nearly out.

The cow gave one huge heave, and the calf was born. Quickly I wiped the mucous from its mouth and nostrils, made sure it was breathing and then detached the ropes from its feet. The calf was fine, but the cow was very still. I pulled the calf over to her and she licked it. The poor old girl was exhausted, but the mother instinct was so strong that she was determined to see her calf was all right. She clambered to her feet and the young calf was quick to lock onto a teat and take the all-important first sucks of her mum's rich milk.

The men were all smiling and the cow's owner was ecstatic! He hugged me! I asked for more water and washed all the blood and slime off me. I asked for some water for the cow, and I gave her an antibiotic injection and some salts to help her pick up a little after her ordeal.

I was taken to the main building and we drank mint tea and had some bread and honey. Before I left I went to see the cow and to my great surprise and relief, she was still on her feet and the calf was suckling. I asked the owner to offer the cow a drink, he ran off and returned with an old bucket, the cow drank it all. It was time to go home.

The return journey was the same; I was on the mule, and the men plus the taxi driver, walked behind. We got back to the taxi across the valley. The moon was huge! I finally got home at 1.30am. Penny was still up and very anxious that I'd been so long! She was worried for my safety... I hadn't given it a thought!

I slept very well that night, but was woken very early by someone banging on the gate. It was the cow's owner; he had a large bag of eggs, and some freshly baked bread and a whole cartload of alfalfa for the animals! Bless him, he must have got his wife to bake the bread whilst he cut the alfalfa and loaded up his cart as soon as he'd got home last night! He was so grateful. He said the cow was fine and the calf, a heifer, was a good calf. Little things like that made everything so worthwhile!

A letter arrived from Milly. She seemed to be enjoying her new job but was missing Watha. She said she would try to arrange a way to get him to Greece! I jokingly replied that Wicked Uncle had offered him a lift to France on one of his shipments of horses for slaughter.

A couple of weeks passed and Milly wrote again. It seemed that because Algeria had been so volatile that it would be impossible to ship him out to Greece or even to England. Correspondence carried on and it eventually seemed that the only was for Watha to leave Algeria would be with Wicked Uncle.

I was asked by Milly to approach him and to ask if it would be at all possible to get the horse to France? From there, the passage to Greece was simple. I saw Wicked Uncle and his brother in the street and asked them to visit the house when they had time. A short time later, they were at the gate. I asked them in and we stood in the barn with Watha and the other the horses and donkeys.

I jotted their minds that they had mentioned the possibility of getting Watha to France, and they immediately said it would be possible. I asked how much they would charge and they gave me a price... one that I felt was very reasonable.

Then I asked if I could go with him: They were quite stunned by this, but said they would ask. They said that if, I was able to go, and I would have to travel in the lorry. I said that would be fine. They said they could speak to their agent in Algiers to get me a passage on the boat. It was left like that as I had to let Milly know the outcome of the conversation.

It was some time later, after several letters to check details that Milly agreed that this course of action would have to be taken. I contacted the Major in London and told him that I had the chance to go on a horse boat to France, and would be able to write a report if he, or anyone else would be interested! He agreed to this.

I told Penny what was going to happen, and spoke again to Wicked Uncle and his brother. We would travel by road to Algiers. The horses would stay the night in their agent's stables; I would stay in a hotel with them overnight. That worried me somewhat!

The following day, the horses would be walked a short distance to the docks to board the boat to Marseilles. Once there, the horses for slaughter would go into lairage for the night, and Watha would go to another yard owned by a friend of theirs! He would be collected by Milly the following day and then driven to Greece by horsebox. If you said it quickly it didn't sound too awful, but it sounded full of pitfalls!

Milly agreed and we fixed for Watha to go with the next shipment that was to be in a fortnight's time. Frantic correspondence with Milly took place, including telegrams!

The time went very quickly, and the day before we were due to go Wicked Uncle and his brother came up for the first payment for the bookings of the boat and hotels, etc. They said they would be at the house at 04.30am, and that Watha would be walked down to their yard to be loaded. I sent a telegram to Milly to let her know that I would be seeing her in Marseilles in 48hours time!

I hardly slept that night. I packed some things into a small bag; I would only be gone two nights. I took my 'Oran Clothes' to wear at Marseilles. I was up and ready and ate breakfast with Penny. She was in a tizzy about being left for two nights, and I think she was worried incase anything went wrong! I was too, but I didn't say anything incase it upset her further.

The two men came and I led Watha off for the great adventure!

The lorry was in the process of being loaded when we arrived. There were sixteen horses in each of three lorries. Watha would be at the back of the third lorry. He loaded easily as the lorry had backed into a dip and there was no need to jump up onto the lorry in the way that had injured him so badly before.

We set off. I was in the cab with Wicked Uncle, his brother and the driver.

It was a five-hour journey and we didn't stop at all. The horses travelled well which was a relief to me. Finally we arrived on the outskirts of Algiers. It was a large but shabby city. The lorry drove on and eventually we saw the sea; the yard was very close to the docks. It was a particularly seedy looking area!

The horses were unloaded, watered and fed. Watha took it all in his stride. Once they were settled, Wicked Uncle and his brother called me to go to the hotel.

It was a dirty place, with no lobby. A man, presumably the owner, came out and greeted us: he leered at me. I was told I was in room 7. Nothing was said about food. The room was tiny and dirty; there was a small bed. A cracked washbasin and a European toilet in the corner! Surprisingly, the plumbing worked.

There was no lock on the door, so the key was unnecessary, I propped the door shut by placing the chair under the handle. It was nearly 10.00pm, so I went to bed. About midnight there was a knock at the door. It was the owner and he wanted to know if I was all right. He said if I let him in he would give me some food. I told him to go away! He returned again later, and got a very curt reply.

I was up at 4.00am having hardly slept and with a very real sense that I might be safer up and dressed!

Wicked Uncle and brother took me to a scruffy roadside café where we had coffee and bread and jam; I was very hungry! Then we left for the stables.
It was a hive of activity. Horses were being fed and then having halters put on and, when they were all ready, they were walked down to the boat. I had Watha and two others and they all went very quietly down the empty streets to the dockyard. It was quite eerie as none of the horses were shod; there was a patter, rather than a clatter of hooves.

We all walked through the dockyard gates and along a quay where a large ship was waiting, a trail of smoke was drifting up from her funnel. The horses amazed me, they were totally un-phased by the huge cranes that were loading cargo into the hold.

The 'Danielle V' was a nice white ship and flew the French flag. The horses were coaxed up a covered gangway and then down a ramp into the bowels of the ship. They were in pens, with deep straw and plenty of hay. The French sailors took great care of them. I was quite bemused to see the disdain with the way the Frenchmen treated Wicked Uncle and his brother. They were led off to where they would spend the time of the voyage.

By contrast, I was taken to the ship's medical room, where I was to sleep overnight. There was a comfortable bed and a bathroom! Luxury! One of the ship's officers knocked on the door and invited me to lunch and dinner in the wardroom. I thanked him. He said I could walk around the ship and I asked if I could see the horses. He said when I was ready to do that I was to ask a member of the crew to go with me for safety, as it meant going down steep steps.

The ship left Algiers about 10.00am, and I watched as we slowly left the harbour. From the sea, Algiers looked very beautiful. It must have been more so in former days.

The Mediterranean was surprisingly rough; I found a crew- member and asked to see the horses; he led me down into the hold and I was relieved to see all the horses eating and looking happy and settled. Watha put his lovely head onto my shoulder; he was fine. Wicked Uncle and his brother were down there, and I got the impression that they had slept there! The French sailor steered me well clear of them.

I had soup and bread and cheese for lunch. The Officers were a jolly lot; the Captain explained that this ship went to many ports in the Mediterranean and carried many different cargoes. After lunch I went to my cabin and slept like a log; when I woke I felt very seasick! It was almost time for dinner. I went along to the wardroom and the Captain could see I was unwell. "We have the very thing for you." He said. "Ail O Lit", he explained that it was garlic in a sauce and very good for the 'Mal de Mer.' I'm not fond of garlic, but I did have some and it was fine. To my surprise, and relief, the seasickness abated!

Early next day the ship entered the port of Marseilles. The final phase of the trip was beginning! We tied up on a dock with some large black sheds alongside. The horses were unloaded and led into the sheds. I said my goodbyes to the Captain and crew, and it was only then that I saw Wicked Uncle and his brother; they had clearly not had a good passage. They were going back on the ship to Algiers but had to deal with the paperwork first.

I went into the sheds, the horses were in large pens, again being fed and watered by Frenchmen. I felt so sad for them, but their handling throughout had been done with great gentleness. I was handed Watha and shown a large door at the end of the shed; I led him away, Wicked Uncle and his brother shook hands and said they would be at the house as soon as I got home for their money. I thanked them.

The heavy door was opened for me and I led Watha out onto French Soil and there, beaming like a Cheshire cat was Milly! It was such a relief to see her! We took Watha to a waiting horsebox and he was driven off to spend a night with a friend of Milly's before setting off, by road to Greece the next day.

Milly and I went off to the centre of Marseilles where she had a room booked in a lovely hotel. We sat in her room, drinking tea, whilst I told her all about the adventure. Later, we went out to find a café for some supper and had a celebratory glass of wine.

The following morning, I saw Milly briefly before I took a taxi to the airport for a short flight to Algiers. I flew in an old Dakota that rattled ominously!

I then took the train to Relizane and enjoyed the walk back to the house. It had been such an Adventure.

Penny greeted me with open arms and told me how very worried she'd been! We sat for ages while I related every last detail of the trip to her. It seemed that all had been well and that there had been no difficult cases in my absence.

The following morning, Wicked Uncle and his brother came to claim the rest of their money. Milly had put it into an envelope and added some more as things had gone so well! They left very happy.

I spent the next couple of days working and writing my report for the Major. It was the first report of it's kind ever written. I wrote of how well the horses had been handled by the crew when loading in Algiers, and that they have travelled very well, despite the rough crossing. When he received it, the Major wrote to say he was delighted with it and thanked me for undertaking the task. I never did tell him that Watha was on that ship! There was a welcome letter from Milly to say that Watha was safely home in Greece with her, and that she was riding him a lot. Dear Watha, we missed him for a long time after his departure.

Life in Relizane continued apace. We had a visit from the Regional Veterinary inspector, and he greeted me like a long, lost friend. He took us to the little café in the town, and, as had happened before, we had really good wine with our lunch. I asked him if they kept it for him, as it didn't seem to be available at other times. He laughed and called the owner to the table. There was a long conversation in Arabic, and the vet and the owner shook hands. "Any time you want to buy wine, you can do so here; just bring a shopping bag, and don't tell anyone"! We thanked him and the owner for that information, and took up the offer at Christmas time.

We passed a jolly Christmas and there were hardly any callers at the gate, so we were able to enjoy a quiet day listening to the radio. We went down to the Catholic Cathedral for a Carol Service, and although it was all in French, we knew most of the carols and sang lustily along in English. No-one seemed to mind. The congregation was tiny; just us, the Spanish family from the patisserie; the hotel owner and a group of Nuns from the Convent.

We had a visit from the Major in the springtime and that passed well. More or less following the pattern of the previous year. He did, however have a proposition for us. Penny had already said that she would only want to do one year in Relizane, or anywhere else; she wanted to return to her New Forest Ponies. I, on the other hand was happy to stay on.

The Major said that he would like me to go to work in Rabat in Morocco! I was over the moon at this suggestion! It seemed the Hamers were leaving, and the refuge needed a new manager. He asked me to find someone to work with; someone I knew well. This was to happen in September this year. The Relizane refuge was not closing, but would be empty for a while until a new person was found. He added that a husband and wife team might work.

Whoever took over a Relizane would need to be made of stern stuff, as it was not a place that everyone would wish to live. I hoped the Major would come to a good decision, and appoint people who would care as much for the work as we had. The Major left Relizane, once again, full of praise for the way things were going. He thanked Penny for all she'd done, and then shook my hand and said he would see me in London!

We would be there until then end of June, so we made plans to continue the work, and then to wind down the number of in-patients as the time to leave approached. Penny seemed to be very happy at the prospect of going home. For me, it was mixed feelings. I had loved Relizane. However, I was going back to Ascot until September and then I was off to pastures new in Morocco. I was hugely excited at this news!

We took in a little donkey that was badly in need of some TLC. She had fallen in the street whilst heavily laden with bags of cement; she was quite badly cut on her head. We were able to dress the wounds, and told her owner that she was to stay until she had fully recovered; we were able to lend him one of the bank donkeys, but only on the condition that he didn't overload him. The man promised faithfully that he would take huge care of our donkey. As soon as he had gone, we trimmed her feet as they were in a very neglected state; this was very common, and our set of farrier's tools were in constant use.

Quite early one morning there was a loud commotion outside, and a fire engine had drawn up by our gate. I went out quickly, not knowing what was wrong; the four firemen took a box out of the back of the tender and, I could see by there actions, that whatever was in the box was dangerous. I went back and got my long gloves. "Madame, c'est La Rage". *Rabies!* The crowd that had gathered stepped back and were jabbering and yelling! Rabies was endemic and every year claimed the lives of animals and humans. They knew only too well the consequences of getting bitten.

Luckily, the box was strong, and we were able to tip the cat straight into the Chloroform box and put the poor thing to sleep very quickly. There are two kinds of Rabies, one is the classic that has the wild eyes and foaming mouth, the other is far more sinister as it's not at all obvious what's wrong with the animal... but it will suddenly awake from it's stupor and bite. This was the type the poor little cat had contracted. Thankfully the fireman knew what the signs were. Once the poor creature was dead the firemen left; but not before they had all washed their hands very carefully.

I went over to Mohammed's shop and rang the Regional Veterinary Surgeon to report the fact that the cat was Rabid. He didn't need to confirm this, and as no one had been bitten he gave us the all clear to dispose of the body and that was to be by incineration. We had no means of incinerating the body, so we made a large pile of wood in the yard and put the body onto the fire; when the fire had died down, there was no sign of the cat. That was the only case of Rabies that I had seen so far, and it had really surprised me how quiet and calm this cat had seemed.

We had a rare visitor, 'Spit' the Camel stayed with us for a week whilst we dressed her back. She was too tall to get through the gate and in via the back door, so we got her in via the yard gates, and once in the yard, she could easily walk into the hall via the high doors. She was a dear, but rather noisy. She gurgled and moaned all day, but was sweet natured. The owner showed us how to make her sit down, and twice a day; we were to be seen coaxing her with the "Hutt! Hutt! Hutt', that his owner had used whilst tapping her gently on the foreleg. Once down it was a simple matter to treat her back.

All the camels we met were Dromedaries, (one hump). They worked as hard as the horses and donkeys. We didn't see very many in Relizane, but they were widely used out in the countryside. When visiting the outlying markets we would often treat camels. I thought they were wonderful creatures.

I was walking home from a day in the fondouks one afternoon, and I saw a lovely Arab saddle for sale in the corn shop. It had obviously come straight off a horse It was a genuine one, with a wooden frame that sat on several layers of felt; the wooden frame was covered with taut hide, and a loose red leather cover, shaped to the frame was on top. The saddle had a very high pommel and a very high back. It came complete with girths and wonderful stirrups that were very ornamental. I asked the price.

After considerable bargaining, I got it for a song! There was a passing carter who offered to take the saddle back to the house. I jumped on as well. I decided to send the saddle home and the following day I wrapped it securely and Penny and I carried it between us down to the post office. That was my souvenir of Relizane!

Once, towards the end of our time, I was out in the street with a group of animals, when a shout went up from down the dusty street. "Touaregs". It was an extraordinary sight. Five men on camels were riding in; they were very dark skinned and were dressed in robes of intense blue. They were magnificent! The people in the street seemed to be in awe of them! They rode up to our gate and stopped.

The owners of the animals we had been treating stood back, and bowed, almost with reverence as one of the men walked across to me. He was much taller than the usual Algerian and had a very upright bearing. He spoke in Arabic and greeted me. I returned the greeting. He explained that they were nomads and had come a long way as they had heard that we were in Relizane. He asked if I would go with them to their encampment about 5 miles away. He told me that he had a mare that was very ill.

I shouted for Penny and told her that we would both go. Mohammed at the shop had found a battered old taxi, and the man said he would come with us in the taxi, and that his men would lead his camel back to the camp. As I understood, the mare had colic, and

they had tried all sorts of medicines to no avail. I
packed a bag with everything I thought we might
need. Off we went.

We saw the tented camp long before we actually
arrived. It was in a dip in the hills and there were
palm trees and some greenery, so that meant there
was water there. The tents were large, made of a goat
hair in a mixture of black and greys, held up by a
series of poles.

There were women at the camp and we fascinated
them! The man led us to the mare that was clearly in
great distress. I feared that she might have twisted
her gut, in which case there was no hope. I examined
her and decided that there was some hope. We
decided first to perform a 'back rake', hoping to be
able to remove some fecal matter by hand. I asked
for water and soap; the man barked an order at a
woman who returned with a bucket filled with hot
water, and some soap; I covered my arm with wet
soap and inserted it into the mare's rectum; she
strained momentarily, and my arm slipped in gently. I
could feel a massive blockage, and after a lot of
manipulation, I was able to break up what felt like a
brick! It was in fact compressed food that, due to
lack of water had solidified. I asked Penny to pour
some water in, using the tube and funnel we had
brought; this helped.

After what seemed to be an age, I had raked out a
considerable quantity of muck. The mare stood, she
was trembling and looked very 'tucked up', but after
she'd walked round led by the tall man, she started to
relax; he went on walking her, and to our huge relief,
passed a motion, as hard as rocks, then another and
another. She sighed and looked much easier. I asked

for a rug to throw over her; within a moment, a goat hair rug was brought, and I popped it over her back. She had stopped shivering.

I surprised the owner by asking for a bucket of warm tea, with plenty of sugar mixed in; he smiled as the mare gulped it down! I told him to keep walking her for an hour, and he gave that task to a young lad.

I think the men were quite impressed at our efforts! We were ushered into a large tent and two cushions were placed for us to sit on. Tea was brought; it was mint tea, and this was poured with great ceremony by the man who had called on us was obviously the 'Chief' of this group of Touaregs.

He said that he and his family would be forever grateful to us for saving his best mare. He asked us to stay for a feast that was, even now, being prepared for us. Little did we realize, but a goat had been slaughtered in our honour, and was being cooked. There was a circle of men, magnificent in their blue robes and white tarbushes.

We are roast goat and couscous with vegetables; as always eating with our right hands; forming little balls of couscous and eating them; it was delicious.

The women were constantly filling and re-filling mugs with fresh goats milk. To this day, not a taste I am fond of! They treated us like royalty, but I felt it was us that were in the presence of some remarkable people with a long heritage.

When we left, all the women stood inside the tent and waved goodbye. The men walked with us to the taxi and as we got into it, each of them shook us warmly by the hand. I felt we had made some fine friends that we would probably never see again. How privileged we had been to be invited into their home and have a glimpse of these wonderful people

It was evening time when we got home, luckily there were no animals waiting for treatments, so we were able to get a quick cup of tea before we set about evening stables, feeding and watering the animals and making sure they were all comfortable for the night. We ate a simple supper and sat chatting about the day we had spent with the Touaregs. Something I will never forget.

It was Penny's turn to do the town Fondouks the next day. It was my turn to stay at home and clean in between callers at the gate. By the time she returned, all the animals would be done for the night and I planned to have a casserole cooking in the oven for her return.

Penny set off about 5.00am. She went to the first fondouk where she found a mule badly in need of our help and some rest; it had a very deep sore along the backbone, parts of which had become infected where flies had entered the sores. She arrived back with the mule and it's owner. We explained that the Mule would have to stop with us, but the owner was adamant that it had to go with him; he was getting very angry.

As usual, when we were in the street outside the house, a crowd gathered; to our surprise, the crowd began to shout at the man who was shouting at us! They shamed him into leaving the mule and pointed out the sores on her backs. There was much, "Tut Tutting", they explained that we would get the mule better; the man capitulated, and the mule and the man, and the crowd all entered the gate and followed us into the hall. Many of the crowd had never been inside before and they were clearly impressed with what they saw; I could hear them saying that the straw beds were excellent and they marveled at the supply of water and food.

Everyone went off happy. We promised that we would try to get the mule back to him as soon as possible, but did warn him that it might be a while as her sores were so deep. Penny returned to her work in the fondouks. The mule's owner came to visit every day, and brought food for the mule and eggs for us.

The one thing that had come out of it all was our amazement of the way the crowd had stood up for us. This was very heartening!

By the time I finally had the mule treated and fed and watered it was almost lunchtime, so I had sandwiches and then a short siesta. Penny returned about 4.00pm, hot and dusty and went for a shower under the hosepipe. We ate the casserole and discussed the day and made plans for tomorrow, along with a few thoughts about going home.

One morning, very early there was loud banging on the gate; it was two of the women from the house opposite. They explained that Algeria was at war! We had no idea, and found out later that the war had been going on for some time. It was a border dispute over the southern Sahara with Morocco; this flared up from time to time, but this time it had turned very nasty.

The two women explained to us that, in the event of soldiers coming to the town, we were to go to them and they would dress us in their clothes and we would be safe. We thanked them profusely, but afterwards decided that we might be better to be seen as British! But how sweet of them! Luckily, the war fizzled out quite quickly!

Life continued apace and we felt we would never be able to wind down enough to be able to pack up and, 'close the shop'. But things did slow down and we were able to turn our minds to packing and also telling everyone that the refuge would be closed until new people arrived to take over, probably in September.

The house was easy, as I'd done it before; we closed the shutters and taped all the window edges up to try to keep the sand out of the place. We told Mohammed what was happening, and though he understood, he seemed very sad at the news.

Luckily on the last week were able to discharge the remaining animals and by great fortune, there were no new ones needing to come in for treatment. We were able to treat everything in the street. Many of the owners were genuinely sorry that we were going. One of them begging us to stay, even going so far as to offer to marry us, (both!). Needless to say, this ploy fell on deaf ears!

I wrote out a huge list of things that I felt might help the new people when they took over. Where to find feed for the horses and so forth.

Penny did the final trip to the bank in Oran and closed the account; whilst there she purchased our tickets from the Air France office; we would leave on June 19th. We had a date to work to and this made things easier. We decided to take the early train to Oran on the day, rather than stay in a hotel in Oran... once bitten!

Tearful Goodbyes were said to Mohammed and his family, and a few of the carters who had gathered. We took the decision to travel to the station on one of the carts; our luggage safely loaded, I locked the house up and, for the last time, I locked the gate and gave the key to Mohammed, who, by then was beside himself with sorrow!

The carter took us to the station door and the stationmaster met us and said he would help us to the platform. We offered to pay the carter, but he threw his arms around us both and wished us good luck. He was soon driving off again, and the stationmaster was fussing about getting our bags loaded onto a trolley by a porter.

The train drew in and we were ushered into our carriage; the stationmaster bade us a safe journey and saluted as the train drew away from Relizane. I felt very sorry to leave.

Three hours later we reached Oran and took a taxi to the Air France Office where we were able to get the shuttle bus to the airport. Once aboard, the plane took off and as we flew over the land and then out across the Mediterranean, I was suddenly quite overcome with emotion. This was so final. But I knew that Morocco would be a very different kind of challenge.

There is a post -script to the story of Watha. Some years later, when working back at the farm in Ascot, I went to London with Milly's sister, Dolly. She drove a trailer as we were off to London's East India Docks to collect a most precious cargo. Watha and Milly were due to dock on the MS. Leo. Watha was coming to England! He was such a wonderful, charmed horse.
That is another story...

Part Two: Photographs

Relizane in its heyday, circa 1950

Relizane in 1963, shabby and poor

The house

Patiently waiting for dressings

A fondouk emptying at the end of market day

Loading up for the long journey home

Touaregs

A dreadful combination for ploughing. The poor horse struggles to keep up and gets very rubbed by the harness

A horse with a serious infection on the front of his shoulder

A woman makes tea in one of the villages

This little donkey is taking home reeds for the roof

Part Three: Morocco

The summer holiday was spent working at Ascot once again with time also spent in Hampshire visiting parents and family, but September was fast approaching.

I was going to Rabat in Morocco. This time, my co-worker was to be Carol, a girl I had known since I was 5 years old. This time I knew we would get on well together.

Carol had also had a good grounding in horses, and she was keen to join me in the new adventure. She went up to London to meet the Major. He had said that as long as I felt she would be able to cope with the work that he was quite happy to send us both out.

I was longing to go back to Rabat. My one-day spent there the previous year had left a lasting impression. I could picture the refuge, and had plans in my head of a few changed that might be possible. It had been one whirlwind of a day, but the place had been on my mind ever since.

Carol and I flew from Heathrow, with our parents there to see us off. My parents were hardened to the fact that I had wanderlust; Carol's parents only knew what Carol had told her, and what I had filled them in with about Rabat and the work.

It was September. We flew via Paris to Rabat. As we came in to land the plane circled over the city and it looked just like twinkling fairy lights, this was going to be our home! When we landed it was dark; we could see little of the airport except for the fact that it was quite small.

Once inside the buildings, we were able to collect our suitcases and then went out to find a taxi. We were going to stay at the rather scruffy little Hotel that we had used last year, that would be fine until we found somewhere to live; and the cheap hotel seemed as good as anywhere to stay whilst we settled in.

The owner, Mohammed, greeted me like a long, lost friend and showed us up to our room that was to be home for the next two months. We went to bed as we'd been travelling for most of the day. It was very warm, even with the window wide open. Very early in the morning I woke to the sound of the Muezzin's call. It is such a haunting sound as it is repeated all over the city. Carole woke and I explained what all the noise was. She peered out of the window and watched the men walking to prayer.

We had asked Mohammed for our breakfast at 6.00am, and it arrived bang on time. Fresh croissants, jam, butter, and strong coffee. I asked where the croissants came from and he told me that they were from the little market nearby. Whilst we ate, we discussed what we would do with our first day. I had a map of the City and we studied it to get some landmarks.

The hotel was a short walk from the huge, wide main street. But behind the hotel, a short way away was the little market place that Mohammed had told us about. That would be our first place to visit. It was a bustling little place with stalls that sold lovely French bread and pies; a little shop that sold everything possible, and several meat and vegetable stalls. We could have bought anything we might need there.

We bought bread and some nice cheese and butter and some tomatoes for our lunch and then turned around and walked down to the main street. We were quite near to the magnificent railway station. The road was very wide with lovely gardens in the middle. We walked down, passing the Royal Air Maroc office, and several expensive looking shops. I noticed that we had already picked up a couple of, 'slick dicks!' I explained to Carole that they were just a part of life.
A little further down was the imposing Hotel Balima, with its terrace right alongside the pavement. People were sitting at tables under Orange trees; they were drinking coffee and juices and just watching the world go by.

We continued right down to the bottom of the street, taking note of a large Chemists shop, the very imposing Post Office and even a Chinese Restaurant! This was far removed from Relizane. We came to a very busy road, with vehicles and people everywhere. Opposite was a huge, long, low market building. We braved the traffic to go and look. This was clearly where the people went to shop for meat and groceries. There were little stalls selling goat meat and some selling camel meat, along with beef and mutton. The vegetable stalls were full to overflowing with good and very cheap produce.

We noticed a bus station nearby. Not the buses that ran about the city, full to the brim with people; these were much smarter looking coaches. They might prove useful!

Having walked all the way down, we decided to walk back up by another very smart street. There were some lovely, expensive looking shops and restaurants. We found a left turn and followed this a very short way and found ourselves outside a big theatre! The road opened onto a large square. In the middle were lovely gardens, and around the outside were some nice cafes and bars. It was quite hot, so we stopped at one and had a coffee, and then went to the centre of the square to have our picnic.

We decided to take a 'Petit Taxi' to the Refuge. These were parked in ranks along the side of the pavement. We climbed into one with the number 227 on its luggage rack. The driver spoke French and I asked him to take us to Akkari. He seemed surprised. "Are you sure you mean Akkari Madame?" he asked in French.

I explained that we wanted to go to the SPANA Refuge. He looked blank! I said, 'Boulevard De l'Ocean", and he still looked perplexed. "Madame, it is a very long road, the road ends in Akkari, and that is not a place where tourists went". I told him to get us to Akkari where we would be working at the SPANA Refuge. He said that he would do his very best to find the refuge, and we set off. I was watching to see which way he took us, and Carol was looking left and right, trying to take in all the sights, sounds and smells of this exciting place.

The traffic seemed to come from every direction, but it all kept moving. There were lots of car horns angrily sounding and policemen on rostrums at every junction. We soon left the big, smart white buildings behind us and were suddenly in the sort of area that bore some resemblance to Relizane. There were donkeys and horses pulling carts, many people on bicycles and lots of really battered old cars and lorries. The driver told us that we had arrived at Akkari. All I could remember was the refuge was right on the coast. I told the driver this information and he turned up a little street near a garage. Ahead of us was a large building. He told us it was the Abattoir. We assured him that we weren't going to work there! We swung right just in front of the building and drove down the road alongside it; suddenly there was the sea. The vast expanse of the Atlantic spread before us. I felt we were very close. The driver turned left and there was the Refuge, a long white walled building; the very last one, right on the edge of the City. This was it!

We pulled off the road onto a sandy area and parked in front of the big but shabby blue wooden gates. I got out and rang the bell. A voice from within asked who it was, and I replied in Arabic. The gate was thrown open and M'Barek threw his arms around me! He was beaming as he helped Carol from the taxi; he greeted her. I asked the taxi driver if he would wait for a while.

M'Barek closed the gate and called his wife and family out to meet us; he introduced them one by one. His wife, Yamina; she was young and very pretty. His oldest son, aged 8 whose name was Mohammed; then the two daughters, Rachida aged 7 and Aziza who was 5... they were all very shy! M'Barek called me, 'Mademoiselle Twiss', and he just couldn't get his tongue around Lewis.

We were invited to tea, and were ushered into an office, and then through a hole in the wall to their home. They all lived, ate and slept in this one room!

We sat and drank Mint Tea. This was a first for Carol and she liked it. Mint tea was always served very hot and very sweet. I told M'Barek that we would be coming to work at the refuge the next day and he seemed pleased at this idea. He then gave us a tour of the refuge.

We went back into the office. There was a desk, and a cupboard full of various medicines and dressings and a large sink with a cold-water tap.
There was a huge window, and outside the window was an arrangement of concrete bars for safety. These were essential protection, but it did give a wonderful view of the Ocean.

We then walked outside and along the corridor outside passing pens with dogs in them. These were the boarding dogs; I noticed there were only 3 dogs. Then on to what we had been led to believe was an 'Operating Theatre'. Someone had clearly conned SPANA, as the only item in this very ordinary stable was a shelf! I understood this had cost £3000! I made a note to report this to the Major when I wrote.

There was one more stable and then a series of yards with shelter. These were yards for horses and donkeys. In one of them was a huge motor scooter! That was for us to visit the village markets! The yards formed a square in the centre of the refuge. The last three yards were open to the elements; M'Barek said these were the dog runs. I made a mental note to ask for funding to provide some shelter from the sun in these runs. On the other side of the gateway was a small room that had a partition in it with straw one side, and hay the other. Next to that were the pens of strays; there were 3 dogs here too. I noted there was a very old toilet of the French sort, two tiles and a hole that would have to change!

M'Barek showed me the little kitchen where he cooked the meat and rice for the dogs. It was spotlessly clean. I asked where Ali was and he told me that it was his day off. I said I would look forward to seeing him tomorrow. I told M'Barek that we would be there at 5.00am.

We set off back to the hotel, my head was buzzing with ideas! The taxi driver was very chatty on the way home, he asked what work we would be doing and seemed quite impressed. He said his name was Mohammed. When we got to the hotel, I paid him and asked us if he would be able to take us out to Akkari in the morning; he was overjoyed! Carol was very excited at the prospect of working at the refuge, and getting to know people. She also needed to pick up some basic French and Arabic quickly. I told her that it would just 'happen', and not to worry about it.

The next day we had breakfast at 6.00am, and then went to the little market for some food for lunch. When we got back to the hotel, there was taxi 227 and Mohammed beaming at us as we walked towards him. He greeted us in a mixture of French and Arabic and off we went. This time, we went a different way, leaving Rabat by the imposing gate known as, 'Bab–El-Had', very close to the King's Palace. We ended up in Akkari at the little garage and turned up the little road, there were a few tiny shops, and we passed by the abattoir once again.

Mohammed the taxi driver dropped us and offered to pick us up again. He had clearly nominated himself to be our very own driver! We asked him to come at 5.00pm. We were finally here and ready to work.

Carol had taken in all the strange sights and sounds and seemed quite happy. It was still lovely and warm, and we had the wonderful sea to look at! The refuge stood on the top of quite a steep granite cliff. There were only rocks below. The drain outlets from the Abattoir was about a hundred yards away and the water was always red there; every day fishermen would sit up on the rocks by the outfall, catching huge fish for their families.

We met Ali, a charming man; he introduced himself as, 'Dakhoudoki Ali'. He spoke only Arabic, but he had such an expressive face it was not difficult for Carol to get the gist of what he was saying.

I thought it would be a few days before the word got round that we were here, but I was so wrong! Within a few minutes of arriving there was a loud knocking on the gate. M'Barek shouted to find out who it was, and a voice replied that he had a sick horse. The horse was soon on the graveled area inside the gate. The carter showed us a wound on the horse's foreleg; it was a minor wound, so between us we cleaned it up and dressed it. The owner went off very happy and promised he would come back in a few days for us to make sure the wound was healing. Throughout the morning we had callers, and managed to patch them all up and send them on their way.

At lunchtime, Ali went home for a break and M'Barek went to his room, presumably to sleep. Carol and I sat outside on a rock, looking across the Ocean as we ate our picnic. I said we would try out the scooter later, after lunch and maybe go for a ride along the coast. The best laid plans!

We went to have a look at the scooter. It was a huge Harley Davison! It was definitely a scooter as opposed to a motorbike, but she was a big beast! I had a license to drive a scooter, so I wheeled it down to the gate. M'Barek had come out to watch us. He told us that it hadn't been used for about 5 years as the last people at the refuge had a car. I couldn't find the pedal to kick start it; M'Barek said that it used to start with a key, and went off to the office to find it.

I got on and turned the key; the engine roared into life... Roar being the best way to describe it! The exhaust belched smoke until the engine had warmed up. I shouted to Carol to jump on the back and once she was settled, I gently opened the throttle by twisting the grip on the handles, very slowly.
The beast leapt forwards and the front end reared up and decanted both of us onto the ground! The momentum carried the scooter forwards until it too came to a halt and fell over. We were all roaring with laughter!

I tried again, and it did move forwards at a sedate pace, and off we went. I hardly dared to change gear or go faster for fear of our lives! It went on, quite sweetly and after several miles we found ourselves at Temara Beach. We thought it wise to turn around there and return whilst we were in one piece. We got back to the refuge and the engine stalled and a cloud of dirty black smoke enveloped us all. It never, ever started again! Ali pushed it down to the little garage, but the mechanic said it was, 'dead'. We left it with him as scrap.

My first letter to the Major told him the saga of the scooter. I also asked if we might put some straw matting on a frame to give shade in the dog exercise pens; he agreed this. I told him about the 'Operating Theatre'.

Ali busied himself painting the big gates, then he started on the buildings; they had just a simple whitewash applied. I imagined the sea would mean having to do this a couple or more times a year. The first week passed so quickly, but we were unprepared for Thursdays! The first Thursday we went to the refuge, there was the most dreadful smell in the air. I asked M'Barek what it was and he told us that every Thursday, the abattoir killed only Camels, and that was the smell! It was really vile, but we just had to carry on. All the other days of the week it was fine... but not Thursdays!

We received a letter from the Major and he had some wonderful news for us. The Charity had been given a Landrover by one of its benefactors, and the Major was going to drive it out to Morocco for us to use. He was clearly very angry about the, 'Operating Theatre' scam, and said he would sort that out from the London end. We were given permission to provide shady areas in the runs for the dogs. We also had permission to get a proper loo. This would make a huge difference.

Weeks passed and we had really settled in, but we both felt it would be much better if we could move out of the hotel and live nearer to the refuge. Now, Carol and I had been in the Girl Guides together, and we both knew how to, 'make do and mend'. We were both growing rather tired of the daily commute to work, but this was put to one side when poor Carol contracted a very virulent stomach bug that laid her low for a couple of days. We put it down to the common bug that many Europeans get on their first trip to North Africa. She recovered and was able to resume normal life.

One morning whilst we were cleaning up the office, I said to her that I had been thinking about us moving. My suggestion was that we moved M'Barek out of his one room, and gave him one entire dog exercise run in which Ali could build a series of rooms. I then said that we could have his room, which led off the office; and that we could sleep in the little brick shed that currently served as a straw and hay shed. It already had a partition, so we could have a side each. Carol thought a while and then smiled. She thought it was the perfect solution.

We thought we would clear out the cupboard in the office, and give the shelves a good wash. M'Barek appeared and he started to clear the shelves, we left him to it and said we'd return when he'd got it all empty. We went out to see to the dogs. All of a sudden there was a shout from the office: we rushed in to find M'Barek armed with a broom yelling and stabbing the broom at something on the floor inside the cupboard. He stooped, and brushed out a dead, pale brown Scorpion! The body was removed, and M'Barek told us that the pale ones were extremely poisonous. We had no idea that there were Scorpions in Morocco.

That evening I wrote to the Major suggesting that we could move into the refuge. I added that this would be a perfect solution as we would always be on hand to deal with callers and problems. Mail to and from the UK took about 3 days each way, and we very soon received a reply from the Major. He expressed concern about the fact that we had no hot water, but he agreed, subject to the fact that we were not to stay there if we felt it was too basic. We were over the Moon.

I had the difficult task of telling M'Barek first. I called him into the office the following morning and told him of the plans. He listened and mulled it all over. He asked if he might have a new dwelling and keep the room next to the office. I explained it was a new dwelling or nothing. He reluctantly agreed, much to my relief. We walked him into the large exercise run and suggested where they might be able to sleep, with a separate kitchen and living room. I could see he was warming to the idea. I asked Ali if he could arrange for whatever he needed to be brought to the refuge by carter, and that he could build it. Luckily building materials were very cheap. Dear Ali, he was very surprised that we wanted to live at the refuge; he considered it far beneath us to do so!

He was also shown where we wanted the new loo, and thought this was quite proper! He said he would paint out the brick shed that was to be our bedroom and put a big lock on the door. The locks and keys were multiplying!

It all happened so quickly. We bought second hand furniture for our 'sitting room', and a gas cooker that would stand on the ledge in the office.

M'Barek seemed pleased with his new home, and more so when we bought him some mats for the floor. Ali surpassed himself with his skills at building, but his greatest triumph was our loo. Painted deep blue inside and pristine white outside. Not only did it come with an electric light, but a lock on the door, it also came with a padlock on the outside, with a key for us both so that no one else could use it! M'Barek took it upon himself to hose it out every morning when he did the kennels.

We moved in! Taxi 227 and Mohammed collected us, and all our baggage from the hotel for the final time. We said our farewells to Mohammed the hotel owner, and off we went. We arrived and between them, Mohammed the taxi driver and M'Barek carried our bags into the little shed that would be our new bedroom! We said goodbye to taxi 227 and Mohammed said he would be sure to see us when we were in town, and he drove off back to the City. We paid him and gave him a good tip, he left us beaming from ear to ear and waving out of the car window. He made us laugh when he shouted out, in Arabic that he was 'The official Taxi to the Donkey Doctors!'

It took us a while to sort our stuff out. We each had a cupboard and a bed, and that was it! The shed had a half, 'stable door', the bottom half locked, but not the top, so Ali went off in search of a suitable lock and came back with new locks for both halves and new keys. He told us it was most important to lock the doors at all times. The very thought of this idea really annoyed me, but Aly was most insistent about this, I had a distinct feeling there was distrust between him and M'Barek.

Ali was very quiet and spoke little, but his face and eyes told a thousand stories. I liked him a lot. He was very dark skinned and explained to me that he was from the Sahara region, but had come north to seek work when he was a lad. He had a problem with his eyes, but he said there was no cure. I guessed he hadn't ever been to a proper doctor.

He was married to Rosella, who was also from the Sahara. They had five children and lived across the derelict land outside the refuge in a huge shanty town called El Mansour. The shanty - town was outside the city limits. He said that he would take us to his home one day.

M'Barek was originally from a small town in the South on the way to Marrakesh. It was called T'let Sidi Bennour. His mother and his aunts still lived there; he told me that he always visited once a year. M'Barek was very efficient and very opinionated. This occasionally led to controversies and I had to stamp my ruling on how things should be done.

We settled in at the refuge very quickly and rigged up a shower in the empty stable; as it was so hot, the long hosepipe that M'Barek used to wash everywhere down always had hot water if it was left in the sunshine, and we used this as a shower! If the stable was needed, we could simply move the hose.

Cooking was easy as we had two gas rings, (Bottled gas). We also had electricity and were able to boil a kettle, but we had no running hot water. We usually ate in our sitting room, there was a small table and chairs, and two beds in there that acted as sofas! This was hardly a life of luxury, but it suited us well.

Work was picking up considerably, and we had a steady stream of customers at the gate. One by one they would step inside for treatment. I was longing to get out to the markets, but for now we were unable to do so as we were a long way from a bus route, and finding a taxi in our part of Rabat was rare indeed, and Taxi 227 was only allowed to drive within the city limits.

I realised that the work in Rabat would be very different to that of Relizane. We would not be besieged with donkeys coming for Market day, as there was no such Market in Rabat. The markets existed, but we would have to travel to them, and the chance of getting animals back to Rabat for treatment was impossible.

We did get a large volume of door callers, but for the most part, these were wounds, and the occasional case of colic. The refuge stables were never packed full as they would have been in Relizane. But the work was very varied, and we were on the go from dawn to well past dusk, with a break at lunchtime.

We both felt that we ought to pay a visit to Meknes, where there was a British man operating a small SPANA refuge. His name was John, and he was an ex- Household Cavalry farrier. He had come from England just after us. His job in Meknes was to train up local lads to be farriers, and the local people doing the job at the time were not at all skilled, and the feet of a hors, or a donkey are so special and need regular work on them to keep them sound.

I wrote to John and had a reply by return from his wife, Jackie, who invited us to their home for lunch the following week. We visited the bus station in Rabat and bought return tickets. The buses looked quite smart, in dark blue livery, bearing the logo, 'CTM'.

The day came for us to go, so we bought some flowers at the market to take with us as a gift, and then climbed aboard. The bus was full of men and women in traditional robes; on top of the bus was a big rack for luggage; I noticed two goats and some chickens also being hoist up, along with several old bikes and some huge sacks of wool!

We left Rabat and began to climb gently. We had never travelled on this road before. It was quite hilly, and we drove through some quite big villages. The scenery was lovely. The road was lined with big Eucalyptus trees, with lots of tiny farms growing vegetables. We passed fields of Orange and Lemon trees and men and women working in the fields. After about an hour and a half, the bus stopped at a small town, and was immediately besieged by young boys selling cold drinks and hard-boiled eggs! We each got some bottled orange juice and a cake to nibble as we drove on.

Along the way the bus stopped to let people off and new ones on. But we had one sudden stop. The driver leapt to his feet, rushed at the man sitting a couple of rows back and threw him off the bus! The driver said in a loud voice, "KIF!" The man had been smoking Marijuana! The driver must have smelt it.

As we approached Meknes, we drove into a large market place, with enormous walls surrounding it, and a magnificent stone gateway. I decided that they must be a gateway into the old city? The bus stopped and people started to get out. The baggage and animals were lowered from the roof. I noticed a tall man; he stood away from the bus and was clearly looking for us!

John was a northerner, and seemed genuinely pleased to see us. He said that he had only been in Morocco for two months, and was finding it hard, as he spoke no French at all! I noticed that he managed very well with a few words of Arabic and hand signals. He told us that we would go straight to the refuge, and then go out to his house. He added that his wife was longing to speak English to someone again!

We walked through the huge gate; this was Bab El Mansour, and once through we were in a very ancient part of the town. It was quiet, with palm trees and flowers. We walked on to a little row of tiny, white houses, and stopped out 72. Bab El Kari. I knew this as it was written in huge letters on the building, along with 'SPANA" and a picture of a Donkey. John banged on the door and a small, wiry man opened it. John told us that his name was 'Izzy', and then John chuckled and said that what he called him! We walked into a little courtyard. There was a Bougainvillea in the centre, which gave good shade and was full of scented blossom. To the left there was a tiny room that John said was an office cum treatment room. To the right was a stall, and in the stall were a mobile forge and an anvil. John explained that he was finding it hard to get started on the training of the boys, but added that his first three were due to start in a few days time. There was a little upstairs room where the guardian lived. He was there to keep the place safe and clean and tidy. That was all there was at 72. Bab el Kari! We were asked to wait for a moment and John returned driving a battered old Citroen 2CV car. He said it was as old as the hills, but it was fine for getting about the town. I was amused to hear John calling the car a 'Trashy Mo'. The French name was a 'Deux Cheveaux'. I had a chuckle.

He was amazed that we had no proper transport in Rabat, but I told him that we were waiting for the Landrover. He drove us out of the old town through another gateway and there were European houses all along the road. He pulled up in front of a bungalow and we all got out. His wife Jackie met us. She seemed very nice, but was homesick!

We had a very nice lunch, and sat talking for ages about work and England, the time passed very quickly. All too soon, we were back in the car, and then back to catch the bus to Rabat. We decided that we would have to go to see them whenever we could; we liked them both very much.

One morning, the postman came with a very grand looking letter addressed to us both. Inside was a gilt edged card inviting us to a Garden Party at the British Embassy! This was exciting, but we felt we had nothing suitable to wear! We felt we ought to go as we were very alone in this big city, and the Embassy was a little bit of Britain!

Digging deep into our cupboards, we both came up with something that would just about pass muster. The day arrived and we stopped work early in order to shower and wash our clothes before sending M'Barek out to find us a taxi. How he managed it was a miracle, but he did and we were off to the Embassy in no time at all.

We entered by the main gate into a beautifully tended garden. We were ushered through the main door and met by the British Consul, Mr Richard Kemp. He ushered us into a grand room and from there through the huge French doors into a really lovely garden. There were a lot of people there, chatting to each other. We knew no one, but suddenly a very nice woman appeared in front of us. "Hello, I'm Kitty Shore, you must be the girls from SPANA?" She chatted to us for several minutes. Kitty had a lovely Somerset accent. Her husband John joined us; he was a big, tall man and immediately we felt at ease. After chatting for some time, they introduced us to the Ambassador, and again to the Consul, Richard Kemp. Both the Ambassador and Richard were keen to stress that they were there for us in the event of any problems we might encounter.

The evening passed quickly, and as we left, John and Kitty both walked with us to the door. "Do come and see us", they insisted, and gave us their address. We promised that we would. The doorman got a taxi for us and we went home, from the grandeur of the Embassy, back to the refuge. It had been an interesting evening, but both of us said that we were glad to be 'home'.

We did go to visit Kitty and John one day. Kitty sent a letter inviting us to lunch. We found a taxi and he drove us to Agdal, a pretty suburb where many Embassy staff lived. We pulled up outside a walled garden with big metal gates. I rang the bell and a maid appeared to let us in. Kitty was behind her and made us feel very welcome.

The garden was lovely, full of orange and lemon trees, with an enormous Passion Fruit Vine that was laden with fruit, running along a long wall. The bungalow was huge. Kitty and John had spent their entire lives with the Diplomatic Service, and had lived all over the world in considerable luxury. Kitty didn't work, but acted as hostess to any visiting diplomats, and they chuckled as they had been given the specific job of looking after any new comers at the garden party! What a great job to have!

We ate a wonderful lunch in their lovely dining room. They had a lovely young Boxer dog called, 'Arnaud', he was lovely and adored John. They had a maid and a gardener.

We very much enjoyed seeing them and invited them over to the refuge to see where we lived and what we did. They said they would love to, and we made plans for the following week.

It was almost the middle of November, but the weather was still warm, but I knew that it would soon get colder and damp, and I knew that we might be cold at the refuge with the sea and the fogs that we would be having. I got Aly to build a fireplace in the sitting room, and we got an electric heater for the office. At the same time, I got Ali to run a power line across to M'Barek's building, as, until then, they had not wanted electricity. We found them an old cooker and a kettle, and Yamina must have thought she had won a lottery!

It was the day of Kitty and John's visit and they arrived in their own car. M'Barek knew they were coming and swept the gates open with great panache and saluted as they drove in. We gave them a tour of the place, pointing out our makeshift shower and our bedroom; then we went into the office and through to the tiny sitting room.

We had prepared lunch earlier, so we were able to sit down and eat. They had brought a bottle of wine. This was something we had often thought about, but hadn't yet managed to get. Kitty told us that the little market, (close to our old hotel), sold it. We made a note to visit the next time we went into the city.

We had a very jolly lunch, and as they left they both expressed some concern that we were living where we were, and at the Spartan conditions that we had. We said we loved it, but Kitty was adamant that if we ever wanted a bath or a shower, or had any washing done to take it over to their house. They also extended a very genuine open invitation to visit at any time. We would!

In no time at all, Christmas was upon us, and with it came a big downturn in the weather. The hot days gone, we were getting a lot of rain and our room felt cold. Undeterred, we went out and bought carpets and more blankets for our beds. At least we were dry and the place was very waterproof, thanks to Ali's maintenance.

Between that visit and Christmas, Carol had another bout of sickness and diarrhea; it lasted for four days, and she was very tired and low at the end of it. She stayed in bed for most of the time. I was concerned, as she had lived in Morocco quite long enough to get used to the food and to build up a resistance to the various bugs. I told her that if it happened again, we would find a doctor. Once fully over it, we started to make plans for Christmas.

We both had parcels and lots of cards from home that we saved to open on Christmas day. We decorated the room with homemade paper chains, and found a piece of fir scrub that we used as a Christmas tree. We took a taxi to the French market on Christmas Eve and found the place looking very festive, as most of the stallholders were French. We bought vegetables and some lovely fruit, splashed out on a bottle of champagne and a bottle of port to give Santa a glass when he arrived with his sleigh, and with lots of good wishes for Christmas we went back to the refuge.

Christmas Day arrived and we had several callers to deal with, nothing too serious. I was on cooking duties, and got cracking on the lunch.

We lit the fire and opened our presents; I think we both felt very homesick. Christmas is not the time to be away from home. We listened to BBC World Service and sang along to the carols. After a lovely lunch, we raised a glass of port to Her Majesty as we listened to her speech. I just knew that Mum and Dad would be doing the very same thing. I had a huge feeling of homesickness that lasted all of ten minutes!

There were no more callers and we saw to our small group of dogs and a couple of mules at the refuge quite early. There was suddenly a car horn tooting outside, and there was John; he had been sent by Kitty to collect us and take us to their house for a meal. There was a momentary panic... but we quickly changed and off we went. We even had a bottle of wine to take with us!

Kitty met us at the top of the steps. We were pleased to see that we were the only ones there, and were able to flop out on their wonderfully soft sofas, with Arnaud the dog piled on top. We ate far too much, and drank too much, but we had the most perfect end to the day. It was gone midnight when John called a taxi for us!

On Boxing Day, we both woke late with a bit of a hangover! We chatted about the events of yesterday, and both felt we should take John and Kitty for a meal... quite where, we didn't know, we would have to keep our eyes open in the city for a suitable restaurant.

Soon after Christmas, I started to feel that we were working far under our capacity, and it was then that a letter from the Major arrived. He was driving out to see us with the Landrover that he would leave with us for our daily work. This was great news. He said he was planning to leave England on 2nd January. He said that it would probably take him 4 days to drive all the way to Rabat. That gave us time to book him a room at the Balima Hotel, and to make sure that everything was in good order.

The day arrived when the Major was due. We made sure that M'Barek was in his best working clothes, and that Ali had his clean overalls on. We were both in the office when we saw the Landrover drive up by the gates. I shouted to M'Barek who rushed out to open them. He saluted the Major as he drove in. We greeted him, and then he ceremoniously greeted M'Barek and Ali. He knew them both well. We looked around our new transport! She was a lovely big, long wheel - base Landrover with a covered cab, with a canvas roof over the back. Perfect! I had huge plans for visiting markets as well as being able visit to Meknes to see John and Jackie.

The Major had a cup of coffee and we showed him round. He was pleased with the improvements, but furious with the 'operating theatre'. He vowed revenge on the people responsible! He planned to stay for just one night and then take the train to Marrakesh where SPANA had a small-animal refuge that dealt with dogs and cats. From there he would fly to Oran and visit Relizane before flying home.

I asked him how Relizane was and he said that it would probably close, as no one was willing to work there any more.

The Landrover was parked safely inside the refuge. We decided to take a taxi for what we hoped, would be the last time, as the Major was treating us to dinner at the Balima. We enjoyed the meal, and the Major was keen to hear all our news. We told him that the Landrover would be so useful, as we would now be able to visit the markets in the countryside.

We left the Major on the steps of the forecourt and where Mohammed and taxi No 227 were waiting, he drove us home. The Major was leaving early the next morning.

The following morning we got up early and took the big Landrover for a run. She was tailor made for the job; as a considerable part of the work would be visiting the weekly markets in remote places, often well off the beaten track.

M'Barek told us that there would be a market at Khemisett in two days time. He said it was a huge market and that it would be a busy day. We looked forward to it! Finally, we could do the real work we had come for!

On Thursday morning, we rose at 4.00am, and M'Barek was already out loading our bags into the back of the Landrover. We planned to set off at 4.45. Us in the front, and M'Barek sat proudly in the back. It would be a drive of about 40 minutes. There was a sliding window in the back of the cab, and M'Barek was able to talk and tell us when to turn off the coastal road to Casablanca.

We arrived at Khemisett, and drove almost through the village when M'Barek said we should turn left; we drove for about a mile and suddenly, the market came into view. It was huge. There were lots of tents and stalls, and two enormous areas where the animals were tethered. There were hundreds of animals, mostly donkeys and mules, with a few camels. Some still wore packs; others had them removed; all the animals were tethered. Carole was amazed at the sight. This was the first time she had ever seen a market. The whole area was surrounded by 'Cork Oaks'; I was interested, as I'd never seen them before. M'Barek said the building in the distance was a Cork factory. M'Barek told me that we should go and see the person in charge of the market. He was in a tent, sitting at a small desk. M'Barek ushered us in, and explained to the man who we were and what we would be doing. The man nodded, and we left.

M'Barek stayed with us as we worked through the lines of animals, treating those that had sores. A few of the owners questioned our actions, but M'Barek put them firmly in their places! By late morning we were very dirty and flagging, we had some sandwiches with us, and we bought a bottle of orangeade. Then we carried on. Carole set into the work with great enthusiasm, and was totally un-phased by the bad sores that some of the animals had and the conditions we were working in.

We worked on until almost 4.00pm, when we stopped as the people were starting to leave. It had been a very busy day. I explained to Carole that we would still be doing this when the weather improved, working under a very hot sun. We got home about 6.00pm, and no sooner had he shut the gates behind us, M'Barek unloaded the Landrover, and was hosing out the back. We both had a shower when M'Barek had finished with the hose and slept well that night.

The following day, after we'd seen to our door callers, none of whom were in any danger, we decided to drive into the centre of Rabat. I had never driven there before. But we set off gently, driving the route that No. 227 used and soon found ourselves right in the centre. The Landrover was right hand drive, and all the local vehicles were LHD, so some maneuvers were slightly difficult. I soon got the hang of it, but hadn't bargained on the interest we would attract!

As I drove up the main street, I approached the huge junction, in the centre of which was a podium of red and white and atop it, a policeman in his grey uniform. He wore a white cap and gloves. He was directing traffic with some theatre, but the traffic was flowing nicely. As I drove up, he put up his hand to stop us. He blew his whistle and climbed off the podium and walked across. I wondered what on earth I'd done wrong, but he smiled at us.

He saluted as I opened the window. "Good Morning Mesdames", he said in French. And then asked where we were from. "England", I replied. He asked what we were doing in Rabat, and I told him. He was most interested. He chatted for several minutes and then saluted and went back to the podium. (All the traffic had been stationary for this time). He waved us on, laughing as we went.

Later that day there was a knock on the gates and another policeman stood there. He had come in a police Landrover, and had rather a lot of braid on his cap.

"Good morning ladies", he said in impeccable French. My name is El Mansour, and I am the Chief of Police". I felt more than a little worried.

"I have come to tell you that your vehicle needs to have Moroccan Plates if it is staying in the country. You can use it for 4 months, but after that you must apply for license plates. That will mean you will have to pay import duty". He told me where to go to set the process in motion. I thanked him for this information, and asked him if he would like to look around.

He peered carefully into every pen and kennel, and we showed him the office and offered him coffee. He declined as he said he should get back to the office.
He walked back to the Landrover where his driver was waiting. "It was so good to meet you. I hope our paths cross again"... and he was gone!

I felt we should check at our Embassy to see if we really did need to change the plates. We would do that tomorrow. Meanwhile a queue had formed outside, so we went out to see to their various problems. One of the carters lived just around the corner, on the way to the abattoir. He asked if we could go to his home as he had a very, very lame donkey. We told him we'd come as soon as we'd finished at the refuge.

We both walked round, with M'Barek carrying our bag of medicines. He seemed to feel it was his place to attend and act as interpreter, in the event of any problems. The carter let us into his little yard. His name was Mohammed, and he and all his family took us to the donkey. The little soul had a very swollen leg, caused by infection from a wound. We cleaned up the wound and dressed it, and gave the donkey antibiotics. I told Mohammed that we would come back the next day to put a fresh dressing onto the wound.

It was a tiny yard, with a couple of doors off it that was his living quarters. In the yard was his grey horse that pulled his cart, a camel and her calf! I love camels; they are so haughty... and sometimes naughty too! I asked Mohammed if he would be available to help if we ever needed a cart for anything... he replied that he would be very pleased.

The following day we drove to the British Consulate to see Richard Kemp. We had met him once, at the garden party. I explained about the Landrover and he said that we could use it legally for 4 months, but after that it would indeed need Moroccan number plates. He added that we would normally have to pay duty for importing it, but, as we were a charity, and working for the people, there may be a loophole, but he wasn't hopeful! He said that we ought to begin the process of registration as soon as possible as it could take a long time to go through the various departments! We had coffee, and he offered us his help whenever we needed it.

He told us that our first port of call should be to go and get the vehicle weighed down at the little port of Rabat-Sale. We thanked him for all his help and left. As we were nearby, we drove to the French market and bought some nice bread and other goodies! We then went on to weigh the Landrover.

The little port of Rabat-Sale is on the mouth of the Bou Regreg River. It was very small, with just one road down and back. As we approached, we saw the weighbridge area. I parked the Landrover and walked over to the little office. A man told us to drive onto the weighbridge. He then gave me a sheaf of papers and told me to park over by a little office, where we would have to get the papers stamped. It was full of lorry drivers, queuing at a desk, where an official was stamping papers. It was my turn. I told the man what I was there for, and, for the only time ever, received a rude reply.

He told me that foreigners should have to wait until the end of the day, and then he would get the paperwork done, if he had time. He was generally very brusque. A man who looked as if he might be French was waiting behind me in the queue. He stepped forward and told me that he would help. He spoke sharply to the official in Arabic, and then winked at me and asked me to hand over the paperwork.

The official, clearly rattled, took the papers and stamped a form that would enable us to leave. I thanked the man for his help, and made a point of thanking the official, and went back to the Landrover and drove home. Not a nice experience, but it was the one and only time this happened.

We went home and had some lunch. Afterwards, I called M'Barek and Ali into the office. I had asked the Major to allow some money to buy then new boots and overalls. I gave them both sufficient money for the purchases and asked them to be sure they got a receipt. They were overjoyed!

I noticed that Ali's outfit cost much less than M'Barek's, and that he brought some change back, which I gave to him. M'Barek cost the exact amount and that's what the receipt said! I vowed to keep a close eye on him.

I told the men that we had to register the Landrover and that it might mean that we would be away for a part of the next few mornings, but that we would deal with all callers before we left. The weather was starting to warm up considerably, so our patients came at anytime from 04.30am. We were always up as it was cool at that time.

We set off to find the Ministry of Finance. It was a large rather shabby modern building in an area of the city that we didn't know. We did have to drive through the main street to get there. Every time we took that route, the Policemen on duty would either stop us to chat, or waved us through like royalty! It amused us no end!

The Import Duty office was separate building that stood alone, right opposite the main Police Station. I parked right outside and we both walked into a shabby little office, where a man was sitting at a desk with piles of paper and files. He was smoking and drinking coffee. He looked up and seemed very surprised to see us! I explained what we hoped to be able to do, and produced the form from the weighbridge. The man said his name was Slimane Ahmed, and that he was the boss of his particular department. He studied the Log Book, and told us the process to change the plates would be lengthy and costly, but added, that as we needed to use the vehicle for urgent work, that he would try to hasten things along.

Suddenly, the door burst open, and the Chief of Police, El Mansour walked in! He greeted us warmly and then greeted Ahmed. "Ahmed my friend, these ladies are to be given every assistance". Ahmed told him that he would do his utmost to hurry things through. We filled in a sheaf of forms, helped by both men, and then took our leave. We were asked to return in three days time.

The weeks went by, each week we had to visit the office of Ahmed, but each time, there was another form to fill out, or another excuse as to why things were going so slowly! We began to despair and contacted Richard Kemp, the British Consul.

He must have contacted Ahmed, as suddenly things began to happen.

We received a letter, written by Ahmed asking us to visit his office. We went as soon as we could get away. Ahmed told us that the Duty was now payable, and quoted an enormously ridiculous figure, far above the value of the vehicle. I was shocked, and told him that I would have to consult London. We left, promising to contact him as soon as we could.

Rather shaken by the thought of losing our transport, we drove down to the Hotel Balima, and sat under the trees on the terrace drinking lovely icy cold freshly squeezed lemon drink. A young man suddenly appeared and sat down at our table; we had no idea who he was, but he told us that his name was Zaoui. He was impeccably dressed in a suit and tie; spoke excellent French and was young and very good looking to boot! He told us that he had been speaking to Ahmed at a meeting in the Ministry of Finance, where he worked. He said that he might be able to speed things along. I suspected that he would ask for money to sort out the problem, instead of which, he was very genuinely offering to help us. We bought him a coffee, and sat chatting for quite some time.

He knew all about us, and our work. I asked him how he knew this, and he told us that his father was a Caïd, one of the Royal Advisors, and very close to the King, and that nothing unusual happened in Rabat without the Caïds knowing! Zaoui asked if he might come to see the refuge at some time. We offered to take him right there or then; and off we all went!

Zaoui seemed to know everyone; all the Policemen waved at him and us on the way back to the refuge. Both M'Barek and Ali seemed in awe of him. We showed him round and offered him some lunch. He stayed nearly all day! He said he would be in touch about the Landrover as soon as he could speak to Ahmed again. I drove him back to the City and he wanted to be dropped off outside the Palace. To my surprise, he walked in through the huge gates, chatting to the guards on duty.

In the days that followed, we waited, as he had told us to do nothing until he had, 'made enquiries'. We threw ourselves in the country markets where we had become welcome visitors. M'Barek was a great asset on these trips. He would hold animals still whilst we treated them, and dealt with difficult owners.

Three weeks passed and we decided to drive into Rabat to see if we could see Zaoui. We stopped at the little market for some provisions and then drove down to the Ministry of Finance. We asked to see Zaoui and were taken along the corridors to his office. Zaoui greeted us and asked for coffee to be brought in. We were there some time; he said that he might have some news in a couple of days and said he would very much like us to have supper with him that evening. He suggested a little café he knew in Agdal, he said it was not very smart, but the food was excellent. We agreed and left, with the arrangement that we would meet him at 7.00pm.

We found the café, situated on a corner and shaded by large Gum trees. Zaoui was already there. He explained that we might need to go to the little shop across the road, as the café sold no alcohol, but they didn't mind us drinking it.

We fetched the wine and to our surprise, Zaoui asked the owner of the café for three glasses. Being Muslim, we had assumed that Zaoui didn't drink. I went over to the shop and got a second bottle.

Zaoui explained that the only things on the menu were brochettes of lamb, served with bread. There was a man cooking some on a charcoal fire and they smelt wonderful. Zaoui ordered us six skewers each, and showed us how to use the bread, firstly to dip into the red sauce, and then wrapping a piece of lamb with the bread, and eating it; the sauce was so hot! But, the whole thing was delicious. At the end of the meal, we had each eaten twelve skewers and two entire loaves of the wonderful flat bread! Zaoui asked the owner to bring the bill, and the owner was gone for just a moment before returning, and when he did, Zaoui paid him and we left.

One morning, there was a knock on the office door. It was Ali; he announced that he would love us to visit his home to meet his family and have tea with them. I said we would be most honored, and he said that we were to visit the following day. He asked if he might drive with us and show us the way.

I was looking forward to the visit, and when the time came, Ali hopped into the back of the Landrover as we drove out of the refuge. It was a short drive to the huge shanty - town where Ali lived. He told me to park near a tiny little shop, and he asked a young lad to look after the vehicle whilst we visited. The lad sat down beside it; I later learned that this was Ali's young nephew.

We walked down dirty little earth paths, some with sewage in them; we turned left and right and eventually stopped outside a blue door. Ali went in and ushered us in, he was beaming as he introduced his family. His wife, Rosella, was very dark skinned and quite tall. She had a wonderful smile; the oldest son, also called Ali was about 16, there was a very pretty girl called Saadia,

And a little baby of about a year old, his name was Mustafa.

Ali's little house was built of brick that had been rendered and white washed, as were all the houses in this little road. It had a roof made of straw, and an earth floor. There were two rooms. We were taken into the main room and asked to sit on the cushions on the floor. Ali carried in a huge brass tray with mint tea glasses and the traditional teapot. The pouring of the tea was done with great ceremony, after chipping off a huge lump of sugar for each glass from a cone of hard sugar. Mint was added to the sugar, and then the green tea. I loved it, very sweet, but very refreshing. Rosella appeared with two plates of cakes that she had made. We ate and drank and chatted and really enjoyed ourselves.

We were shown the other room. It was a bedroom where they all slept. There was a large bed made of scraps of timber, with neatly folded blankets on top. I guessed the children slept on the floor. There was a small cupboard and this was opened to show us the contents. It never ceased to amaze me that people on such low incomes could bring up families, but they managed well.

It was March and the days were getting quite hot again. We had started to drive to the beach for a swim during our lunch break. This worked well, and was a great improvement on the hosepipe shower! We usually went to the little beach at Temara, until we found the wonderful beach at Sidi Boukanadel, on the other side of the city and that was approached by a long road, and many flags of different nations flew along the tops of the dunes. It had once been known as 'La Plage des Nations'.

It was always quite deserted; there was a tiny café near the little slope down to the beach where we parked, but there was never a soul there, just miles of beautiful white sandy beach. The sea was wonderful; with huge Atlantic rollers slapping onto the sands and the undertow then swept the sea back out again. It was great to swim in. We got quite good at riding in on the huge waves, but just occasionally we would miss the moment and get caught in the roll of the wave and be tumbled over and over, and deposited on the beach; by the time you got to your feet, the sea was a long way away! We always took M'Barek with us as he insisted that we would not be safe alone, so he would sit and guard our belongings, dressed in his overalls and wellington boots!

About this time, Kitty and John invited us to lunch. There was another English woman there. Her name was Maureen, and she was a nursing sister at the huge Hospital Avicenne. She normally worked in Switzerland and spoke fluent French. She had been in Switzerland so long that she had almost forgotten her English. We liked her a lot; we guessed she was probably seven or eight years older than us. She was rather shy at first, but we made it our goal to get her out of her shell! The hospital was on our way home from Kitty's, so we dropped Maureen off. We told her that we would collect her the next day and show her the refuge.

When we got back to the refuge, there were a couple of callers and their horses that needed dressings. Then we saw that all the inmates were well and hosed out the kennels whilst M'Barek applied anti-tick fluid to the runs. Ticks were a big problem in Morocco and could grow to the size of a large grape if they had a good blood feed. Every day we combed through all the dogs' coats in an effort to find and remove the dirty things before they fed. We sometimes got one on our legs, particularly after market days when we would be walking around in the scrubland all day. They were easy enough to remove. A blob of spit, and then twisting them clockwise would soon cause them to let go. There are many ways to remove ticks, but this method never failed and never left the head embedded in the skin to cause an abscess. I learned this trick from Milly when I first went to Algeria with her.

We thought that Maureen might like to come with us to the beach one day. We met up with her, totally by accident when we were shopping at the little French market. She said she's love to come, as she'd never been to the coast since she arrived in Rabat. He said the she would be free on Sunday, so we made plans to pick her up from the hospital at 10.00am the following Sunday, and that we'd take a picnic and get her home again sometime in the afternoon.

The rest of the week was a very busy time. There were a lot of dogs in the kennels; some strays and some boarders. The French people used the kennels when they went home on leave.

One morning a large car arrived, it contained two large dogs of no particular parentage. The driver introduced himself as Monsieur Didier. He explained that he would shortly returning to France for good, and would like to leave his two dogs with us until he was settled back into his new home. He wanted to see the kennels.

We showed him round, and he asked us if we would be willing to take the dogs, and added that they would like to live together. I explained that this would be no problem whatsoever. He agreed the terms, and said he would pay 3 months fees in advance and then pay the rest by money order from France. He seemed quite genuine, so I agreed. The dogs would be coming the following week.

We made a fuss of the dogs, 'Laika and Tasha', as they were shut back into the car and M.Didier drove off waving as he went. I told M'Barek that they could use the big kennel by the office, as it was large enough for both dogs.

We went into Rabat to see if we could buy some dressings; luckily, the chemist shops sold a huge variety of things. We chose the one down near the big market. I went to the Chemist, and Carol went over to the market for some vegetables.

As I left the shop, I saw Zaoui across the road. He had already seen me, and was crossing over. He told me that we should all go out again, to the café at Agdal. I told him we'd love to, but insisted that we paid this time. We arranged to meet him there at 6.30pm.

That evening, we got to the café before Zaoui, the owner recognized us, and gave us a table against the roadside railings. I left Carol there and I went across to get some wine. When I returned, Zaoui had arrived, and he was carrying a big paper package. He put it onto the table and said, "Open it!" It contained a set of Moroccan number plates! They were for the Landrover... we were both quite stunned! I asked how much we owed him, and he said that he had pulled in a few favours and no payment was required. He pulled an envelope from his pocket and told us that these were the registration documents. We were to remove the UK plates as soon as possible and get the new ones onto the vehicle. I said it would be done first thing in the morning! We had a very jolly meal!
We asked Zaoui if he'd like to come to the beach with us on Sunday and, at the same time, meet Maureen? He said he'd be delighted, and would wait at the Palace gates just before 10.00am.

The next day I drove up to the local garage and within minutes, the new plates were on... we were fully legal! I drove over to the Hospital and found Maureen, and asked her if she would like to visit Meknes the next time we went; she jumped at the chance. We wondered if Kitty might also come. I left it with Maureen to ask when she next saw Kitty and John. I drove home to find Carol busy treating a queue of carters. I quickly went out to help her, and told her about the planned trip to Meknes.

We planned to go to visit John and Jackie the following week, as long as work permitted. We were mainly able to count a Friday as a good day as the men were at prayer; it was their 'Sunday'.

One job that I hated doing was to have to put down the stray dogs that had been with us for too long. The City had a stray collection service that was carried out every evening. A horse drawn cage was driven around the city, and the men with it would catch any stray dogs. These dogs were taken to the Abattoir where they were put down straight away. The killing was by electrocution, which is outlawed in many parts of the world now.

We were often asked to take in strays, but there was very little chance of finding homes for them. A French lady who ran a Florists shop in Rabat ran the local SPA, (Society for the Protection of Animals), and she tried to find homes for the dogs. It was impossible to go on collecting dogs, so we had to make a decision about which ones would have to go. I loathed having to make the decision.

Each Thursday afternoon, I would do the deed, always by lethal injection, which was very quick and caused the dogs no worries.

Sunday arrived and we were going to the beach! I asked M'Barek if he would come and act as guardian;

he jumped at the chance. After seeing to all the inmates and a couple of door callers, we packed our stuff into the back of the Landrover and drove over the Hospital to collect Maureen, she seemed genuinely excited! We told her that Zaoui would be joining us, and we drove into the City to collect him from the Palace gates. He and Maureen chatted happily all the way to the beach, Maureen sat in the front with us, and Zaoui in the back; he was able to chat through the open sliding window.

We had a lovely time; we swam in the huge breakers, and then ate our picnic under the big yellow parasol that we'd bought to shelter from the sun. All too soon it was time to go home. We dropped Zaoui off and then Maureen; we promised to take her again, whenever she was free, and we continued to do this.
We went out for meals on occasions, and shared brochettes at the little café in Agdal; Maureen was coming 'out of her shell' very nicely! We took her to a market one day. She was bowled over at the sight of so many animals, and the way that we just waded in and did our work. She was fascinated by all the little stalls and was absolutely aghast at the dentist pulling teeth just sitting on the ground!

It transpired that she had been in Morocco for nearly eight months, and had not been paid! This sounded like a job for Zaoui, so we all met up for a meal and she explained that she was under contract to the Government, and that all her papers had been sent to the Ministry of Finance. Zaoui promised to look into this matter, and he said that he would like to meet up again in a week's time. We agreed to meet at the little café in Agdal.

During that week, we drove up to Meknes with Maureen. We gave a tour of the old part of the town with John's help. There are interesting caves and a huge ruined area that used to house 1,000 horses. Again, we had lunch at John's house and he and Julie said they would drive down to see us one day. I left details of an easy route through Rabat that would find the refuge very easily.

We all met up at the little café in Agdal for supper and we asked Maureen if she'd heard any news? She said she was resigned to the fact that it would be a long wait for her salary to arrive. Now, I don't know what took place during that week, but Zaoui arrived at the café, and with a huge smile, announced that he had looked into the matter, and that Maureen should check her bank balance. We had a good meal, and we dropped Maureen off and then Zaoui. He explained to us that the money had been paid in full! We thanked him profusely, and again, he said he'd been delighted to help.

One morning, Carol and I were in the office writing letters, when M'Barek came in looking very serious. "Madame, my mother is old and sick, and I must go to see her". I said that of course he should, and then an idea entered my head! We could do with a couple of days off... what if we took M'Barek to his village, and then drove on down to the South to take Ali to see his family? I put this to Carole and she was very excited at the prospect of a long trip. I called Ali and he came into the office, wondering what he'd done wrong!

This dear sweet man wept when I told him what the plan was. He was overjoyed. He told me that his mother and father were very old, and that he never thought he'd see them again. Then he said that he would go down and return with us as there was no other way for him to get back to Rabat. I bought a good map and we plotted the route. We thought we'd take the gas rings and some bottled gas with us, and plenty of food and water. The next time we saw Maureen, we asked her if she'd like to come with us, adding quickly, that it would be very basic, no hotels and not much hope of a good shower, to our surprise, she leapt at the chance! We fixed a date for the following week that would be suitable.

We began to plan in detail. Every night after work, we would get the map out. The plan was to go to M'Barek's village first and drop him off. He could stay away for several days and return by coach. He seemed very happy with that arrangement.

We would then drive on down the coast to Agadir, the city that had been decimated by a major earthquake in 1960. Then we would cut inland and cross the High Atlas Mountains by the Tizi-n-Test pass, and once across them, head down towards the Sahara, to Zagora. Ali's parents lived near there. He said he didn't want to stay there, but he'd just love to see him family. He would return with us. The return route was over the Atlas Mountains via the Tizi-n-Tichka Pass, to Ouzarzate, and then on to Marrakesh and on to Rabat. We planned on it taking three full days, maybe four, depending on what the roads were like. I was the only driver.

We had to make arrangements for the welfare of the inmates of the refuge whilst we were away. M'Barek's son, Mohammed was perfectly up to the job, and his cousin, Ahmed, who stayed with them often would help out. I asked Mansour, the Chief of Police to call in, just to keep them on their toes! He readily agreed to do this.

We told all the door callers that we would be away for a few days, they would pass the word to their friends, and hopefully, no - one would come hoping for treatment. I made Mohammed and Ahmed promise that they would open the door to callers... at the same time, hoping there would be none!

The day before we were due to leave, there was much packing to do! I went off to do the food shopping and to fill the Landrover with fuel and get the tyres and oil checked. Carol packed the clothes into soft bags to save on space. M'Barek lashed the gas cylinder firmly to the Land Rover's frame, and stowed the gas rings. We filled large plastic containers with water. The two men would sit in the back, and the three of us would sit in the front. A Landrover is a wonderful vehicle, but the central seat in the front means sitting with one's legs astride the gear lever! I suggested that Carol and Maureen should change places regularly.

In the morning we had breakfast, checked on all the inmates and at 6.30am, in the relative cool, we set off to collect Maureen. She was standing outside the hospital with her bag. We loaded into the back, and Ali and M'Barek sat on top of things, they seemed quite happy. We were off on a big adventure!

We travelled via the coast road for a while and then joined the main road to Marrakesh; our first destination, T'let Sidi Bennour was a small village, off the main road about 80 miles from Rabat. We followed the sign and turned off onto a dirt road, and continued for about 10 miles when we arrived at the village. M'Barek showed us the way to his home. It was a little square house, made of grey blocks. M'Barek went ahead to find the family. We were greeted warmly and given tea and cakes. The oldest lady in the house seemed to be M'Barek's aunt, H'alti M'Bareka; she grinned at us toothlessly the entire time we were there!

Anxious to press on, we excused ourselves, and M'Barek saw us off. He would stay there for three days.

I was more than a little worried that we had not seen a garage that sold diesel since we had left Rabat! However, just as we got back onto the main road, I spotted one ahead; there was only one pump but luckily, it was diesel! I filled up and we turned off the main road to Marrakesh, and set off towards Casablanca.

We had never been to 'Casa', yet it was only an hour from Rabat. We drove on south, leaving the many large white buildings of Casablanca behind and on our way to Agadir. Casablanca in Arabic is 'Dhār Baeda', which means the "White House".

The road was good, bordered by large rock formations in many places. We saw a few lorries and cars, and sometimes, along the edge of the road we'd pass a donkey or horse pulling a loaded cart... . seemingly in the middle of no-where.

We drew close to the City of Agadir. I remembered the dreadful scenes of destruction from the 1960 earthquake that we'd seen on TV. Most of it seemed to have been rebuilt with huge white buildings where there had been rubble.

We decided to stop and did so a few miles beyond Agadir. I just pulled off the road. There was a handy crop of rocks and bushes close by! Ali set up the cooker to make tea and get some food cooked. One by one we nipped behind the rock. It was only moments later that we were joined by a small gang of children! It never ceased to amaze me that in the most remote of places, people would appear from no-where to see what we were doing!

I made tea, and we had bread and some lamb chops. They tasted wonderful after such a long drive. We ate oranges and then packed up and drove off; the bemused children running along behind us laughing and waving.

We had to cross the Atlas Mountains; the road suddenly turned into a rough, stony track and snaked its way higher and higher up into the mountain. This was the Tizi-n-Test pass. The scenery was awesome, but I had to concentrate hard as there were some really alarming bends, and the road just fell away on one side of us! The track was stony and quite narrow.

The climb seemed endless, but it was very beautiful but stark. We reached the top of the Pass and started to descend. I drove even more carefully as the track was slippery, loose stones and small rocks were sent tumbling down the steep slopes beside us! We passed several vehicles; the ones ascending had the right of way, as it was so steep that if they stopped, they would never be able to get going again. The road was quite narrow, and passing was difficult in some places.

We stopped briefly for some tea and cake, and then drove on, hoping to find a suitable place to stop for the night. The descent was getting less severe, and we turned a bend to find a lovely valley down below. We decided that it might be a good place to stop for the night. There was even a little stream!

Our camping place was perfect. We sat in the stream and washed off as much of the dust as we could, it was cool and very clear. Ali went off alone to pray. We were going to sleep in the Landrover! Ali said he would sleep underneath it; Carol, being the shortest would lie across the front seat, she would keep all our purses and money and lock the doors, and once the back was emptied out, there was plenty of room for Maureen and I to stretch out.

We had pies and some lovely melon for supper; Ali lit a fire, he told us that it would keep us safe, as there were mountain Lions. I think we were all tired and dusty from the journey. We sat around the fire for a while, insisting that Ali joined us. When we retired to bed, Ali insisted that the two of us in the back slept with our heads right into the vehicle and our feet at the back... when I asked why, Ali replied that bandits might come! I was too tired to care!

The next day we were all up before dawn. Ali was praying across the way. We all went and had a mini-wash in the stream, and managed to clean our teeth. We ate breakfast of tea and coffee and bread and jam; packed up and off we went.

Our target was the town of Zagora, from the map we worked out that it would take us all day to get there. We drove along the river for some time before the track turned off and then we were in another valley, this one had hugely steep sides, there was no river. We passed a couple of battered old lorries, and were seeing camels and donkeys. There were few horses on this stretch.

We were far down in the South of Morocco. There were beautiful pink coloured hilltop fortresses and tiny villages; we came to several places where the land was lush and there would be a little settlement of houses. People waved as we passed. We stopped at one village, as there was a garage that sold diesel from a tank mounted on the back of a lorry! As far as we were concerned, it was 'any port in a storm'. We boiled the kettle and sat drinking tea and coffee and we had some biscuits. There were eyes watching us from every angle! We were soon on the road again, waving as we left them.

We had lunch at a little roadside stall that was selling fresh bread and hard-boiled eggs, and fresh tomatoes. The Landrover intrigued the stall owner. When we left, I started the engine and it roared into life, the stall owner was clapping with glee! We were driving due south, and the landscape was changing; the rocks and hills were behind us. There were no trees, but every now and then we would come to a place that was verdant and had a well. I supposed it was a sort of oasis.

We drove on towards Zagora. We were all tired and very dusty from the long, sometimes very bumpy journey. It was 7.30pm and getting dark. We had a battered old reel-to-reel tape recorder with us, and as we drove along the plain we could see the lights of Zagora across and down to the right. The Beach Boys sang, 'God only knows'. That has stayed a great favourite, and whenever I hear it, I am driving along in the dark to Zagora.

Ali was clearly getting very excited. He said his home was outside Zagora, just a few more miles. We drove on. Now we were really off road and into the start of the Sahara Desert. Ali asked me to stop; he jumped out and sniffed the air, or maybe he was looking at the stars; he asked me to continue but to turn slightly left. We continued along, stopping every several minutes for Ali to decide where next. I must admit we were beginning to get a little concerned. We were in the desert, not a light in sight, and no road either! Ali asked if he could sit on the bonnet and direct from there. He climbed up and sat on top of the huge spare wheel that was screwed down to the bonnet. We drove on, turning slightly here and there. It was getting very late, almost midnight! We had driven miles out of Zagora.

Suddenly, Ali sat up and clapped his hands! He pointed straight ahead and, in the headlights, I could just see a little cluster of tents. He asked me to stop and he ran ahead. There was much shouting and then I saw him beckoning us forwards. I parked alongside a tent.

Ali was overcome with joy as he introduced us to his mother and father, aunts and uncles and children. He held his parents hands as he looked around him.
We were shown into a tent and tea was prepared for us... bear in mind that it was the middle of the night, and we must have woken them up! A little fire was lit to boil the kettle. I noticed another fire being lit outside. We sat and drank the tea gratefully. Ali said we were to sleep in this tent, but first we had to eat. We sat with Ali and the family. Dear Ali was so full of emotion to be with them all again. After quite a wait, a huge dish was brought in.

Amazingly, since our arrival, a goat had been killed and cooked, and one of the women must have made couscous... in the days a laborious method of rubbing flour and oil until the couscous was in the form that we know it today. A huge mound of it was on the dish, with some vegetables, and the meat from the goat on top. We tucked in, as we hadn't eaten since teatime! Finally, more tea and we then slept on the floor with our sleeping bags. It was 4.00am!

We woke to find the camp all up and busy. There was a large herd of goats, a couple of camels and two dogs. We wandered off to find somewhere to use as a loo!

We were given fresh flat bread and fresh Yoghurt, made from the milk of the goats; it was an absolute feast.

The plan was to stay there until the afternoon and then set off for home. Number one task was to get to Zagora before we ran out of diesel! The women in the camp were bemused by us and, by our pale skins. They told us stories of how they lived and where they travelled to during the year. It seemed that they moved around a large area in the south. They must have been dreadfully poor. One woman was making bead necklaces. She told us that she sold them in the little markets. We all bought one, only too pleased to offer her well over the price she stated.

Before we left we were treated to more food: we left them all waving as we drove out of sight. What a privilege it had been to meet them. Ali was quite tearful for a while, but then he cheered up and was full of smiles. He guided us back to Zagora where, thankfully, we found a garage and filled up, we stocked up on orangeade and some bread and butter.

Restored in every way, we drove on, leaving the scrub of the desert behind us and starting to pick up the foothills of the Atlas again. We were driving home by the other pass over the mountains, the Tizi-n-Tichka pass. That night, we stopped in a valley; above us was a large hill fort, beautiful against the skyline, the walls washed with a soft pinky - yellow hue. We cooked some eggs and fried bread, and had another melon for desert.

I don't think any of us needed much rocking to get to sleep.

The following morning, we awoke to the sound of voices and watched a large herd of camels pass by; they were driven along by two young lads, who smiled cheerfully at us when we greeted them. They were bound for a market in the hills. We watched until they were out of sight, and then went to wash our faces in the little stream that followed the foot of a rocky outcrop.

We ate bread, and some honey, and then we set off again. The road followed the rock and the stream for several miles and then we started to climb. The road snaked it's way up and up, in places so steep that I wondered if we would make it, but the Landrover made light of it. The scenery on this pass was quite stunning; there were more tiny villages as we went along. We paused briefly at the top of the pass to take some photos, and then set off on the descent. Going carefully incase the wheels slipped on the surface.

We passed several lorries; this was quite a feat as it meant getting very close to the edge to let the other vehicle pass. The road was narrow and steep; it was important not to stop the vehicle going up the incline, so we always gave way.

The road snaked down for some time, and then began to flatten out. Below us, to our right was a river; just one more bend and we would be at that level.
I felt the Landrover slip, and guessed that we'd got a puncture! I stopped and we all clambered out... the front right tyre was very flat.

There was no point in wasting time. I gave Ali the job of unscrewing the spare wheel off the bonnet of the vehicle. He got it off with some difficulty, and leant it against the side of the Landrover. Meantime, we were all unloading the back of the vehicle, as the tools were in a compartment under the floor.

I got the jack fixed up, then I loosened the wheel nuts, and Ali pumped the handle to raise the front of the vehicle, when there was a yell from Maureen! "The Wheel! The Wheel!"... We turned to see the spare wheel gently rolling down the slope towards the river! The movement of the jack must have dislodged it!

Carol and I leapt over the edge and scrambled down the slope, just in time to see the wheel plop into the water! Luckily, being so heavy, it came to rest on the reeds at the edge. We were able to get it out, but not without getting into the river first! By the time we had it out, Ali had reached us, and he then rolled the wheel back up the road to the Landrover, as we would have had a dreadful job to get it up the slope.

The rest of the wheel change was problem free; Ali screwed the flat tyre wheel to the bonnet and we loaded up and drove on... hoping that we would get home without further mishap. Maureen had found the entire incident very comical, and chuckled happily. We turned a big bend down by the river and were overjoyed to see the track turn into a proper road! It should be plain sailing all the way to Marrakesh.

We drove into Marrakesh about 4.00pm. Civilisation again! We got the car filled, and left the tyre at the garage to be mended whilst we went to look for some food. We didn't go near the busy part of Marrakesh, but we settled for a little pavement café. We had coffee, and then some chicken and salad.

I was keen to get home. It would take 3 hours. We collected the mended tyre and set off; we should get back to Rabat about 9.00pm.

The road between Marrakesh and Rabat was excellent and it seemed no time at all before we were turning off onto the little coast road. We took Ali home first. I told him to take the next day off, but he insisted that he would be at work. He gave us all a hug and a thousand Blessings as we left him to tell Rosella all about the trip.

As we drove up to the hospital to drop Maureen off, she said that she had never, ever dreamt of doing such a trip, but she had enjoyed it so much. We promised that we would pick her up the following night to go to the little café in Agdal.

Then we drove home to the refuge. Mohammed opened the gates and they seemed surprised to see us home so quickly. M'Barek was still away.

We left most of the stuff in the Landrover, but we did unload the gas bottle and rings, as we'd need them in the morning. We both showered under the, still warm hosepipe and fell into bed exhausted. What an adventure!

In the morning I woke early and left Carol asleep whilst I went to make some tea.

I took her a cup and we sat in the bedroom and drank it. After getting dressed I asked Mohammed if everything was all right, he said that all was well, except for the two dogs of M.Didier; he said they were very 'very naughty'!

I walked to their pen, and sure enough, the two of them rushed at the gate, baring their teeth! I told Mohammed that we would sort them out later; he could easily hose out their run and fill their water bowl without the need to go in. I would take on the job of feeding them later.

We unloaded the Landrover, and Ali arrived. He carried some fresh bread that Rosella had baked. He hosed out the Landrover and then washed all the desert dust off! Carol and I had a fairly leisurely breakfast and then saw to the inmates. We had several door callers, so we got them sorted and then went into Rabat, as the cupboard was bare! I drove to the Little Market and we stocked up on everything we needed.

We went to the Balima for a glass of Lemon pressé, which was so refreshing on a hot day. Out of the blue, Zaoui arrived and joined us. We sat there for a while recounting the exploits of the past three days. He was amazed that we had gone so far! He asked us if we would go with him to dinner at a friend's house the following week. We said we would love to, and arranged to pick Zaoui up at the Palace gates. We also asked him to join us in Agdal when we met Maureen. He said he would be delighted. We set off for home.

The following morning, M'Barek returned. He told us that his old aunt, H'Alti M'Bareka, had returned with him and was staying for a while.

I explained that the two French dogs were being difficult and he said he would deal with them. But from that day until the day the dogs flew back to France, M'Barek was the only person that could go into their kennel, but always carrying a stout pole!
Early one morning, there was a lot of noise outside the gate. M'Barek opened the gate, and there was a lorry with several men and a bull on the back! The lorry was not a cattle lorry, just an ordinary one, with a 'fence' around the sides to keep the bull enclosed! The driver explained that the bull had a potato in its throat, and was struggling to breath. Carol and I hopped up onto the back of the lorry, and it was obvious that the bull was in considerable distress. I could feel the outline of the potato with my hands, and I tried to get my hands below it to ease it back up. This didn't help.

I decided to try to reach it from inside the mouth. The men held the bull and I opened his mouth and slid my hand down... I could feel the potato! All efforts to grasp it were in vain. Carol went into the office and returned with our bottle of cooking oil. I tipped a small amount down the bull's throat, hoping the potato would dislodge and move either up, or down. Again I tried to manually push the potato upwards by pressing each side of it. We both tried to get the potato to move: I feared for the bull's life.

All of a sudden, the bull became very agitated, gave a huge bellow and the potato flew out, a long trail of mucous followed, and the poor bull coughed for some time. I sent M'Barek for a bucket of water for him. The men on the lorry were all bemused that a woman had done the job! I was thankful that my inept method had worked. They were laughing at me, as I was very disheveled and covered in mess of one sort and another! There were handshakes all round before the lorry departed. Carol and I went back in, and we both needed a shower, as we were both really filthy!

Later that day we went to the little market and dropped in on Kitty on the way home. She was delighted to see us, and made us tea and we sat in her garden and drank it. She wanted to know all about our trip to the South. She said she'd already seem Maureen, who had told her all about it, and how much she'd enjoyed seeing some more of the country. Kitty was amazed that we'd all returned in one piece and unscathed! Before we left, she invited us to supper later in the week and added that Maureen would be coming too. We would look forward to seeing them all.

When we got back to the refuge, there was a letter from the Major. It was a long letter, and told us that there had been a huge move by the Charity in the UK, to obtain second-hand 'Snaffle' bits. ('Snaffles' are one of the kindest bits that a horse or pony could use.). The idea was to ship them out to us, and that we would be able to give every horse and donkey that we met a good quality bit, that would be kind to their mouths.

At that time, all donkeys wore a circular bit of metal, with a piece of metal welded on that stuck downwards, behind the chin; the reins would be attached to this piece of metal; A sharp tug on the reins would raise the metal and it would go into the under jaw of the animal, often cutting them. Horses would be bridled with anything from bits of wire, through all varieties of bit, some very severe.

The first assignment of bits was due to arrive at Casablanca Port the following week! The letter went on to say that the Port would notify us, when the bits arrived, and that we would have to go and collect them. Some of the bits were for Meknes, so would collect them all and then deliver to Meknes when we could.

The evening of our dinner date with Zaoui at his friend's house arrived. We picked him up from the Palace gates and he told me to take the coast road.
We drove past Temara beach when he said I should turn off at the next little road. As we did so I could see some massive iron gates ahead of us, and a high brick wall, with broken glass set all along the top of it. Who ever lived there was clearly quite wealthy. I stopped at the gates and a man in uniform came out of a doorway. Zaoui told him that we were the guests of the owner, and we were beckoned on. The driveway was lined with palm trees, and a well-tended lawn extended the entire way. I stopped in front of a large house.

The front door opened immediately, and a tall man walked out and greeted Zaoui like a long lost friend.

Zaoui introduced us to the man whose name was Mohammed. We were ushered in and we all sat on low cushions in a circle, on the floor. Mohammed explained that he had known Zaoui and his father for many years and that he had heard of our work and us. From the back of the room, three servants appeared carrying trays of food, which were set in front of us.

There was a large brass tray that was loaded high with couscous and vegetables, and on top of the pile were three whole legs of slowly roasted lamb. Mohammed invited us to eat, and we ate in the Muslim way, using only our right hands. The food was quite delicious. There were some very sweet cakes for dessert, all dripping with honey. As soon as we'd finished eating, a servant offered us a bowl of lemon water to rinse our sticky fingers in.

It was a very pleasant evening, Mohammed was the perfect host and we had all chatted happily. As we left I noticed a picture of the King of Morocco, Hassan V, but it was a different photo to any others I'd seen that hung in public buildings.

I commented to Mohammed that this was a rather nice picture and he beamed back at me, "It is my cousin"! Zaoui and Mohammed laughed heartily, as we had absolutely no idea! It explained the big gates and the high walls, the large house and the servants! We left for home, but not before asking Mohammed to visit the refuge one day. He said he would love to. We took Zaoui home, still bemused at the evening we'd spent!

The following morning, M'Barek did the stables and dogs and we attended to some door callers. We had some breakfast, and then set off to Casablanca, with

M'Barek in the back, to collect the bits from the port. Casablanca was about an hours drive down the coast, and we were soon on the outskirts. It was a big city, and it really was 'white'! I had no idea where the docks were, so Carol sat with the map on her knees to make sure we got there. We went through the main part of the city and it looked very modern and smart, and expensive. Then we turned off and the surroundings became much shabbier as the docks could be seen ahead of us.

I drove in through the gates and a policeman promptly stopped us. Once I'd explained what we were there for, he directed us to a building right by the dockside. We drove on to the large building. I parked the car, and Carol and I went into the office, I was clutching the letter they had sent. The office was full of men, and they all stopped and stared at us. Probably wondering what on earth two women were doing there! I handed over the letter, and the man went out to a back room and brought a file. He took out the documents and stamped the pages. (How they loved their rubber stamps!) He told me to drive to the other end of the building and we would be met, he handed me one of the pieces of paper. Within 10 minutes we were on our way home, with three big wooden crates of bits, one for Meknes, and two for us.

During that week we gave a new bit to each door caller and took a large box of them out with us to the markets. The owners were delighted, and handed over their old bits to us quite readily. From then on, we always had a box of them in the Landrover to give to any owner that we came across.

Two weeks later we repeated the trip to Casablanca, and collected more crates. John and Jackie came down from Meknes to collect theirs, so we took them out for lunch in a restaurant in Rabat. They were very impressed by the city, and also enjoyed seeing the refuge. The big crates just wouldn't fit into the 2CV, so we emptied the contents into old corn sacks, and we managed to cram them into the car!

I was delighted to hear that the idea of a Farriers School had begun to take off. John said that he now had five young lads who were learning his skills. Poor Jackie continued to struggle with the language and the heat and the huge differences between living in the UK and living in Morocco. It really was a totally different way of life for her; she found it very hard.

They set off for home quite late in the day, as we waved them off, we told them to keep in close touch. I told John that we would take the next crates of bits up to Meknes, but Jackie was keen to come down to see us. We promised a trip to the beach next time they came.

Life in Rabat continued, we were very busy each day, but we hadn't escaped all the excitement of the forthcoming World Football Cup. We followed the progress each evening on the BBC World Service, and England seemed to be doing very well. On the day of the final, Germany were to play England; M'Barek was very bemused at us as we sat in the office listening to the match as it was broadcast live. Imagine how we were cheering when, at the last minute the final England goal was struck, and the game was won! We were elated.... . Neither of us even liked football, but it was the only thing that made us feel at home!

That evening, we drove into Rabat and much to our surprise the England victory was the talk of the place! We went to the Balima for a coffee and as we drew up, we parked next to a rather battered old van with UK plates, and it was covered in Union Jacks! We went up onto the terrace and it was quite obvious whom the owners of the van were! There was a group of Cambridge Medical students, celebrating noisily and singing football anthems; they asked us to join them and during the time we were there it transpired that they were touring North Africa, and had only arrived in Morocco the day before.

They had driven down to Gibraltar and caught the ferry to Tangiers and then driven down to Rabat. They said that they were camping, but had no-where to stay that night, so we said they would be welcome to use the refuge. They accepted the offer and promised they would leave after breakfast. When we left, they followed us back to the refuge. It was still quite early in the evening and seeing the Ocean, they asked if they could swim there; we told them that it was very dangerous and they would do better going to Temara, just a few miles away. We went along too, and they all swam and sat on the beach for ages. Carol and I just sat on the beach and watched.

When the boys came out of the sea, they were all limping and clearly in pain... they had trodden on the spines of the Sea Anemones that come in close to land at night, the boys were clearly in agony. We had no idea that this happened, we had never even seen any Sea Anemones! As it was dark, I thought the best thing was to head home, where we might be able to help them.

They all sat on the floor in the office, and Carole and I used tweezers to extract the big sharp spikes of the sea anemones from their feet. Some of them snapped off and we had to leave these. We bandaged and plastered as best we could! The boys all slept in the van.

The next morning we all had breakfast and then they all unwrapped their feet; some were fine but others looked very sore. We gave them some cream to take with them, but it was obvious that some of the spikes would eventually fester. They set off during the morning their next port of call was to be Marrakesh. It was so good to meet them all. The 1966 World Cup has some rather unusual memories for us!

A couple of afternoons after their visit, we were outside the refuge dealing with a donkey that had been in an accident with a car. Luckily it was not badly hurt, and we were able to dress its wounds. A car drove up. A man in a Djelleba got out and walked over to us. He introduced himself in French and told us that his name was Ben Slimane. He was late middle aged, short and quite rotund; he had no teeth, and lisped when he talked. He asked if we could go with him, as his 'racehorse' was very sick! M'Barek insisted that he came along, 'incase we needed help'.

The man explained the symptoms, and I packed the things we were likely to need into my bag. Carol brought hers too.

We drove off in the direction of the hospital, following the car, and it turned down a little dirt road right beside the main gates. The road skirted the boundary of the hospital and we suddenly found ourselves passing by little gardens, almost akin to allotments!

After a while, we turned right and drove across to a small cluster of buildings. In one of them was a beautiful grey horse, being held by a very worried looking man. The horse was shaking and very agitated, Ben Slimane asked the man if there was any change? It appeared not. The horse clearly had colic. I asked if they had given him anything; they said they hadn't! I decided to see what was going on inside his back passage, and got my arm oiled up, so it would pass easily inside. I found a huge 'brick' of compacted food, and managed to remove it, along with a whole lot more. This happened a lot. Horses were fed a lot of chopped grass and hay, and it used to go solid and cause colic, sometimes it was fatal.

I asked Carol to prepare a drench. This is a liquid that is poured down the throat from a bottle. The neck of the bottle is wrapped so that there is no chance of the horse getting cut. Carole administered the drench whilst I held the horse's head high. After a short time, all the oily drench had gone, and we waited.

I told the groom to take the horse out and to keep him moving, and on no account was he to stop to let the horse eat anything, or to roll as this could prove fatal. They went outside and we all followed, watching carefully.

After about 15 minutes, the horse staled, (pee'd), and then he walked on. That was a good sign. About 15 minutes later, the horse stopped and emptied himself, at first passing big blocks of compacted food, then more normal ones. I crossed my fingers, as I thought he would be all right. We walked back to the stables and I asked the owner if there was a chance of a bucket of warm water. He sent the groom off with a bucket and he returned quite quickly. I gave the warm water to the horse, and he drank noisily. He looked tired and was still shivery, but his eye looked much brighter.

I told the owner that I wanted the horse fed carefully and to make sure there was always water in his stable. He promised faithfully, and told the groom to take care of the horse... or else! As we stood looking at the horse, the owner raised his hands to Allah in thanks, and then turned to me and hugged me! Then Carol and then shook M'Barek's hand, he asked if we would return the next day to see if the horse was alright. I said that would be fine, but that we would drive ourselves.

The owner said that the horse was very famous. His name was, 'Intestat', and he was a very big winner of races. I told him that he would not be able to race for a while, until we were sure he was fully better. He was clearly very fond of the animal. He drove us back to the refuge and there was more hugging and hand shaking!

The next day, Carol and I returned to see Intestat, Ben Slimane and the groom were there, waiting for us. "He is well! He is well! Praise to Allah" shouted the groom.

The horse looked to be fine, and he was relaxed and eating. I noticed a big bucket of fresh water in the corner. Ben Slimane asked if we ever went to the races?

I told him that we had no idea there was a racecourse! He said he would take us one day, when Intestat raced again. That would be fun!

Again, much hugging and thanking! We left him and drove to see Kitty, as we were so close. She was in good spirits. We had tea and lovely scones and cream! I asked her if she would like to come up to Meknes when we next went? She said she'd love to, as she had never been.

Ben Slimane became a frequent visitor to the refuge, in one way it was good to see him as he always came with freshly cut Alfalfa for the horses and donkeys. One day he arrived with a huge, heavy flat package, he gave it to me and said it was for saving his friend's life. I opened it, and it was an enormous brass tray that had been hand beaten. It was elaborately worked. I felt quite overwhelmed!

I accepted the tray, and he looked so pleased as he left! It was an absolute work of art of considerable quality.

We were so involved with our work and life in general that we suddenly realised that we had gone past the point where we should really have gone home for the hot summer! It had crept up on us quietly, and it didn't occur to us to pack up and go home... . getting hot was part of the job, and we really enjoyed it.

I wrote to the Major to ask if we could stay in Rabat through the year and he was happy for us to do so, just as long as we were happy to stay put... we were!

Chatting to Carole one day, I broached the subject of asking our mothers to come over to visit us. This seed grew and grew, and before we knew it, we had hatched a plan! We each wrote home to see if they would like to come. They were so excited and said they'd love to come, and that my older sister wanted to come too! So, plans were set in motion.

One morning, when in Rabat, we went to look at hotels, and found a little one down by the market. It was nice and quiet, with a little shaded courtyard, and seemed perfect. When we told Kitty and John our plans, they were horrified, and quite adamant that the two mums and my sister would stay with them! They insisted that they had plenty of room and that they would really love to have them to stay.

When we wrote home, we both told our families that they would be staying with John and Kitty. We each had a letter back to say how much they were all looking forward to coming! We felt we ought to do some homework, as we would take them out to eat at least three times during their time with us.

We took Maureen and Zaoui went to the Chinese Restaurant at the bottom of the main street, expecting it to be a Moroccan take on a Chinese eatery; but we were wrong! We climbed the stairs from street level to the first floor and entered a lovely room, decorated in Chinese style, and a beaming Chinese lady greeted us in French! It was a surprise! The waiters were also Chinese.

The food was exquisite, we ate several courses, at first with chopsticks, but we soon changed to knives and forks. 'Madame Chinese', as we came to know her, was charming and attentive. We went to pay the bill and were given a glass of rice wine each. Over the next few months we ate there about every two weeks.

Madame Chinese was always very pleased to see us. We took Maureen several times and, like us, she loved the place.

It was going to be a while before our mother's and my sister Betty arrived, and we threw ourselves into work each day as usual, although we were constantly thinking of things we could do with them. We decided that they might like to see the side of Morocco that a normal tourist might never see; the day-to-day life of the people.

At that week's Souk at Khemisset, we were told that there was to be a 'Fantasia' that night. It was to be held on the land where the market took place. We decided that we would stay on and see some of it.

Earlier than usual, the hundreds of animals, fully laden with the goods at the market started to leave. The little stalls and clutter started to disappear, and some much larger, goat - skin tents were erected at one end of the area. M'Barek told us that these tents belonged to the local Sheik. He was the local dignitary, and held in respect by one and all.

Fires were lit, and kettles and cooking pots were set over them. A few goats were tethered nearby, and we imagined that they were destined to the pot! There was clearly going to be a feast. About 6.00pm we became aware of a great many people arriving, mostly on foot, but many on donkeys and some in really battered old cars. They all lined up and formed a huge square area; the tents filled one entire side. The area in the middle was vast! We saw some horsemen riding in our direction, and it wasn't until they were much closer that we realised they all carried long, ornate rifles and wore traditional dress. There were a lot of women there too; they seemed to gather together on one side of the square.

A man approached us and spoke to M'Barek, he had been sent across by the Sheik to ask us to follow him back to the Sheik's tent. M'Barek was not invited and he stayed by the Landrover. We went with the man and were ushered into one of the goatskin tents and found the floor carpeted, and spread with cushions. A tall man stood up and told us that he was the local Sheik, and greeted us. He told us that he had heard of the good work we had been doing at the Souk since we had arrived in 'His Village', and we were invited to sit and watch the Fantasia in his tent. We were offered tea, and we sat down.

The Sheik explained that the Fantasia was an event that happened often during the summer months. It was a display of horsemanship and dated back many centuries. Just then, a huge plate of food was placed in front of us, and the Sheik told us to eat; it was couscous with vegetables and goat meat. I must say that is was delicious, and most welcome at the end of a busy day.

The meal ended with those delicious little cakes, dripping with honey. Then the Sheik stood, and beckoned us to follow him. Outside the tent was the empty square, surrounded by a big crowd; the end facing the tent was now occupied with the horsemen. At the sight of the Sheik, four of the horsemen started to gallop straight at us! They thundered along, and when they were so close to us, they pulled their horses to a stop and fired their guns as they did so! There was a big cloud of dust and smoke from the black powder of the guns. The women were ululating, as they would have done when their men were in battle; it was a very high-pitched screech, their tongues would trill; it was a wonderful sound that made the hairs on the back of our necks stand up!

As the horsemen withdrew, another four were thundering towards us; the crowd were cheering, and again, right in front of us, they screeched to a halt and the guns fired in the air! The festivities continued for a good two hours, then, as suddenly as it had happened it was over. We thanked the Sheik, who told us that we must always be his guests whenever there was a Fantasia in his province. We had really enjoyed seeing the spectacle. M'Barek was waiting for us; he had a splendid view from the bonnet of the Landrover! We got home much later than planned; we saw to the in-patients and went to bed after a shower to get rid of the day's mess and dust. Neither of us could sleep for ages.

At the weekend, I asked M'Barek if Yasmina and the children would like to go to the beach. He was amazed, as they had never been to a beach! He said they would love to go. Then I asked Ali if Rosella and his children would like to go the following week, he too was very excited at the thought.

M'Barek had been to the beach on many occasions, but had never paddled in the sea! We watched with great amusement as he took Yasmina down to the water and they paddled! Yasmina held her robes up to stop them getting wet. The children were in the water, splashing each other and squealing with delight as the waves broke gently over their knees.

Yasmina was amazed when Carol and I took off our clothes and revealed our swimming costumes, and even more amused as we ran down to the sea and strode out to the big breakers to swim and dive through the huge waves. We had taken a picnic, and some bottles of Coke that we had after our swim, and before we left for home. Dear Yasmina, she talked about that day so often!

When we arrived back at the refuge, there was a little party of men at the gate, they had arrived in a pick up truck, and a donkey was standing in the back of the truck. I drove in and M'barek went to see what the problem was. When he walked back in, he looked very serious. "Trouble Madame!" and he explained that the donkey had been bitten by a dog and had Rabies!

M'Barek was wonderful in a crisis, and in no time had found a stout stick which he offered to the donkey. It grabbed the stick in its mouth, and that allowed us to get it off the truck and quickly into a stable. The men left very quickly, they knew the score and that the poor animal would die. We left the donkey in the stable; the Rabies was quite advanced, and there were streams of saliva pouring from its mouth. We could do nothing until the following day, Monday. I told M'Barek that no one was to enter the stable, or touch the animal until I had seen the vet at the abattoir in the morning.

We both went several times during the night to look at the poor creature. It was tormented and in a dreadful state. Once, it had dropped the stick, and was trying to rip its belly open, violently biting itself. I put a broom in and managed to drag the stick close to the door. I put some rubber gloves on, picked the stick up and gave it back to the donkey; it held it in its mouth again. It was such a distressing sight.

The next morning, I drove to the abattoir and found the vet. I explained what we had and he agreed to come at once, he jumped into the Landrover and we returned to the refuge. When he saw the donkey he said it was near to death. We couldn't kill the poor thing as he said it was important to retrieve the brain intact, as soon as death occurred. He told us to send word to the abattoir as soon as it died, and he would send some men down to take the brain. He also said that they would remove the body and dispose of it. That was a great relief to us!

Fortunately for all concerned the poor, tortured beast died during that night. I sent M'Barek up to the abattoir, and he returned with two men who deftly removed the donkey's brain using a hammer and chisel! They placed it into a big jar. They told us that the carcass would be removed as soon as they could get a vehicle. It seemed strange. The poor creature's brain would be sent to the Wellcome Foundation at Pirbright, Surrey England, as it was the World's leading Rabies Vaccine Laboratory. When I was at Ascot Farm, before joining the Charity, I knew the Pirbright area very well! Small World.

The men returned with a lorry and quickly had the donkey on board. I told M'Barek not to touch anything in the stable, or to walk where the body had been dragged onto the lorry. Carol and I set off to get the strongest disinfectant we could find, and returned with two large drums of evil smelling black liquid.

We all set about the job of cleaning everywhere, and hosed and scrubbed; luckily, the stable was made of concrete blocks and had a concrete roof. So once it was totally hosed, we scrubbed it with the black disinfectant. I then asked M'Barek to build a fire in the stable, and we made a huge fire, and let it burn out. More hosing followed, and Ali was asked if he would paint the stable out when it was dry. It was such a heart - rending episode. I will never forget the look in that poor tortured donkey's eye.

Christmas was approaching and we made sure that we had plenty off food and were going to get some wine on our next trip to the market in Rabat. However, Mansour, the Chief of Police, who arrived in his Landrover one morning, beat us to it. His driver and another policeman who had followed on a motorcycle were ordered to unload the back of the vehicle.

To our surprise, off came a huge carboy filled with red wine! Mansour said it was confiscated wine that had been produced illegally by a Muslim farmer. It was carefully carried in to the office and gently sat onto the desk. It was huge, and must have contained at least five gallons of wine! The two policemen withdrew to their vehicles, but Mansour stayed. "I will take some wine with you" he said.

Getting the wine out of the carboy was difficult, but he said we should fill a jug. We all had a glass of the most delicious red wine. I was highly amused at the Chief of Police, himself a Muslim, drinking the confiscated wine of a Muslim farmer! Following this visit, El Mansour became a fairly frequent visitor, and when the wine had nearly gone, he produced another!

We asked him and Zaoui to the refuge on Christmas day, and we had a great time. We cooked a chicken and did some roast potatoes and vegetables. We ate one of my mother's Christmas puddings that she had sent me. The wine flowed and we had a very jolly day.

On Boxing Day, we dealt with our work before we smartened ourselves up and set off to Kitty and John's for yet another huge lunch. We collected Maureen on the way. Kitty had produced a wonderful feast! We had a roast lunch, then a wonderful fruit salad, made with every conceivable fresh fruit, and then we had mince pies and liqueurs! Another very jolly day! We spoke a lot about our parent's and my sister's visit. Kitty and John had it all worked out! We could start to make plans as they were coming in March before it got too hot.

It was back to work the following day. We received a telegram from M. Didier in France to tell us that he would like his two dogs sent over by air to Paris, where he would collect them. I told M'Barek who was very relieved, as both dogs were really unpleasant to have to deal with each day!

We bought two wooden airline crates from the airline office, one for each dog, and I bought their tickets to Paris out of the money that M.Didier had sent. They were booked to leave two days later, the plane left at 08.00am and we would drive them to the airport.

The following day both dogs were bathed. Now, due to their ferocity, a 'bath' would have been out of the question, so M'Barek did them with the hosepipe; he even managed to get some shampoo onto them! When they had dried, they both looked very presentable and they looked very well in themselves.

We had a steady stream of callers at the gate throughout the day, luckily only one needed to stay with us for intensive treatment for a badly infected wound to the hip. The owner explained that he had been fighting with another man, and the horse had got in the way and received a nasty knife wound! We managed to get the wound cleaned out and dressed. The horse was fine otherwise.

The following morning we were up and busy very early. At 06.00, M'Barek, with a huge smile on his face, managed to manhandle both dogs into their crates, and slammed the grille door with great aplomb! We got the crates into the back of the Landrover, and M'barek sat with them. The airport was on the other side of the city, about an hour's drive away.

We were directed to a big shed, where the crates were off loaded, the paperwork stamped, and we watched with a sense of great relief as the two crates were placed onto a trailer and towed over to the Royal Air Maroc plane that stood ready on the apron. We watched as it took off, I think were all relieved. We then returned to the refuge, stopping on the way for some shopping at the little market.

That evening we received a telegram from a very delighted M. Didier. He had his beloved dogs home, they had travelled well and were sitting with him! This sometimes happens, when dogs are devoted to one person, no – one else will do. In their case they turned aggressive, but as soon as they were reunited with their owner, they were quite normal!

At the next market we attended, something stung me on the forearm. It was very sore and extremely itchy, but I put something onto the sting that took the pain away. We got on with our busy day, and arrived home dusty and dirty, and in my case, with a swollen arm. We used the hosepipe to shower, and wrote up the daily notes and went to bed.

The next morning the sting had subsided, and no longer itched, so I ignored it. We went into Rabat for some food from the market and I also wanted to pop to see Kitty to ask her if she might like to accompany us next time we went to Meknes. She said she would love to come, and we fixed up to go in a couple of day's time, Maureen would come as well. We could drop in at the refuge to see John, and then descend on Jackie. We would take food with us, so there was no extra burden on her.

When we got back to the refuge, El Mansour was there, with his Police escort. M'Barek was always slightly edgy when he saw the policemen... Ali used to laugh at this. The purpose of the visit was to invite us both out for a meal. He said we could choose. We opted for the Chinese restaurant. He said that he would collect us at 7.00pm. I did wonder if he might turn up with a Police escort again! He left, and we carried on looking after our patients and treating any door callers. It was quite a hectic day.

At 7.00pm, El Mansour arrived in a smart taxi, and Zaoui was with him. We set off to the City. Madame Chinese was very pleased to see us; she had never met El Mansour, but welcomed him warmly. We had a lovely meal, with some good wine. I rather guessed that we were being propositioned! However, I managed to forestall any advances by saying that we should get home, as one of the in – patients needed a dose of antibiotics. They seemed quite all right with that, so we all set off back to the refuge.

We all went to see the horse, and I gave it a shot of antibiotic, I was relieved to see it looking a lot happier. Then we went in to our sitting room. El Mansour attempted to put his arm around me, and I

166

had to stop him in his tracks. I told him that he was very kind and that he had become a good friend, but that is all he was. (I knew full well, that somewhere in the Countryside he must have a proper home and a wife, and probably children. To his credit, he never tried again, but we did remain good friends.) After rather a lot of the confiscated wine, the two of them went home in the taxi... it had waited for ages, but it was more than the driver's life to abandon the Chief of Police on the edge of the City!

The days and weeks flew by, and it was only a week before our family members were due to arrive! We were very buoyed up by this, and made plans of what to do, and where to go. We had made sure that Kitty and John were still happy with the arrangements; they were nearly as excited as we were!

The day of their visit arrived. We went into Rabat early and bought lots of flowers from the little market, these were for Kitty and John. We stocked up on things to eat, and fresh vegetables. They were due at 4.00pm, and we were going to collect them from the airport. We were just beside ourselves at the thought of seeing them all again, also to showing them round the sights. We left the refuge at 2.30pm, filled the Landrover up on the way, and arrived with 20 minutes to wait. I went to the little office to check the arrival times, and there was Zaoui! He explained that he wasn't staying, but he felt that he might 'ease their passage'. He spoke to the man on duty, and said he was returning to the City. He added that he looked forward to meeting our family.

We watched the plane come in to land, and it drew up quite close to the building. A man in uniform walked over to us and asked us to follow him. He whisked us out onto the tarmac, and as the door of the plane opened, he went up that gangway and spoke to the steward. There was a small delay, and suddenly my Mother and sister, and Carol's mother stood at the top of the gangway! The man led them down, and beamed with delight as we threw our arms around them.

He then led us all into the building and into an office. He said the baggage would soon be with us, and sure enough, a young lad appeared with all their suitcases! The man stamped the passports and we were ready to go. No one else had been allowed to get off the plane until we left! How wonderful when 'strings' can be pulled that can achieve such lovely things!

As we drove through the City, they were looking every which way... nothing can prepare you for the different sights, sounds and 'smell' of North Africa. We drove on and arrived at Kitty's, and both her and John were on the steps to greet us all.

We all sat for a while, chatting and drinking tea, when Kitty decided that they might like to see their rooms and maybe shower to cool off after their journey.

Dear Kitty had prepared a sumptuous feast for us all, and the wine flowed. We all discussed plans, and we left them all, sitting out on the verandah, under the stars, with the wonderful scent of Bougainvillea. We had arranged to pick them up at 9.00am, and then we would take them on a tour of the City, and also to the refuge. We found it very hard to sleep that night.

We were up at 4.00am and made sure that everything was in order at the refuge. We treated a couple of animals at the gate, and then set off to collect our visitors.

As I pulled in to Kitty and John's driveway, I could see them all waving at us. They said they had enjoyed a wonderful breakfast, and had slept very well. Mum was amazed that the Passion Fruits had been picked from the vine in the garden, and they had the juice with their breakfast! We told Kitty that we would drop them back in the evening, and that we planned to take them out for a meal first. I told Kitty that we had booked a table at the Chinese Restaurant the following night and that we really wanted her and John to join us. She said they would be delighted.... Kitty had no idea there was a Chinese restaurant in the City.

We got the two Mums into the front of the Landrover, and Carol and my sister Betty climbed into the back. We had got some cushions for them to sit on.

I drove them into the City, and we started at the bottom of the big, wide main street. I drove slowly along, and we pointed out all the landmarks. We were approaching the top of the street, close to the Palace, when I slowed down, as there was a big junction, controlled by a policeman on his podium. He raised his arm and signalled us to stop, and to my Mum's horror, climbed down from the podium and walked over to us. He saluted me and shook my hand, I introduced our visitors, and they were all wondering what on earth we were doing! He wished them a very happy time, (they understood no French at all!), climbed back onto his podium, and waved us, and all the other traffic that was stationary behind us, forward with a flourish of his arm. My sister was roaring with laughter at what had just happened!

I drove them along the coast road that skirted the entire City, and they had a fantastic view of the Atlantic Ocean. We stayed on the road all the way to the refuge. When we arrived, I tooted the Horn, and M'Barek appeared, saluted and opened the gates for me to drive in. I was watching their reactions as they climbed down from the Land Rover. I introduced them to M'Barek and Ali and I heard M'Barek shout for Yasmina, and she and all the children appeared and shook hands with the visitors. We went into the office, put on the kettle, and Carol took them into out sitting room. We drank tea and chatted until lunchtime.

There was so much to ask, and so much to tell. For lunch we ate little pies from the little market, and fresh bread and butter with bananas. It was quite hot, but they asked if they could see the refuge, so we went outside and M'Barek walked solemnly with us, opening doors and holding some of the in - patients, he was in his element.

They were so amused that we needed a key to access the loo. I had to explain that everything was locked and unlocked all the time. They were a little taken aback at our bedroom, but we explained that it was very cosy and that we were able to shut the top door if it got cold in the winter.

We all clambered back into the Landrover and I drove out to Temara Beach. We sat and drank mint tea under the straw roof of the little café and watched the ocean for an hour. At Temara the rollers were less wild as in the centre of the little bay was a small rocky outcrop that stopped calmed the incoming rush of water. I promised that we would go to the beach at Sidi Boukanadel, where Betty could swim with us in the huge surf.

We took them to the little café at Agdal for supper, and Zaoui joined us for supper. We had wine and they ate the fiery sauce without batting an eyelid!

When we had finished the meal we gave Zaoui a lift home to the Palace Gates, and dropped them back at Kitty's. I think they were all ready for bed.

The following morning, we collected them at 8.30am, and we drove all around the outskirts of the City before turning into the main street. I parked at the Hotel Balima and we had coffee and a pastry each before we had a little walk around the shops. They were all amazed at how smart the big shops were. We then drove out to Akkari and we walked around 'our' part of town. They were quite fascinated by the change, and also how friendly the people were towards us.

We had lunch at a little café down at the Port of Rabat Sale. The café was right on the quay, so we watched the fishing boats unloading and setting off again. From there it was possible to walk through the oldest part of the City, The Medina; this was a real jumble of tiny streets, just wide enough for a couple of donkeys to pass.

People stared at us, as it was very unusual for foreigners to walk in the Medina. There were little stalls selling spices, others selling carpets and Copper and Brass. It was full of colour and people. We walked for half an hour and eventually came out in the big market at the bottom of the main street! From there we took a taxi back to the Port to collect the Landrover.

We drove back to the refuge and were told that no callers had been,checked on all the dogs and went to shower and change.

We left the refuge, as it was time to return to Kitty and John's for our visitors to change and for Kitty and John to come out with us to the Chinese Restaurant. We drove into the City in convoy, Kitty came in the Landrover, and Carole and her Mum went with John. We got to the restaurant and Mrs. Chinese made us all feel very welcome. She was delighted to meet our friends and family.

We had a wonderful meal. Kitty and John had spent some years in the East, and were absolutely bowled over by the authenticity of the food. We had a really fun evening! We drove back to Kitty's house and said that we would return in the morning, but at 8.00am, as we were driving up to Meknes.

We went home and were soon in bed. The breakers could be clearly heard crashing against the rocks. There was a storm in the early hours, but we slept through most of it.

The morning dawned sunny and bright and was very soon warm, all signs of the night's rain were soon dried up. We saw to the animals, and left to collect the 'Mums'. They said the storm had been amazing, with huge flashes of lightning. We told them that we often had them, but the day would be hot. We drove out of Rabat after stopping at the little market for provisions for our lunch with John and Jackie. They loved the journey and marveled at the little farms, and the groves of Oranges and Lemons.

We stopped high in the hills and had a drink and some biscuits. We were in the middle of no-where, and were soon being watched by a crowd of children! This amused the family no end. We drove on and through the huge gate at Meknes to show them the refuge at Meknes.

There was no sign of John, I guessed he'd gone home to help Jackie, and we drove on to find them both at the bungalow. We had a good lunch with them. I was quite perturbed at how tired Jackie looked. John was worried too, and in a quiet moment he told me that she wasn't at all settled and that they were thinking of going home. John said that he was not very happy either. I think they both found life so different to what they were used to, and were unable to adjust. I was very sorry to hear this.

We drove back to Rabat and called in at the refuge to have a tidy up, and then off to meet Zaoui at the little café in Agdal. Zaoui was there before us, and welcomed us all. He was impeccably dressed, as ever. We ate the wonderful brochettes and hot sauce, with fresh, flat bread, and drank wine. It was a super evening! I think the Mums and Betty were sorry it was over, but we drove them back to John and Kitty's. When we left they were all drinking on the terrace!

The following morning we went off to the beach at Sidi Boukanadel. We took a picnic of little pies and snacks from the market, and put a couple of bottles of wine into the basket as well. We took the big sun umbrella and blankets to sit on. The Mums and Betty were bowled over by the length of the beach, with not another soul in site! M'Barek had insisted that he should come to guard us.

The two Mums donned their costumes and paddled in the huge Ocean. The breakers were very big, but Betty went out in them with Carol and I took photos before joining them. We had a wonderful day.

On the way home we stopped for supper at the little café, they had said that they loved it and were quite happy to return. The owner greeted us all like long lost friends! The many greetings and the hand shaking fascinated my Mum: she would chat away to the man in English all the time that he was giving his welcome speech. We told them that the following day we would go to the market at Khemisset, and warned them to bring a hat and lots of sun – screen, and to wear things that wouldn't show the dust too much.

We were up early to pack the Landrover for the market, then, with M'Barek on board, we set off to collect the family. We drove them to the market and arrived there about 9.00am. The place was already bustling! Carol and I went about our work, and I told M'Barek to show the Mums and Betty all around the place, so they could see all the little stalls.

Along with our work - bags, we'd taken some soap and water to wash off the morning's grime. We were both very proud how quickly our visitors got the knack of popping behind a bush, or a rock for a 'comfort break'!

We sat under a huge Cork Oak and ate our lunch. The Mums and Betty were so excited at having seen all the stalls, particularly the dentist and the doctor!

Just as we were coming to the end of our lunch, a man approached us. He said he was the local Sheik's man, and asked us to go with him to meet the Sheik. We all went, and the Sheik appeared from inside his huge tent. He greeted Carole and me first, and I introduced him to our Mums and Betty. He greeted them very warmly, and invited us into his tent for mint tea.

I could see my Mum and Betty were completely overwhelmed by all this, I think Carol's Mum was dumbfounded! He clapped his hands, and cushions appeared from the back of the tent. We sat down and he poured the tea.

"I am glad to see you. There is to be a Fantasia tomorrow night; it will be held here, and I would much enjoy having you all as my guests"!

We had understood what he said, but, of course, or Mums and Betty hadn't a clue. I told them that when they left that they should thank him, in English, but I didn't mention the Fantasia. We told them that we would collect them at 9.00am, and that we would go and swim at Sidi Boukanadel, then have lunch at the refuge, and after that we would find something nice to do! I mentioned our plans, including the Fantasia, to Kitty. She thought the Fantasia sounded fun, but didn't really want to go.

I always found it a little strange that Kitty and John never mixed with the locals. I suppose after a lifetime of a very sheltered life in the Diplomatic Service, they had all they needed. I felt they missed out on so much!

We drove straight home to Kitty's and we left them there to shower and have supper. We went home, very excited at the prospect of tomorrow. We told M'Barek that he should come with us, but I knew the Sheik wouldn't invite him into the tent. M'Barek knew that too and was quite happy to go and watch.

The next morning, we had no callers, so we were able to leave early and get provisions for a picnic. Then we drove into Rabat proper and went to the Post Office for some stamps, and on to Agdal to collect our visitors.

We went to the beach at Sidi Boukanadel and the tide was right in and high. The breakers were quite magnificent; we just sat and gazed at them for a while and then changed into our costumes and went into the sea. The two Mums stayed right on the very edge, but Betty and Carol and I were soon out in the massive waves. It was fun to ride them in until they deposited you on the beach! If you got the timing wrong, the wave would tumble you, like clothes in a washing machine... and then dump you on the beach.

We stayed until lunchtime and decided to go back to the refuge and have our picnic. I drove home through the City, stopping briefly to get some medicines at the chemists. When we got back to the refuge, we took our picnic basket across the road and sat out on the rocks, the ocean was so vast and beautiful to watch. Occasionally a fishing boat would pass by, way off shore, as this was a dangerous, rocky place.

We had a few callers in the afternoon, and were much photographed by our visitors as we went about our business. I told M'Barek that we would need to leave at 5.00pm, so he set about seeing to all the in-mates.

We drove to Khemisset and were soon pulling into the market area. It was deserted, but in the distance, I could see the tents of the Sheik's entourage. I drove over and parked close by. M'Barek stayed with the Landrover. The Mums and Betty were intrigued!

The Sheik must have seen us coming as he was waiting for us at the tent door. Again, we were all greeted and ushered in, he led us into the tent, and then straight out again, through a side that had been opened up. Outside the tent on the other side were three Camels sitting down... He beckoned to the Mums and Betty to climb aboard! Their faces were absolute pictures! There were all wearing summer dresses, and had some trouble getting onto the camels, that were sitting down patiently. The sheik was beaming and chivvied his men to help! Then the lads leading the camels issued the words, "Hat! Hat! Hat", and the three camels started their cumbersome way of standing up. Suddenly, the Mums and Betty were up, high up on the camels. The boys led the camels away and were gone for a considerable time before we saw them again. They arrived back smiling and laughing. Carol's Mum said that her camel has gurgled all the way!

"HAT! HAT! HAT"! Shouted the boys, tapping the camels' forelegs with a stick.

The Sheik laughed as the camels sat down again; a camel sits in three stages, first by kneeling on the ground and putting it's head down on the ground, (people often fall off at this stage); then it rocks backwards onto it's haunches and finally settled. The

Mums and Betty were roaring with laughter as they clambered off.

The Sheik was clearly delighted at their achievement. We went into the tent, drank tea and whist we sat there, we noticed that many people were arriving and forming the huge square. We were brought a massive platter of roast lamb and couscous. We all ate, and the Sheik was trying to teach our visitors how to roll up the couscous into a little ball using only the right hand.

The meal ended with the honey cakes; very rich and very messy, but so delicious. The women brought water for us to wash our sticky fingers. The Sheik stood and ushered us outside, where a group of cushions had been placed. We sat down and the Fantasia began. Row after row of horsemen charged at us and firing their long muskets at very close quarters; it was noisy, dusty but just so incredible to all be a part of this ancient tradition.

Betty and the Mums took many photos, and at the end, were invited back into the tent by the Sheik. He very solemnly shook hands with us all; he threw his arms around our Mums and Betty. We thanked him for his hospitality, and for giving our visitors such a fine time. He said that we were his honored friends and that we were welcome at any time. We drove home on cloud nine; we had all had an unbelievable evening!

There were just two days left. We asked the Mums and Betty what they would like to do or see. We had been invited to Zaoui's for a meal on the first of the two nights, and on the final night, we were having a farewell meal at Kitty and Johns.

To our surprise, they all said they would love to see Casablanca. So off we went!

It was no time at all before we were in the City, with its big white buildings. I had only ever driven to the docks, but we thought the main streets might be better.

The centre of the City was very smart, with some very expensive looking shops. We parked and went for a coffee at a pavement café. The owner was French, and produced an amazing selection of cakes and pastries for us to chose from.

I asked him where the beach was and he gave me directions to the beaches, but added that the 'public beach' was further along. Until we got there, I didn't quite understand what he meant.

All along the 'front' were private beaches, 'Copacabana', 'Paradise', 'Honolulu', etc. Each beach was fenced off and they appeared to be owned by the hotels that stood on the opposite side of the road. We stopped at 'Monte Carlo Beach', and Carol went into the Hotel to see if was possible to sit on the beach. It transpired that as long as we bought a drink or food, we could sit on the beach! We parked up again, and walked down to the beach. No sooner had we set foot on the sand, a waiter came out of a little brick kiosk to take our order. We decided that it wasn't everyday that we sat on a beach in Casablanca, so we ordered a bottle of Champagne. An old man appeared with some comfortable chairs and we spend a very happy time there.

We drove home, stopping at Temara for a sandwich and a coffee. Then back to the refuge. There were several animals and their owners waiting, so carol and I dealt with them and the Mums and Betty went off into our room to tidy themselves up before we went to Zaoui's for a meal.

We had been told how to get to Zaoui's home, but he said that he would meet us at the Palace gates incase we had any problems. We drove into the City, taking our visitors on a different route, in fact giving them a really big tour of the place, and finally towards the King's Palace. Zaoui was waiting for us. He walked over to the guards at the gate, and the barriers rose; Zaoui got into the Landrover, and we drove into the Palace grounds. It was very beautiful, the walls and buildings all in pale green and white, with huge flower beds; we turned sharply right, only to be stopped by more guards; Zaoui leaned out and they recognized him, the barriers opened, and we drove on, stopping close to the side wall of the Palace.

Zaoui helped the Mums and Betty get out of the vehicle, and then bowed, and welcomed us to his Father's house. We briefly met his Father, resplendent in his white Caïd's robes; he was tall, with a white beard. He made us all feel very welcome.

We were ushered into a smaller room, where Zaoui's three sisters were waiting, all giggling and shy. They proceeded to dress the Mums and Betty in proper Arab dress! They were clearly very amused at the outcome; then we all went through and sat around the adjoining room on cushions. Zaoui's Mother appeared, she was very beautiful; she greeted us like long lost friends, and greeted us with the lovely Arabic words, 'Welcome, my house is your house'. She dismissed the daughters who returned carrying an enormous bowl of couscous, this time, not with vegetables, but with plump raisins and nuts, she poured some olive oil over it and then sprinkled sugar over the top. Then in came three huge legs of slowly roasted mutton and finally, a small bowl containing a fiery sauce.

Zaoui told us to eat, and was quite amazed when they managed to make little balls of the couscous. He laughed when we told him how they had learnt the knack. The meat was really succulent, and it was dipped into the fiery sauce. I loved this variety of couscous. I found it far nicer than the vegetable kind that tended to be rather soggy. When we had eaten our fill, the platters were removed, and another huge plate arrived with massive pie. Zaoui explained that this was 'Pistilla', a great delicacy in Morocco; it was made with pigeon and very flaky pastry and lots of chopped nuts. We all took a small helping it was quite delicious! There was a lull before another plate appeared with a huge honey cake on it. By then we were really full. It had been just wonderful.

Zaoui then told us that he had a little treat. He said we were going to a 'place he knew'... all very secretive. We said our very fond farewells to his sisters and mother, and climbed back into the Landrover. I drove through the gates and Zaoui told me to drive to the big square in the City; we stopped outside a café called, 'La Jour at Nuit', ('The Day and Night'), a little coffee shop that we had often stopped at. Zaoui took us through the door, but the name of the place had changed to 'La Lanterne Noir', ('The Black lantern), seeing my expression, Zaoui explained that this café had always had one name for the day, and one for the night; we went upstairs to a large room that had tables all around the walls; there were quite a lot of people there.

We sat at a table, and Zaoui ordered drinks, we all had wine. Within minutes, the lights dimmed right down and music could be heard, then, into the middle of the room walked a woman who proceeded to dance to the music; she was a belly dancer! Zaoui explained that she was the most famous in Morocco, and he wanted the Mums and Betty to see something very authentic. They just loved it!

It was very late when we got back to Kitty and Johns, but they were on the terrace, and we left them all there drinking gin and tonics, no doubt relating the day's events.

The final full day arrived all too soon. We collected our visitors at 8.30am and drove into the City for some sightseeing. I parked at the 'Tour Hassan', a huge tower, build in red stone, very high and square. The top was flat. We paid the guardian and began the long walk to the top; there were no stairs, but a very wide ramp that went ever upwards. When we reached the top it really was flat, and none of us were brave enough to go to the edge to see the view across the port of Rabat-Sale and the river. We clung to a post in the centre for dear life.

From there we visited the pretty gardens at Chellah on the edge of the old part of the City. We spent some time there before going off to have coffee at the little café that we'd visited the night before for the Belly Dancing. The owner was pleased to see us and asked if we had enjoyed the dancing. He didn't charge for the coffees. Then we visited several of the big shops. They all bought souvenirs of their visit. We called in at the Royal air Maroc office to check the flight times and they were fine. Then we drove on to have lunch on the terrace at the Hotel Balima. We were all very pleased to see Zaoui; he ate with us and we told him about the morning's sight – seeing. He said that the ramps inside the Tour Hassan were to allow horses and riders to get to the top, and added that the bravest jumped off. I have no idea if this was true, but Morocco did have a very bloody past, and it wasn't all that time ago that heads of traitors were displayed on the gates leading into the City!

When the meal was over, he said his farewells to the family. I think he had enjoyed seeing them every bit as much as they had enjoyed his company. As he left he told us that he would like us to meet him at the café in Agdal the following night and we could raise a glass to our family who, by then would be back in England.

We went to the refuge afterwards, and they took more photos of the place, from the road, looking across the sea, of gate visitors, and of M'Barek and his family. They promised to send some photos to him. We tidied up and left for John and Kitty's for the farewell meal.

It was very late when we got back to the refuge. We had enjoyed a wonderful evening. The Mums and Betty had bought a joint gift of a bronze camel for John and Kitty. They were delighted and placed on a sideboard. Kitty said they had really enjoyed having them to stay and that if they ever returned, the bedrooms would be ready and waiting. Quite a lot of wine and Champagne was drunk!

The plane was leaving at 9.30am, so we collected our visitors at 7.30am and drove through the City, across the river and out to the airport. Once again, Zaoui must have a hand in the events, as we were allowed through to say our goodbyes at the foot of the gangway of the aircraft. We laughed, we cried and we waved as the plane taxied away and took off. I think we both felt a mixture of elation and sadness. We went back to the refuge, stopping only to get some bread at the little market. Luckily, the day was very quiet. We were able to deal with the callers, and generally relax. It had been the most wonderful time.

The following morning, we were jolted back to reality when a letter arrived from The Major. It stated that there was concern amongst the various animal welfare organizations about the trade of Tortoises between Morocco and Great Britain.

We had no knowledge of this! The letter went on to say that the tortoises were caught in the hills, crammed into tea chests, and sent to the UK, the only other thing in the tea chests were tomatoes. Many of them died on the journey.

The Major asked us if we could supply the names of any dealers working in this trade, and also if we could visit the docks at Casablanca to see for ourselves. The Chief Vet at the Port had been informed that we would visit, and had promised his help. It all sounded very interesting. We told M'Barek and Ali that we would be away for a day. M'Barek was a little miffed when we said we would travel alone, he felt it was his duty to be with us. I explained that we were meeting the Chief Vet, and he seemed happy with that.

I got film for the camera and we let the Chief Vet know that we would be in Casablanca the following morning; he advised us to be at the docks by 7.00am as there was a consignment due to leave on a ship bound for London. He said he would meet us at the Port gates.

We set off early the following day. It seemed strange to be doing something so very different! When we got to Casablanca I drove straight to the Port. The Vet was there, he introduced himself as Dr. Mohammed Ashir. He seemed very nice; he then introduced us to the Chief of Police who was there to ensure that we were not threatened by anyone. He said that his friend El Mansour from Rabat had spoken highly of us.

We all drove down to the quayside in procession, with the Police vehicle in front.

The crew of the ship were looking very suspiciously at us, but the Policeman went up the gangway and we followed; he asked to see the Captain.

We were taken down into the hold, where there was a mixed cargo. In one section were about 12 crates. The vet asked the Captain to open one crate. A Crewman levered off the lid. Inside was a pathetic sight: there was a huge number of Tortoises, quite young ones, sitting on a huge pile of tomatoes; the crate was full to the brim, with no air whatsoever.

The Policeman ordered the crates to be removed from the ship; there was rather a lot of arguing, but eventually the Captain relented. The crates were carried off and placed on the quayside. I asked what would happen to them, and the Vet said they would be released into the wild; I suggested that we could easily take the crates and set the creatures free as we got to a suitable place. He agreed to this, and barked an order to some crewmen to load the Landrover. We asked who had sent the Tortoises, and the Policeman said that this matter would be investigated, with vigour. I asked if we could see the Manifest where the details would be listed. From this I was able to get one name and a partial address, but it was a start.

We stopped on the way home and released the Tortoises on sloping ground that had some tree cover, the sort of habitat they liked, poor little things. We got back to the refuge, all was well; we showered and started to compose our report for the Major. We had no typewriter, so it was several pages of longhand I put the reel of film into the envelope. We drove into the City and dropped it into the box at the Post Office.

A couple of days later we received a letter from the Major who was delighted with the Report. He said that copies and photos had been passed to the relevant organizations. This was the very first move in getting the trade in Tortoises stopped. (It was some years before it was finally made illegal).

That night poor Carole started another bout of her problem. I told her that we would get to a Doctor is it went on for too long. Luckily we had the name and address of a Doctor that Maureen had told us about.
The following morning Carole was incapable of working and stayed in bed as much as she could, but had to scurry to the loo frequently. We drove to the Doctor's surgery late in the afternoon. Carole was in with the doctor for an age, and when she emerged she was clutching a bag of medicines. She paid the nurse for the treatment and we set off for home. She told me that the doctor had taken tests and that she was to go back to see him in two days time. In the meantime, she was to take the medicines and drink lots of water.

It was some relief to find Carol very much improved the next day. I did the work and she stayed in and cooked and did the bookwork. In the cool of the evening we both drove into the City and went to the little market for our shopping; the little market stayed open until very late, the little lights on each stall were very pretty. We stopped for a coffee before driving home.

We went to the beach the following lunchtime and Carol was clearly very much better. On the way home, as we turned up the little road opposite the garage we both noticed a poster at the little cinema. It was the Beatles in, 'HELP!' The rest of the poster was in Arabic, but it was definitely the Beatle's film. We felt we should go and see it, even if it was in Arabic, we could sing along to the music.
The film was due to start at 8.00pm.

We went home and did some work on all the dogs; removing the odd tick, and giving them a run in the yard. There were a lot of callers at the gate during the afternoon, but we were finished by 6.30pm. We changed and set off to the cinema, not really knowing what to expect.

The cinema was tiny, and apart from two men, we were the only ones there. When the film started we were thrilled that it was in English, with Arabic subtitles. We new every word of every song, and had both seen the film before. I think we grinned like Cheshire cats, all the way through. It was just wonderful!

When we called at the Doctor's surgery the following day, Carole was told that she has Amoebic Dysentery. Caused by an amoeba in the gut, she had been told that it was very common in North Africa. There was no proper cure at that time, but if she were careful, she would be able to control the problem sufficiently to enable her to work.

We went off to the beach at lunchtime. Carole had packed some bread, butter and some cheese and salad. We set off and M'Barek came with us. I think he considered it his job to look after us in every situation. The beach at Sidi Boukanadel was deserted as ever.

We swam and then sat and ate. Carol was rather quiet and I guessed she was mulling over the problems of her illness. On the drive back, she said that she really ought to go home. I wasn't surprised, but I was concerned.

Her reasoning was that as long as she was in Morocco, there was always a strong possibility of the problem returning. She felt she might have a better chance of good treatment back in the UK. We chatted late into the night, finally falling asleep listening to the ocean.

The next morning, we were off to Khemissett and as we had to collect some nails for Ali, I took the route out through the edge of the City. As I drove along, I could see a crowd ahead and slowed down; M'Barek told us it was an accident, and I stopped. He jumped out of the back, and as he did so we both saw a grey horse on the road. It must have slipped and fallen, it's cart was on it's side and there were oranges everywhere.

A group of men were shouting and hitting the horse, trying to get it to its feet. M'Barek grabbed our bags and we pushed in to stop the men. When the crowd saw us, I heard someone shout that we were the 'Donkey Doctors', and to let us look at the horse. The men who were hitting the horse stopped, and Carol and I were able to get down to the stricken animal.

I asked if anyone had a knife and a man rushed forwards, I asked him to cut the ropes that that attached to the horse to the cart. The cart was pushed away. The horse was alive and was able to move his legs. We needed to get the horse sitting up and I asked if anyone near had a couple of straw bales. Within moments, two men returned carrying one each. M'Barek took the horses' head and Carol and I rolled it slightly over and then we all pushed, the man slipped the bales of straw in place. Once it was sitting up the horse looked far more alert.

We let it sit for a moment and then we gently got it to it's feet; the horse was a bit shaky, but alright apart from a couple of nasty scraped to his legs, and his head was bleeding where he'd hit the road. I asked the owner to move the horse to see if he was able to walk, and he seemed to be coping. I told the owner to walk him slowly to the refuge where we would see to his wounds. M'Barek and several member's of the crowd repeated these instructions to the owner. He said he would go at once. As we got back into the Landrover, people who wanted to shake our hands besieged us. Quite amazing! We drove back to the refuge, doing a little detour to get Ali some nails.

We had time for a coffee while we waited for the horse to arrive. There was a knock at the gate and the horse stood there, with his owner and a large number of the crowd. We let them all in while we dealt with the horse. Luckily, there was nothing more than superficial wounds to patch up. I told the owner that he must not work the horse for a couple of days and he said that he would keep him safe. The horse was led away, with the crowd following. I think they had enjoyed the whole event.

We then went off to Khemisset, later than planned, but still with plenty of the day left to get a lot done. During that day my arm swelled up; it was the same place that was stung some weeks before. By the time we'd finished, my arm was very achy. We went home and when we had showered I had a good look at the swollen arm. Exactly where the sting had been was a deep red mark. I could see that it was infected.

The next morning my arm, below the elbow was very swollen, and the site of the sting looked very angry. Luckily, we were going to Kitty's for supper and Maureen would be there. During the day it got much worse, and it was very obvious that it would need to be lanced.

When we got to Kitty's, Maureen took one look at it and confirmed that it should be lanced to drain the pus. She said I should go to a doctor, but I said that I was sure she'd done it many times before. She had, but then said she had no instruments. Carol laughed and went out to the Landrover and returned with her bag. It contained everything Maureen would need. So while Kitty and John sat with Carol on the terrace, sipping cold drinks, Maureen and I went into the laundry room and she deftly dealt with my arm. It felt instantly better, and even more comfortable once it was dressed. We joined the others for a much needed drink.

One morning the post came and there was a gilt edged card. We assumed it was an invitation to another Garden Party, but we were so wrong! There was a letter inviting us to visit H.M.S. Tiger, a Royal Naval ship that was paying a courtesy call to the Port of Casablanca. The Officers had invited us, along with other British subjects living in Morocco. It sounded as if it was one of those opportunities not to miss. The invitation was for 3rd October, just one week away.

That week we were very busy with callers, none of them had serious problems, but they all took time to examine and treat. I was quite sure that some of them simply because they enjoyed the experience! We never minded this as it meant that they knew we were here and they trusted us.

We both got our 'tidy' clothes to wear for the visit. It was time to leave for Casablanca. We remembered to take the invitation, as it was also a Pass to enter the docks.

We arrived at the Dock Gates and were sent on to where the ship was moored. She was huge! We were allowed to park right alongside and were accompanied up the gang -plank where we were met by an officer. He took us on a tour of the ship, which proved to be very interesting. We stood on the huge bridge before he took us to the Ward Room where we were to have drinks. Here were a handful of other people there and they chatted to us. The Officers were very attentive and they mingled amongst us.

We'd been there a short time when a uniformed man knocked at the door and asked for the Captain. A brief discussion took place between the two men, and the Captain turned to face us all. He told us that he had just received a signal from the Admiralty and that the ship had been asked to make haste to the Mediterranean. He apologized and asked us all to leave so the ship could be readied for sea.

As I left, the Captain took me to one side. "Madam, Is the Landrover yours?" I told him it was, and he then asked if they might borrow it for a short time? I said yes, and Carol and I followed him. He saw us ashore and asked one of the crew to get into the Landrover. It was then used to hoist a large black car up onto the deck! Once the car had been safely stowed, the Captain thanked us profusely and we left.

Two days later we were listening to BBC World Service and we heard that major talks were being held aboard H.M.S. Tiger in the Mediterranean. The Prime Minister, Harold Macmillan, was holding talks with Mr. Ian Smith who had declared Rhodesian Independence from Britain. Zimbabwe was born, and we had been involved in a very small way!

It was October and it was just starting to get chilly and it rained quite often. We lit the fire at nights to take the chill out of the sitting room. I made sure that M'Barek and Ali had a warm jacket each to work in as the winds off the sea could be quite chilling. We also made sure that we had plenty of jute sacks ready as they worked wonderfully as rugs for any inpatients.

One morning there was a shout at the gate. M'Barek opened the door and let a man in. Neither of us recognized him. It was Ben Slimane, the owner of Intestat the racehorse. He was beaming at us with his new set of dentures! Until then, we had only ever seen him toothless. The new dentures were truly dreadful and gave him a smile that was beyond description! I think he had come solely to show us the new teeth. He must have paid a lot for them, but they were so bad!

He stayed a while and we sat in the office and gave him coffee and chatted. He said he had decided to leave Intestat until the following summer before he raced again. He told us that he was being very careful with the horse and that he always had a big bucket of cool water in the stable with him. He left us, still with that awful tombstone effect grimace.

Christmas was once again nearly upon us and we had a steady trickle of cards from friends. We both received parcels from home. Carol's Mum had sent a cake and some crackers. My Mum had sent a pudding and some chocolates and also some decorations from the tree. We also had a parcel from Betty. It contained tins of ham and all sorts of goodies to eat. We would have a lovely time!

On the day we had our usual roast chicken with all the trimmings, followed by the pudding, then later tea and cake! We also had a fine carboy of wine to drink, thanks to El Mansour! Zaoui came for part of the day; he shared lunch with us and had some cake. He went home about 6.00pm. I asked M'Barek to find him a taxi.

On Boxing Day we went for lunch at Kitty and John's and Maureen was there too. Once again, we had a wonderful meal and then a lovely curl up in the huge armchairs. Arnaud slept on top of me; a Boxer dog is quite weighty!

We were so fond of our friends, and towards the end of the day, Maureen told us that her contract was nearly finished, and that she would be returning to Geneva in three months time. We were all utterly stunned.

On the way home that evening, Carol said that she would like to return home before it got too hot. She had been mulling over her illness and had clearly reached a decision, probably nudged on by Maureen's announcement.

I wasn't surprised at the news, and I could see that she was dreading another bout of illness when it gets so hot.

The next day I wrote to the Major to inform that that Carol would be returning to the UK before it got too hot, and I explained the reasons. Carol was relieved that she had finally made a decision. We drove to Kitty's with some flowers to thank her for a wonderful meal, and to tell her Carol's news. She was very sorry, but understood exactly why Carol was going.

We were quite busy during that week, and no more was said about going home.

We returned home from Khemisset on the Thursday to find a letter from the Major. He said he was very sorry to hear about Carol's illness, and that she should plan to return in May, before the very hot weather. He went on to say that I should try to find someone to take over Carol's position. I could think of no one. I would have to think long and hard. I was due home for some leave, but I would stay on until the end of June.

One evening, after a very busy day, and just as the sun was setting across the ocean, I walked across the road and sat on the rocks to watch the sea. I felt quite overcome with emotion. I was in love with the place, the Country and its people. This worried me somewhat, as it would mean I would probably stay here forever. Both Maureen and Carole were going, and the thought of starting again with someone new was not something I really wanted to do. Just then, Mohammed the carter passed me in the half-light, he was on his way home. He raised his arm and shouted a friendly greeting as he drove by. I returned the greeting, and just sat, looking out across the vast ocean until I went back to the refuge and told Carol that I had decided to return home, but that I would wait until the Major had found two people to take over the refuge.

In the morning I wrote to the Major to tell him of my decision. I suggested that I returned in late June. That would give him plenty of time to find suitable people. We drove into the City to post the letter. We stopped for a coffee at the Balima and sat quietly. I don't think either of us could believe that we were going.

When we got home there were several callers. One man wanted some medicine for his wife! One old man had walked there with a donkey and it's foal; the donkey was in need of its feet trimming. This was always such a hot job to do!

The third caller was a regular, one of the local carters. His horse had developed a sore. Luckily he had brought it in good time and a dressing and some extra padding was all that was needed.

The following day we were meeting Maureen and Zaoui and going for supper at the little café in Agdal. We were busy with callers most of the day and even missed our swim because of the number of visitors. We showered under the hot hosepipe before changing in the evening. Having made sure that all the inmates were all right, we set off to collect Zaoui and Maureen. We told them both of our decisions; Maureen understood, but poor Zaoui was very upset. Once he'd heard our reasons he was much calmer. He understood why Carol was going, but he said that if I loved the place so, how could I bear to go? We all drank a little too much that evening!

The next morning we were both up at the crack of dawn, it was always a little cooler at that time, but the sun soon rose and it became hot very quickly. We did the morning rounds and planned the day. Carol was going to stay at the refuge to deal with callers and I was going to get the Landrover serviced at a garage in the city. I was also going to shop for medicines and food. I also planned to visit Kitty and tell her all the latest happenings.

The Landrover was serviced in no time, and I drove on into the main street to the chemist to stock up on dressings and some medicines. Then on to the little market and I got some goodies for us, and a large bunch of flowers for Kitty.

I arrived at her gate and the gardener opened it. He grinned and told me that 'Madame' was at home.

Kitty was thrilled with the flowers. She made coffee and we sat out on the verandah. I told her that we would be going, Carol in May, and me in June. She said she had a feeling this might happen. Dear Kitty, she was so understanding. She knew how much I adored Morocco, but she told me that to stay would be wrong. She said I was missing a part of my life in the UK that could never be lived again. When I left her, I was quite at peace with myself.

When I arrived back at the refuge, Carol was outside dealing with a rather fractious mule. Between the owner and M'Barek, the mule seemed to be sufficiently restrained for her to deal with a wound on its neck. I drove in and she followed a short time later. I told her that I'd been to see Kitty; she was pleased, as she didn't know how to broach the subject.

We went to the beach for a swim at lunchtime. We sat on the beach, under the sun brolly and ate some fresh bread and cheese. M'Barek sat by our clothes to make sure they weren't stolen. This always amused us, as there was never a soul there!

Later that day I wrote a long letter to the Major. It took me an age, as I wanted to get it exactly right. In the evening we drove into the city and posted it at the big Post Office. I think we were both feeling very low about it all, but I knew that it was the right decision.

In the early hours of the night, I heard knocking at the door. M'Barek had heard it too and was shouting to see who it was. Outside the gates stood a man with a horse, it was covered in blood. We got it inside the gates and the man said that there had been an accident. It transpired that the poor animal had been hit by a lorry. The owner explained that the lorry was travelling very slowly, but it had a noisy engine and had frightened the horse, who had been hurt when he ran into some railings.

We cleaned the blood up as best we could, and found two deep wounds at the top of each foreleg. M'Barek told the owner that the horse would have to stay with us, and the owner readily agreed. We felt it wise not to stich the wounds as there had been penetration downwards. It was important to let the wounds drain. In the event of infection, we might have to make an opening at the bottom of the wound, but we hoped that it wouldn't come to that. We dressed both legs and led the horse to one of the pens. M'Barek gave it water and we fed it. We both went back to bed.

The following morning, the wounds looked quite healthy, so we applied fresh dressings. The horse was very sweet natured and was certainly enjoying his food. We went to Khemisset that morning. The market was quite busy and we only just got through all of the animals before they started to leave. We returned home. The horse was fine, but a little stiff which, considering the accident, wasn't really surprising.

The weekend came and went in a trice. The horse was recovering very well indeed. His owner called daily to see him and to give thanks to Allah for his remarkable recovery. The postman brought a letter from London.

The Major wrote a very nice letter, saying how very sorry he was that we were both leaving. He added that he would start to look for suitable replacements and would let us know in good time. He asked if I would be willing to stay until they had settled into the job.

We took Maureen and Zaoui to the little café that evening. Zaoui told us that he would bring Mohammed, the King's cousin to visit us the next day, he said they would arrive about 11.00am, and I told Zaoui to invite Mohammed to stay for some lunch.   As we drove home we discussed what we could cook for him. In the end we thought that a proper, 'Sunday Lunch' would be just the thing!

The next morning we both drove to the little market with a long shopping list. We managed to get everything we needed. We finally bought some strawberries and a pot of thick cream.

The rest of the morning we were both busy. I cleaned and Carol cooked and prepared vegetables.   I went round all the dog pens and checked on the other in-patients. The horse with the injured legs was dong very well. I told his owner that he might be able to go back to work the following week.

At 11.00am there was the sound of a car outside. M'Barek opened the gate and immediately jumped to attention and saluted! Mohammed and Zaoui got out and greeted us. M'Barek was completely phased by our new visitor; he knew exactly who he was and it made us laugh to see M'barek bowing as he ushered our visitors around the place to show them all the animals.

We went into through the office into our little sitting room.   Luckily, we some really good wine left in the carboy, so we drank and we ate and we laughed the afternoon away. Mohammed said it was the first time he had ever eaten English food, and that it was very good. They left about 4.00pm. As they got back into the big car, M'Barek was very careful to open the doors for them. He saluted as they drove off. We had really enjoyed having them.

The injured horse made remarkable progress and he went home with his very happy owner three weeks after he came to us. The wounds had completely closed and we made sure that he took sufficient wound powder home with him to dust the wounds with each day. The owner was delighted and proudly walked the horse back to his home in the shantytown.

We had been asked to visit Kitty and John as they were planning a farewell dinner for Maureen; they wanted to know if we'd like to go in with them and buy a nice gift to present to Maureen. Of course we agreed, and I told Kitty that Maureen had always admired a lovely statue of a horse that was on display in one of the expensive shops in the main street. We all went to look at it.

The statue was lovely; we had seen it before, but Kitty and John had never been told about it. Every time we passed the shop with Maureen she commented on the horse. It was an Arab horse, and was held by a man in traditional clothing. We enquired about the price and we all felt it would make a perfect gift. John paid there and then, and we said we'd give them our share when we next saw them.

On the night of the dinner we collected Maureen from the gates of the hospital. She was excited as her contract only had one more day to run. She was then going to stay at Kitty and Johns for a day before flying home to Switzerland.

The meal was a great success, we toasted everything we could think of and all drank a little too much.

When John gave Maureen the gift she was overcome, but managed a tearful speech. We dropped her back at the hospital gates about midnight and said our sad goodbyes. We would miss her enormously.

It would only be a matter of weeks before Carol departed, but in the meantime there was work to do. We continued with our weekly markets and were kept very busy with callers at the gate. It was starting to get quite hot again, so we each bought a new straw hat from the little man that weaved baskets and hats from rushes and straw.

Another film came to the cinema, this time it was Norman Wisdom in, 'A stitch in time'. We went to see it and were thrilled to find that it was all in English with subtitles. We really enjoyed watching it, as it was so funny. That, sadly was the very last film that we were able to watch. All the rest were in Arabic.

There was a dreadful commotion at the next market we went to. A fight had broken out between two groups of men and there were fists flying at first, then knives. Nobody was hurt, but one of the men had slashed one of the donkeys belonging to one of the other men. We hurried over and shouted at the men to stop and calm down. M'Barek waded in and very officiously told them to go away!

The donkey was bleeding a lot and half it's right ear was missing. It kept shaking its head and blood was spurting everywhere. I managed to hold the two edges of the ear tightly together and the bleeding eased and finally stopped. As soon as I slackened my grip, it started again! It was about 30 minutes before we had it fully under control. I bandaged the ear and made sure that the cut sides were well padded. I asked M'Barek to tell the owner that the donkey would have to go home with us to Rabat.

The owner said we should take him, but the only way to get him home was in the back of the Landrover! M'Barek sat with him, holding him with a rope. I promised the owner that we would return the donkey the following week and that he would be fine by then. We set off for home and I drove very carefully with our precious cargo.

Considering the mode of transport, the donkey behaved impeccably and we got home safely. We carefully got the donkey out of the back of the Landrover and settled him into a pen. I decided that his ear would be best left alone for the night.

The following morning we took the bandages off and the ear looked fine. The bleeding had stopped and there was a good crusty scab all around the ear. I dressed it with Boracic and Iodoform powder; it was wonderful for wounds and also kept the flies off. The donkey enjoyed his week with us.

When we returned to the market the following week, the owner was waiting for us at the gateway. He was thrilled to see the donkey, free of blood and with the wound healed up. He bought us some eggs for our troubles and told us that Allah would look after us both. For reasons unknown, the market was very quiet and we drove home in the middle of the afternoon, as we'd run out of customers.

There were a few callers at the gate, so we saw to them before going inside to get cleaned up.

There was a letter from the Major to say that he'd found two suitable replacements to take over from us. Two young women who were both used to dogs, and one of them was used to horses. He said they would be coming out in June and asked me if I could book them into the little hotel that we had stayed at when we first arrived?

There was also a letter from the farm at Ascot to say that they were really looking forward to having me back again. The letter also contained lots of news about the animals, particularly the Jersey cows that I was so fond of. I was looking forward to seeing them all again too.

I wrote to the Major as soon as we'd visited Mohammed's little hotel in the City. He was happy to let the room for the two new girls for as long as they needed it.

I also asked the Major to send them out with a whole list of things that we were unable to get in Morocco, in particular, worming powder and tick treatments that worked.

Carol had just a short time left in Rabat. We drove into the City to book her flight home. She would fly from Rabat to Paris, and then on to Heathrow. I think she was longing to get home to see a doctor in the hopes that there was a cure for her illness. We called in to see Kitty on the way home. She made some tea and we sat on the steps in the garden. She said that she would give a farewell dinner for Carol nearer to the time she was leaving. We went home with some lemons from her tree.

When we got back to the refuge, a very agitated M'Barek and Ali met us! There was a snake in one of the dog pens, a big one. We went off with them to have a look, and sure enough there was a large snake, asleep in the sunshine. I just hate snakes and Carol and I kept well back. M'Barek and Aly armed themselves with some bin lids and a stick each and managed to get the snake to coil around the stick and then they both ran out through the gates with the creature. They dropped it far away from the refuge. I have no idea what sort of snake it was, but it had gone, thankfully. I must admit that we checked our bedding that night!

In the three weeks that were left before Carol departed we were very busy. We visited markets three days each week, and we had many door callers. Most of the latter were straightforward wound dressings, but every now and then we would have something a little more out of the ordinary! One day an elderly man appeared with a donkey and told us that it had, 'Swallowed a serpent'! We were bemused!

M'Barek questioned the man and eventually he told us that the donkey had been working in the fields and there were snakes. The donkey drank some water from a ditch and the man said there were snakes there too. I asked if he'd actually seen the donkey swallow the snake, and the owner shook his head, he hadn't seen. Then I asked him when this had happened and he said that it must have been four months ago! By this time a small group of people had surrounded us, and the old man continued the story.

He said that once the donkey had swallowed the serpent, it must have bitten her inside, as ever since then she had been behaving strangely. The little group of people were hanging on his every word. When I asked what he meant by behaving strangely, he said that she had got fat and was greedy and lazy. Suddenly the penny dropped! I asked him if she could be pregnant?

He thought and then he smiled and said, "Allah be praised!".

Happy with the diagnosis that we'd eventually stumbled upon, he was happy. The group of people that were around us started telling him that he was stupid for not knowing. He only smiled and went on his way.

Carol started to pack, luckily she only had a few clothes left that were good enough to take home, so her suitcase would be light. She wanted to take a souvenir home with her, but didn't know what to get. The problem was solved by Zaoui; who arrived carrying a lovely copper kettle that had been made in Fez. Carol was thrilled with it and said that it would always remind her of a wonderful time in her life.

The evening before she left, Kitty and John gave us a wonderful meal. They gave Carol a beautiful book of photos of Morocco as a farewell present. There were some tears as we left that night. I drove home through the city to give Carol a last look.

The following morning there were no callers. We had breakfast and it was time to leave; we packed the Landrover and Ali and M'Barek and all his family lined up to say goodbye to 'Mademoiselle 'Arol'. It was very sad, as they had all been such good friends. We left them standing outside the gate waving as we drove off to the airport.

When we got to the airport we were ushered through into a little room and there was Zaoui. He had wanted to be the last to wish Carol luck. He walked to the aircraft and gave her a huge hug. Poor Carol, she just burst into tears, but had to go up the gangway into the aircraft. Zaoui and I watched it take off and then I drove him back to the city. We stopped for coffee at the Balima. Zaoui was very upset about us leaving and he told me that one day it was his dream to go and live in England. I had to get back to the refuge and he had to put in an appearance at work. We agreed to meet up later at the little café in Agdal.

I felt so lonely for a few days, but life went on and I threw myself into my work. I knew that it wouldn't be all that long before I would have to leave; the thought filled me with excitement and sadness in equal measures, but for most of the time I was far too busy to think about it.

The Major wrote to tell me that he had interviewed two young women who would be flying out on June 1st. That was just two weeks time! He told me that they were friends and one was an occupational therapist who fancied a change; the other had worked for a large dog and cat rescue organization. He felt that they would be well suited to the job.

I told M'Barek and Ali that I would be leaving as soon as the new people were settled into the work and knew there way around. Ali cried, huge fat tears rolled down his face, and for one dreadful moment I thought that M'Barek would do. They both said how sorry they were. I told them both that they were to treat the ladies with as much respect as they had shown to Carol and I. Ali nodded and M'Barek said he would. I made a mental note to drum it into the heads of the new girls just how devious M'Barek could be.

I saw Kitty that week. She was shopping at the little market. We sat at the café near the market and had coffee. She told me that I was to pop in whenever I felt the need to talk to someone. I was very grateful for that. She said that Maureen had written and was settling back into her nursing in Geneva. I told Kitty that I would write her a long letter. I drove her home and dropped her at the gate, then I returned to the refuge and wrote pages of news to Maureen.

A further letter from the Major gave more details. The girls were called, Catherine and Sue. Sue was the one that worked at the rescue kennels. He told me that they could live at the refuge once I had left, but only if they really wanted to. (He felt it was too basic).

That afternoon, I took M'barek with me and we set off to find some new bedding for the stable and horse yards. Luckily we only had to drive a short way and then it was a case of haggling until a good price was secured. I was quite good at this by now, and I told M'Barek I would do the deal. He smiled and stood by, waiting for me to ask for his help. We found a merchant who had some nice straw. I asked the price and he quoted way over the odds. I offered far under the asking price, adding that the straw was not top quality. We finally agreed a price that was very good for both of us. I spat on my hand and shook his. Deal done. I think M'Barek was impressed! On the way home he told me that I was almost an Arab. That made my day.

I drove into the city to see to the hotel booking for the new girls. Mohammed assured me that he would look after them well. I told him the dates and he said the room would be ready. I went on to the little market and got some salad and bread. I really fancied a coffee at the Balima. But I realised that being alone would not be good.

As I passed the Balima, I saw Zaoui sitting drinking coffee, so I stopped and joined him. We chatted for some time. I told him about the new girls that were coming and said that we should all go to the little café one evening so they could get to know Zaoui. I told him that he would always be most welcome at the refuge. He said that he had two tickets for a concert that was taking place the following evening. "Would I like to go?" I accepted as I'd never been to the large theatre in Rabat.

The concert was by the wonderfully talented singer/songwriter, Jacque Brel, an icon in his native France. The concert was simply wonderful. I had never dreamed of seeing him on stage.

On the day of the their arrival I went off to meet the girls at the airport. I was getting used to being allowed to go airside and meet them. First impressions are often the right ones. I felt that Catherine would cope with anything, Sue was younger and might take time to settle. I drove them back to the city and dropped them at the hotel. I arranged to pick them up at 6.30am. I saw the look on their faces. "6.30am?" I explained that it would be so hot by 8.00am that it would be a good time to see the refuge. I also told them to wear suitable clothes as we would be working, adding that they must wear a hat. The Major had sent them in June, so they would spend the hottest months in Morocco. I hoped they would cope with the heat. It was fine if you didn't have to work in it. Only time would tell.

The following day I was up at 4.00am and did the stables and kennels with M'Barek. I told him that I was leaving at 6.00am to collect the new ladies. He said that he would be ready to greet them. I had some breakfast and drove into the City.

They were waiting outside the hotel. They had not slept well, and they thought the hotel was very basic, but they said they could cope with that. I drove them through the main part of the City. They were amazed how grand the building were and how expensive the shops were. Then I turned off towards Akkarri and they saw how the ordinary people lived. They both said they were horrified at how thin the horses were. I explained that this was the norm and that they would see much thinner animals when we went out into the countryside.

I turned off the road and M'Barek already had the gates open, I drove in and welcomed them to their new workplace. They got out of the Landrover and I introduced them to M'Barek and Ali and M'Barek introduced them to Yasmina and the children. We went into the office and I made tea. We sat and chatted for ages. They wanted to know about the work and how we financed it. I explain that their salaries would be paid into the bank in the city, and that there was a separate amount each month for running the refuge. I told them we only ever drew half of the money at a time and drew more out when we needed it. We went on a tour of the refuge.

We were full at that time. All the kennels were full and we had about 10 dogs boarding with us. I explained that every Thursday it was necessary to destroy the dogs that were never going to find homes. We moved on to the horses, donkeys and mules. They looked at them all as I explained why they were all with us. I also stressed the need to get them well as soon as possible for without their animals the families would suffer.

I showed them the bedroom and they seemed a little surprised, but Catherine said she thought it might be quite fun. They both loved the sight and sound of the sea. That morning it was very calm. I told them that when it got stormy the waves hit the rocks with enormous speed.

At lunchtime I drove them to the beach at Sidi Boukanadel and we swam before eating our bread and cheese. They were very amused at M'Barek sitting with the pile of belongings wearing his overalls and wellington boots! I explained that he wore them all day, every day, even when the heat soared.

I dropped them back at the hotel after lunch to give them tome to have a rest and take a walk down into the city. I said I'd collect them at 6.00pm and we would go to a little café for a meal. I told them not to dress up as this café was out of the main part of the city and very casual.

I went home to find several animals waiting for me. I got them all to enter the refuge and stand in the shade and once they were all in, I got my bag and worked through them all. It was only minor wounds ad M'Barek and I soon had them on their way.

I saw to the inmates before setting off to collect the girls. They were already out in the street and we drove off to Agdal. I went over to get some wine and left them at a table taking in the sights. I saw Zaoui arrive and introduce himself. They looked a little worried at being approached by a young man! I introduced them and we had a very jolly evening. We ate brochettes and had wine and later coffee. I drove them all back to the city. When we stopped to let Zaoui out they were amazed to see him enter the palace gates! I explained that he lived there. I told them that they would see a lot of Zaoui and that he was invaluable for sorting out problems.

The following morning we were going to Khemisset and I told them I would collect them at 5.00am. They looked horrified, but I explained that work usually started at 4.00am simply because you could get a huge amount done and avoid having to work in the hottest part of the day. I told them that we normally wore sandals to work in as it got so hot and dusty. I drove home through the city and along the coast road. The ocean was a beautiful silvery colour in the moonlight.

In the morning M'Barek loaded the Landrover and we set off to collect the girls. We then drove to Khemisset and as we pulled off the main road both girls said they were amazed we ever found the place. I explained that the markets had occupied the same places for centuries and that everyone knew about them.

I showed them how to walk along the lines, slipping a hand under each pack to check for sores, and what to do if they found one. After a couple of hours we stopped and M'Barek took them around all the stores, Poor Sue was aghast at the dentist who, at the time of their visit was doing a nasty extraction!

As we drove home in the afternoon they asked lots of questions, and I answered as best I could. I told them to always take M'Barek as he was so good at dealing with the men and was second to none at restraining unwilling animals whilst they were treated. Sue asked if there were, 'proper' dentists and I assured her that in Rabat there were good French dentists and doctors, and a hospital.

We went to the refuge first and they enjoyed a shower under the hosepipe. We did the dressings on the in-patients and I made tea. I made some supper and we sat and ate it before then I ran them back to the hotel. I think they were absolutely exhausted!

The next day I collected them and we dealt with door callers. Though they were both used to horses, they hadn't done much veterinary work, so I tried to teach them as much as I possibly could before I left. We also spent some time going through the drugs in the cupboard and their used. I explained the treatment books and the accounts book that every purchase was listed in. I also explained that the Major liked a letter each week and it should keep him up to date with the week's events.

We drove into the city and I took them into the bank to introduce them to the manager, and from there we went to the Post Office to show them where they could ring home from the public phones inside the building. I drove them to the embassy to meet Richard Kemp. He welcomed them and said he was always there is there were problems. Finally we went to Kitty's who had asked me to take them for tea. They both loved having tea and scones surrounded by orange and lemon trees, with a lovely Boxer dog to play with.

I dropped them back at the hotel. They said they would find a little café and have something simple for supper. They were doing very well and I had already begun to think they would make a go of it, but that they would need a little more time and help. I planned to take them to Meknes the following day.

I woke at 3.30am to a big storm. I got up and saw to the animals; when it rained hard it was lovely warm rain, and I used to love to work wearing wet clothes! I did the in-patients and told M'Barek that we were going to Meknes. I told him that he was to stay at the refuge and gave him a list of jobs to keep him busy.
I changed, had breakfast and left.

The girls found the drive to Meknes very pretty and interesting. We arrived at Bab el Kari and the place was empty. I gave them a quick tour of the nearby ruins and then drove on to John and Jackie's home. John was there and he looked very miserable. Over a coffee he said that Jackie had gone back to England, as she was so homesick. He was just packing up and going too. This came as a great shock! I asked if he had let the Major know and he said only a few days ago. I imagine the Major must have been very annoyed and upset.

Poor John, he said, "I've had it up to here with this place. I've never been so lonely in my life, and I am going in the next few days!" He had calmed down considerably by the time we left, but he was set on leaving.

We drove back to Rabat in the cool of the early evening. It had been a strange sort of day! The following day I had a letter from the Major. He told me that John was leaving and that the Meknes refuge would remain closed until he could fin a suitable couple to run it. This saddened me, but there was little else to do. It would be very hard for people fro England to just arrives and start working; then I remembered that Milly and I had done just that when we first went to Relizane!

The weeks passed very quickly. I let the girls take the Landrover and M'Barek to Khemisset to see how they managed. On their return M'barek was full of praise but added that they got very tired and had to keep stopping. I explained that their new life was very different to working in the UK, and that they would be fine in time. I had spent the day packing up some of my bits and pieces.

The following day I bought my airline ticket home. I was going to fly from Casablanca straight to Heathrow. I wrote to the Major to say the girls were coping well and that I had booked a departure date. I got Ali and M'Barek into the office that day and told them that I was going home. Both of them were in pieces! Ali was crying and M'Barek was, for once, very quiet. They both said how very much they had enjoyed working with me, and that they hoped I had liked their work. I told them both that they had been so good and worked so well and that I would never forget them.

That evening the girls and I picked up Zaoui and we all ate at the little café. I told them I had bought my ticket and would be leaving in just 10 days time. Zaoui told me afterwards that he knew I would be going, but that he was heartbroken!

We had a nice meal ad afterwards we all went to the Balima and sat under the trees drinking coffee until way past 11.00pm.

The next morning we were busy at the refuge when a Police Landrover drew up. The girls looked quite taken aback when the policeman greeted me like a long lost friend. I took him into the office and introduced to the girls. He sent his driver and M'Barek to his Landrover to unload another carboy of red wine!

I explained to the girls that this happened from time to time! I told El Mansour I was leaving and he said how very sorry he was.

When he had left M'Barek and Ali knocked on the office door and entered like naughty schoolboys. They wanted to know if they could both go to see me off at the airport. I hadn't thought about it, but immediately said they could. The next time we saw Zaoui he also asked if he could go to Casablanca with me! I asked the girls if they would mind staying at the refuge as the Landrover was going to be full to bursting. Then I realised that if I took the Landrover, how was it going to get back again?

That problem was answered a few days later when El Mansour visited the refuge. He said he had solved the problem. He too would drive to Casablance, but in a police Landrover; He added that he would take his usual driver, plus a second to drive our Landrover back to the refuge. Perfect!

The next few days were a blur as I tried to show the girls everything they might need and to tell them all they might need to know. I showed them where to get the Landrover serviced, and where to buy straw and animal feed. I did everything I could possibly do to ease their passage into their new job.

One day I went to see Kitty alone. John was there and we sat and chatted for ages. John said that he was due to retire in a couple of years time and that they would return to the UK before that and that he would work at the Ministry of Defence for a while before he actually retired. They invited us all to dinner the night before I left.

The day before I was to leave I got Ali and M'Barek into the office and gave them some money each; I think they were expecting to be told off! I also told them that they were to wear smart clothes the following day for the journey to Casablanca.

The rest of the day was spent going over problems the girls felt might arise. I told them to let M'Barek help them, but to be very firm with him. Any other problems should be addressed to Zaoui or Kitty. I had done all I could.

That evening I picked the girls up and we drove to Kitty and John's home. We ate a sumptuous meal and all too soon it was time for farewells. I hugged Kitty and John for an age. They had been so good to me throughout my time in Morocco.

I dropped the girls back at the hotel and went home to bed.

I had arranged to collect the girls at 5.30am, as I had to be at Casablanca for 10.00am. I had a last look around the refuge, said goodbye to the in-patients and finally to M'Barek's family. Yasmina was in tears. I was trying to be brave. It was so hard.

I wished the girls good luck, and they would need a big slice of that. El Mansour and Zaoui arrived in a Police Landrover, plus the spare driver; M'Barek and Ali looking very smart in their Djellebahs and white tarbushes loaded the Landrover and we were off! I drove and Zaoui and El Mansour sat in the front. M'Barek and Ali were in the back with my suitcases. The Police Landrover drove ahead.

We got to the airport in good time and El Mansour got me through customs in no time at all. He had somehow pulled rank and got us all into a small room that opened onto the tarmac. Everyone was very subdued. A man in uniform asked us to make our way to the aircraft and we must have looked such an odd bunch; there was Ali and M'Barek in traditional dress; El Mansour in his Police uniform and Zaoui in a suit. We stopped at the gangway and I said my goodbyes. Firstly. to Ali and M'Barek, then El Mansour and finally to dear Zaoui. They were all in tears and I was trying so hard not to cry. I could see them all waving as the plane took off and as it did, I was unable to control myself any longer.

How I had loved my few years in North Africa. How I loved the people and how much I'd learned from them all. It was the most incredible experience that I wouldn't have missed for the World!

Part Three: Photographs

Entrance to the Rabat Refuge

M'Barek holding an injured egret

Our patients arrived in many ways!

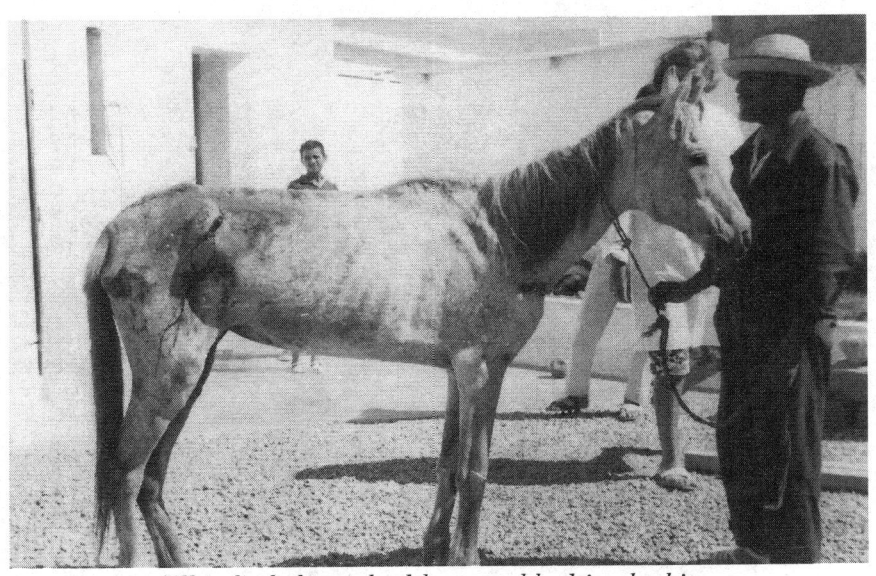

This little horse had been stabbed in the hip

The Rabid Donkey biting into its pole

Carol doing some running repairs on a donkey

Treating a bull with a potato stuck in its throat

Examining a cow in a village

Arriving for the Fantasia

Almost ready

The end of the charge

Watha leaves Athens to return to the UK

Tailpiece

I settled back into a happy life at the farm. I met a member of the Household Cavalry and we married in 1970. Phil and I have a son called James. I continued working with horses.

Carol married the year after us. She is now free of health issues and has two sons.

Maureen retired but stayed in Switzerland. I kept in regular touch with her. She died in 2005.

John and Kitty returned to the UK in 1969 to live at Aldershot. We saw them often. John died in 1998 and Kitty in 2003.

Zaoui married Catherine and they lived for some time in Scotland. I have sadly lost touch with them both.
Watha, Milly's horse from Relizane eventually came to the UK. He and Milly travelled together by ship from Athens. Milly's sister and I met them at The East India Docks in London.

Watha became a common visitor at the Arab Horse Show where he used to raise money for horse charities abroad. He was the most wonderful horse. He died of old age, a miracle in itself. This horse was truly blessed!

Milly moved down the West Country, her wandering days finally over. She got herself a Llama to keep her on her toes!

Mules

in the

Mission House

By

Judy Wright

To Margaret,

x Judy.

RB
Rossendale Books

Published by Lulu Enterprises Inc.
3101 Hillsborough Street
Suite 210
Raleigh, NC 27607-5436
United States of America

Published in paperback 2013
Category: Memoirs
Copyright Judy Wright © 2013

ISBN : 978-1-300-73138-2

CONTENTS

Stories

Poems

INTRODUCTION

'Eclipsed', Matt Whyman
'The Land Ironclads', H.G. Wells

Most war stories deal in harsh realities. However, some are wildly imaginative. H.G. Wells wrote 'The Land Ironclads' as a work of science fiction at the end of the nineteenth century and through it created a harsh reality of his own. Two decades later, Winston Churchill wrote to the author during the First World War, thanking him for providing the idea that formed the basis of the tank.

We must all hope that Matt Whyman's story is not so prophetic, set as it is against the backdrop of a world in turmoil after the moon has been blown up by a missile.

An interesting comparison could be made between these two stories by looking at how the individual experiences of characters and the theme of war are used to reveal more about each other.

ECLIPSED

Matt Whyman

I missed the moment that the moon exploded. Like so many people, I was fast asleep when it happened. According to my friend Maisie, whose neighbour works a night shift, it looked just like a mothball fragmenting into the void.

The morning after, I discovered my father staring out of the kitchen window. He was barely blinking. On the radio a news report claimed that America was demanding some explanation from the Soviets. At a time when the world lived in fear of a nuclear strike from one side or the other, it seemed like an act of madness for Russia to launch a lunar attack. My father didn't appear to be listening, however, and at first I didn't realize the enormity of what was being broadcast. It was only when I sneezed on account of my hay fever that he noticed me.

'Sleep well, cupcake?' he asked.

'Sure,' I told him, looking around. 'Where's Mum?'

As he pressed his lips into a smile, I noticed his eyes shine over. 'She'll be back later,' he said after a moment. 'I promised her I'd tell you that.'

At school I found everyone talking about the same thing. At first I thought I was the victim of a grand hoax. How could the moon just cease to exist? I had only been alive for fourteen years. Considering a lifetime without it seemed unthinkable. I remember that first day was clear and bright. The sky, as blue as a lagoon, had not a cloud in sight. During a special assembly, our headmistress explained that with the loss of the moon we faced a time of great uncertainty. Nobody knew for sure what effect its disappearance would have on everything, from the ebb and flow of the oceans' tides to the rate at which the earth revolved. Still, she assured us that nature would adapt and survive, as would mankind.

Throughout each lesson that followed, we kept turning our attention to the window. Even the teachers couldn't resist looking, despite the fact that there was nothing unusual to see.

Come dusk, as we made our way to our homes, stars began to prick the twilight. I kept looking up and around. I wasn't sure what I was hoping to spot. The moon might have sailed through every night sky for billions of years, but sometimes clouds, tall buildings or trees conspired to cover it up. Everything just looked so normal up there, so peaceful and serene. I saw no smouldering remains or hole torn out of the heavens. Had I spent the day in my own company, without news or gossip, it would not have struck me that anything was different. Still, as an urgent breeze picked up all the litter in the streets, I couldn't help feeling that perhaps we had taken things for granted.

'Come and sit with us, cupcake. There's something we need to discuss.'

I had found my parents facing one another at the kitchen table. Like everyone, they appeared a little shell-shocked and bewildered. They looked up when I came into the room. As soon as my father invited me to join them, I realized I had just killed a conversation.

'What's the latest on the moon?' I asked, noting the television switched on in the corner. The sound was muted, but the footage of the rockets climbing into the sky looked ominous.

'The moon?' My father paused and gazed at me. It left me feeling like I hadn't returned home in years. 'I'm not sure,' he said, and cleared his throat. 'What did they tell you at school?'

I drew a chair from the table and sat with them. 'The

Russians are claiming a test firing went badly wrong. That's what our form teacher told us before the bell rang. They're suggesting the target coordinates were changed as an act of sabotage by the United States.'

Mum clasped her mug with both hands. Not once did she take her eyes off it. 'The last time I looked at the moon,' she said, 'it was on the wane.'

I glanced at Dad, confused by her comment. 'Mum,' I said, 'it isn't coming back.'

Outside, the wind had strengthened so much that it began to moan and whistle. Only then did I notice that the curtains had been closed against the night sky. I looked at my dad, and found his focus upon me once again.

'This isn't about the moon,' he said. 'It's about us.'

Until they told me Mum was moving out, I really hadn't known that my parents had been having problems. As it turned out, I don't think my dad had either. Sure, Mum would sometimes say that he loved his work more than he loved us, but we'd never taken her seriously. Looking back, I suppose this was her way of quietly convincing herself that the changes in her heart were for the best. I didn't cry when Mum revealed that she'd met someone else. I just nodded when she promised me that everything would be OK, and stared at the table when Dad began to weep.

'I should go,' my mother said. 'I would ask you to come with me, Lottie, but space is an issue and this is only for the very short term. Your father and I have a lot of sorting out to do, but we've agreed that you come first. Once we sell this house, we'll have enough money to provide you with two places you can call home.'

'But I don't want to move,' I said. 'And I don't want you to go.'

My mother rose from the table. She circled behind my father, touched his shoulder for a moment and then headed for the door. When she opened it, the howling I could hear out there sounded like another world entirely.

The first few nights were the worst. I suppose we had to get used to the loss and what it meant for us all. The winds struck at sunset and only calmed as dawn broke. In the darkest hours gusts would rampage across town and country with such violence that I couldn't sleep. The experts explained how this was due to the absence of a gravitational pull. As I looked at the impact around me, it seemed more like the loss of a calming influence.

On the television Dad and I watched endless news footage of tidal surges and oceanic whirlpools. It looked to me like God had got fed up with us all and decided to pull the plug. All my favourite programmes were replaced by reports about emerging changes to our planet. Birds flocked in unusual directions, clouds formed strange new shapes, and dogs howled after midnight as if plagued by a frequency beyond our hearing.

Even people behaved differently. Many panicked, with riots taking place as far afield as Reykjavik, Moscow and Rio de Janeiro. I also heard from Maisie that her neighbour had switched to a day shift on account of all the late night looting. As for me, I found my hay fever disappeared completely.

At home our cat reacted badly to the situation. It didn't help that Mum was the one who had always taken care of him. After she left he went hungry for several days because Dad and I completely forgot to feed him. Worse still, the high winds really spooked the poor thing. Instead of spending his nights out on the prowl, he chose to stay indoors. Even with the calm that came at daybreak, he would pop out only for a very short time. Then he'd crash back through the cat flap as if chased in by a snarling dog.

"What's frightening him?' I asked on one occasion.

My father considered this for a moment, watching the fur on the cat's back settle. 'Change,' he said finally. 'It's an unsettling time for us all.'

Throughout this period, while most governments appealed for calm, the two superpowers continued to raise the temperature. In an address to the world President Reagan not only denied all involvement in the moon strike, but even went so far as to suggest that the Russians had been attempting a surprise attack on American defence satellites. One which had ended in a cosmic disaster for us all. As each side had primed their nuclear arsenal to take flight, I asked if we should prepare a fallout shelter. In response, Dad turned to me as if emerging from a dream, and said it was too late for that.

***

I was at school when Mum first returned to pick up some things. I knew she had been here as soon as I walked in. Her perfume hung in the air and the cat was at his bowl, finishing a treat of canned tuna.

Then, late last night, she came back again. I was in bed when I heard the key in the lock. Normally at that hour I'd have been asleep but, what with the high winds, I was wide awake.

I heard her close the door against the gale, and then her voice calling softly for my father. I wanted to get up and see her. I really did. I was just worried that by padding downstairs, somehow I would scare her away. A moment later, my parents were speaking in the kitchen.

It struck me then that Dad hadn't shown any anger about the situation. He wasn't like the president, whose emotions were quite clear each time he made a broadcast. Reagan didn't shout or beat the desk with his fist, but you could see it in his face. From a tension in his jawline to the way his eyes pinched when he outlined the American position. My dad didn't carry that kind of fire within him. Once he had stopped weeping, there was nothing left.

As I listened to them from my bed, it sounded as if my mother was doing all the talking. At one point I even heard some words.

'I'm sorry,' she said. *'I'm just sorry'.*

***

The storm that night was more ferocious than anything we had experienced. It raged so hard against my window that I was too scared to climb out and peek through the curtains. I just pulled my duvet over my head, and prayed the house would not be blown to bits.

Now, as sunrise sees the winds subside, I look out and catch my breath. Trees have come down everywhere, bringing power lines with them, while somewhere in the distance I can hear a voice droning through a megaphone. Weirdly, though, the street is deserted. I switch on my radio, if only for some company, and that's when I hear about the emergency measures.

'*Dad!*'

Grabbing my dressing-gown, I rush across the landing to the main bedroom. If the government really have ordered troops onto the street, there'll be no school today for sure. I don't pause to knock. I throw open the door and then stop in my tracks.

I'm surprised to find the cat curled up at the foot of the bed. My father is sound asleep, but what leaves me reeling is the sight of the woman in his arms. Her head is resting upon his shoulder, with her palm flat on his chest. She opens her eyes and looks at me. At first, we just gaze at one another.

'We've been ordered to stay inside,' I say eventually, blinking back tears. 'It's chaos out there.'

Just then, from somewhere over the hills, we hear the crack of gunfire. The sound takes a moment to decay, as if refusing to fall silent.

'Things will never be the same again,' says Mum in barely a whisper. 'All we can do is hope that we're over the worst.'

THE LAND IRONCLADS

H.G. Wells

I

The young lieutenant lay beside the war correspondent and admired the idyllic calm of the enemy's lines through his field-glass.

'So far as I can see,' he said, at last, 'one man.'

'What's he doing?' asked the war correspondent.

'Field-glass at us,' said the young lieutenant

'And this is war!'

'No,' said the young lieutenant; 'it's Bloch.'

'The game's a draw.'

'No! They've got to win or else they lose. A draw's a win for our side.'

They had discussed the political situation fifty times or so, and the war correspondent was weary of it. He stretched out his limbs. 'Aaai s'pose it *is*!' he yawned.

'*Flut!*'

'What was that?'

'Shot at us.'

The war correspondent shifted to a slightly lower position. 'No one shot at him,' he complained.

'I wonder if they think we shall get so bored we shall go home?'

The war correspondent made no reply.

'There's the harvest, of course. ...'

They had been there a month. Since the first brisk movements after the declaration of war things had gone slower and slower, until it seemed as though the whole machine of events must have run down. To begin with, they had had almost a scampering time; the invader had come across the frontier on the very dawn of the war in half-a-dozen parallel columns behind a cloud of cyclists and cavalry, with a general air of coming straight on the capital, and the defender horsemen had held him up, and peppered him and forced him to open out to outflank, and had then bolted to the next position in the most approved style, for a couple of days, until in the afternoon, bump! they had the invader against their prepared lines of defence. He did not suffer so much as had been hoped and expected: he was coming on, it seemed with his eyes open, his scouts winded the guns, and down he sat at once without the shadow of an attack and began grubbing trenches for himself, as though he meant to sit down there to the very end of time. He was slow, but much more wary than the world had been led to expect, and he kept convoys tucked in and shielded his slow marching infantry sufficiently well to prevent any heavy adverse scoring.

'But he ought to attack,' the young lieutenant had insisted.

'He'll attack us at dawn, somewhere along the lines. You'll get the bayonets coming into the trenches just about when you can see,' the war correspondent had held until a week ago.

The young lieutenant winked when he said that.

When one early morning the men the defenders sent to lie out five hundred yards before the trenches, with a view to the unexpected emptying of magazines into any night attack, gave way to causeless panic and blazed away at nothing for ten minutes, the war correspondent understood the meaning of that wink.

'What would you do if you were the enemy?' said the war correspondent, suddenly.

'If I had men like I've got now?'

'Yes.'

'Take those trenches.'

'How?'

'Oh – dodges! Crawl out half-way at night before moonrise and get into touch with the chaps we send out. Blaze at 'em if they tried to shift, and so bag some of 'em in the daylight. Learn that patch of ground by heart, lie all day in squatty holes, and come on nearer next night. There's a bit over there, lumpy ground, where they could get across to rushing distance – easy. In a night or so. It would be a mere game for our fellows; it's what they're made for. ... Guns? Shrapnel and stuff wouldn't stop good men who meant business.'

'Why don't *they* do that?'

'Their men aren't brutes enough: that's the trouble. They're a crowd of devitalised townsmen, and that's the truth of the matter. They're clerks, they're factory hands, they're students, they're civilised men. They can write, they can talk, they can make and do all sorts of things, but they're poor amateurs at war. They've got no physical staying power, and that's the whole thing. They've never slept in the open one night in their lives; they've never drunk anything but the purest water-company water; they've never gone short of three meals a day since they left their feeding-bottles. Half their cavalry never cocked leg over horse till it enlisted six months ago. They ride their horses as though they were bicycles – you watch 'em! They're fools at the game, and they know it. Our boys of fourteen can give their grown men points. ... Very well –'

The war correspondent mused on his face with his nose between his knuckles.

'If a decent civilisation,' he said, 'cannot produce better men for war than –'

He stopped with belated politeness.

'I mean –'

'Than our open-air life,' said the young lieutenant, politely.

'Exactly,' said the war correspondent. 'Then civilisation has to stop.'

'It looks like it,' the young lieutenant admitted.

'Civilisation has science, you know,' said the war correspondent. 'It invented and it makes the rifles and guns and things you use.'

'Which our nice healthy hunters and stockmen and so on, rowdy-dowdy cowpunchers and negro-whackers, can use ten times better than – *What's that?*'

'What?' said the war correspondent, and then seeing his companion busy with his field-glass he produced his own: 'Where?' said the war correspondent, sweeping the enemy's lines.

'It's nothing' said the young lieutenant, still looking.

'What's nothing?'

The young lieutenant put down his glass and pointed. 'I thought I saw something there, behind the stems of those trees. Something black. What it was I don't know.'

The war correspondent tried to get even by intense scrutiny.

'It wasn't anything' said the young lieutenant,

rolling over to regard the darkling evening sky, and generalised: 'There never will be anything any more for ever. Unless –'

The war correspondent looked inquiry.

'They may get their stomachs wrong, or something – living without proper drains.'

A sound of bugles came from the tents behind. The war correspondent slid backward down the sand and stood up. 'Boom!' came from somewhere far away to the left. 'Halloa!' he said, hesitated, and crawled back to peer again. 'Firing at this time is jolly bad manners.'

The young lieutenant was incommunicative again for a space.

Then he pointed to the distant clump of trees again. 'One of our big guns. They were firing at that,' he said.

'The thing that wasn't anything?'

'Something over there, anyhow.'

Both men were silent, peering through their glasses for a space. 'Just when it's twilight,' the lieutenant complained. He stood up.

'I might stay here a bit,' said the war correspondent.

The lieutenant shook his head. 'There is nothing to see,' he apologised, and then went down to where his little squad of sun-brown, loose-limbed men had been yarning in the trench. The war correspondent stood up also, glanced for a moment at the business-like bustle below him, gave perhaps twenty seconds to those enigmatical trees again, then turned his face toward the camp.

He found himself wondering whether his editor would consider the story of how somebody thought he saw something black behind a clump of trees, and how a gun was fired at this illusion by somebody else, too trivial for public consultation.

'It's the only gleam of a shadow of interest,' said the war correspondent, 'for ten whole days.'

'No,' he said, presently; 'I'll write that other article, "Is War Played Out?"'

He surveyed the darkling lines in perspective, the tangle of trenches one behind another, one commanding another, which the defender had made ready. The shadows and mists swallowed up their receding contours, and here and there a lantern gleamed, and here and there knots of men were busy about small fires.

'No troops on earth could do it,' he said. ...

He was depressed. He believed that there were other things in life better worth having than proficiency in war; he believed that in the heart of civilisation, for all its stresses, its crushing concentrations of forces, its injustice and suffering, there lay something that might be the hope of the world, and the idea that any people by living in the open air, hunting perpetually, losing touch with books and art and all the things that intensify life, might hope to resist and break that great development to the end of time, jarred on his civilised soul.

Apt to his thought came a file of defender soldiers and passed him in the gleam of a swinging lamp that marked the way.

He glanced at their red-lit faces, and one shone out for a moment, a common type of face in the defender's ranks: ill-shaped nose, sensuous lips, bright clear eyes full of alert cunning, slouch hat cocked on one side and adorned with the peacock's plume of the rustic Don Juan turned soldier, a hard brown skin, a sinewy frame, an open, tireless stride, and a master's grip on the rifle.

The war correspondent returned their salutations and went on his way.

'Louts,' he whispered. 'Cunning, elementary louts. And they are going to beat the townsmen at the game of war!'

From the red glow among the nearer tents came first one and then half-a-dozen hearty voices, bawling in a drawling unison the words of a particularly slab and sentimental patriotic song.

'Oh, *go* it!' muttered the war correspondent, bitterly.

II

It was opposite the trenches called after Hackbone's Hut that the battle began. There the ground stretched broad and level between the lines, with scarcely shelter for a lizard, and it seemed to the startled, just awakened men who came crowding into the trenches that this was one more proof of that green inexperience of the enemy of which they had heard so much. The war correspondent would not believe his ears at first, and swore that he and the war artist, who, still imperfectly roused, was trying to put on his boots by the light of a match held in his hand, were the victims of a common illusion. Then, after putting his head in a bucket of cold water, his intelligence came back as he towelled. He listened. 'Gollys!' he said; 'that's something more than scare firing this time. It's like ten thousand carts on a bridge of tin.'

There came a sort of enrichment to that steady uproar. 'Machine-guns!'

Then, 'Guns!'

The artist, with one boot on, thought to look at his watch, and went to it hopping.

'Half an hour from dawn,' he said. 'You were right about their attacking, after all. ...'

The war correspondent came out of the tent, verifying the presence of chocolate in his pocket as he did so. He had to halt for a moment or so until his eyes were toned down to the night a little. 'Pitch!' he said. He stood for a space to season his eyes before he felt justified in striking out for a black gap among the adjacent tents. The artist coming out behind him fell over a tent-rope. It was half-past two o'clock in the morning of the darkest night in time, and against a sky of dull black silk the enemy was talking searchlights, a wild jabber of searchlights. 'He's trying to blind our riflemen,' said the war correspondent with a flash, and waited for the artist and then set off with a sort of discreet haste again. 'Whoa!' he said, presently. 'Ditches!'

They stopped.

'It's the confounded searchlights,' said the war correspondent.

They saw lanterns going to and fro, nearby, and men falling in to march down to the trenches. They were for following them, and then the artist began to feel his night eyes. 'If we scramble this,' he said, 'and it's only a drain, there's a clear run up to the ridge.' And that way they took. Lights came and went in the tents behind, as the men turned out, and ever and again they came to broken ground and staggered and stumbled. But in a little while they drew near the crest. Something that sounded like the impact of a very important railway accident happened in the air above them, and the shrapnel bullets seethed about them like a sudden handful of hail. 'Right-ho!' said the war correspondent, and soon they judged they had come to the crest and stood in the midst of a world of great darkness and frantic glares, whose principal fact was sound.

Right and left of them and all about them was the uproar, an army-full of magazine fire, at first chaotic and monstrous and then, eked out by little flashes and gleams and suggestions, taking the beginnings of a shape. It looked to the war correspondent as though the enemy must have attacked in line and with his whole force – in which case he was either being or was already annihilated.

'Dawn and the dead,' he said, with his instinct for headlines. He said this to himself, but afterwards, by means of shouting, he conveyed an idea to the artist.

'They must have meant it for a surprise,' he said.

It was remarkable how the firing kept on. After a time he began to perceive a sort of rhythm in this inferno of noise. It would decline – decline perceptibly, droop towards something that was comparatively a pause – a pause of inquiry. 'Aren't you all dead yet?' this pause seemed to say. The flickering fringe of rifle-flashes would become attenuated and broken, and the whack-bang of the enemy's big guns two miles away there would come up out of the deeps. Then suddenly, east or west of them, something would startle the rifles to a frantic outbreak again.

The war correspondent taxed his brain for some theory of conflict that would account for this, and was suddenly aware that the artist and he were vividly illuminated. He could see the ridge on which they stood and before them in black outline a file of riflemen hurrying down towards the nearer trenches. It became visible that a light rain was falling, and farther away towards the enemy was a clear space with men – 'our men?' – running across it in disorder. He saw one of those men throw up his hands and drop. And something else black and shining loomed up on the edge of the beam-coruscating flashes; and behind it and far away a calm, white eye regarded the world. 'Whit, whit, whit,' sang something in the air, and then the artist was running for cover, with the war correspondent behind him. Bang came shrapnel, bursting close at hand as it seemed, and our two men were lying flat in a dip in the ground, and the light and everything had gone again, leaving a vast note of interrogation upon the night.

The war correspondent came within bawling range. 'What the deuce was it? Shooting our men down!'

'Black,' said the artist, 'and like a fort. Not two hundred yards from the first trench.'

He sought for comparisons in his mind. 'Something

between a big blockhouse and a giant's dish-cover,' he said.

'And they were running!' said the war correspondent.

'*You'd* run if a thing like that, searchlight to help it, turned up like a prowling nightmare in the middle of the night.'

They crawled to what they judged the edge of the dip and lay regarding the unfathomable dark. For a space they could distinguish nothing, and then a sudden convergence of the searchlights of both sides brought the strange thing out again.

In that flickering pallor it had the effect of a large and clumsy black insect, an insect the size of an ironclad cruiser, crawling obliquely to the first line of trenches and firing shots out of portholes in its side. And on its carcass the bullets must have been battering with more than the passionate violence of hail on a roof of tin.

Then in the twinkling of an eye the curtain of the dark had fallen again and the monster had vanished, but the crescendo of musketry marked its approach to the trenches.

They were beginning to talk about the thing to each other, when a flying bullet kicked dirt into the artist's face, and they decided abruptly to crawl down into the cover of the trenches. They had got down with an unobtrusive persistence into the second line, before the dawn had grown clear enough for anything to be seen. They found themselves in a crowd of expectant riflemen, all noisily arguing about what would happen next. The enemy's contrivance had done execution upon the outlying men, it seemed, but they did not believe it would do any more. 'Come the day and we'll capture the lot of them,' said a burly soldier.

'Them?' said the war correspondent.

'They say there's a regular string of 'em, crawling along the front of our lines. ... Who cares?'

The darkness filtered away so imperceptibly that at no moment could one declare decisively that one could see. The searchlights ceased to sweep hither and thither. The enemy's monsters were dubious patches of darkness upon the dark, and then no longer dubious, and so they crept out into distinctness. The war correspondent, munching chocolate absent-mindedly, beheld at last a spacious picture of battle under the cheerless sky, whose central focus was an array of fourteen or fifteen huge clumsy shapes lying in perspective on the very edge of the first line of trenches, at intervals of perhaps three hundred yards, and evidently firing down upon the crowded riflemen. They were so close in that the defender's guns had ceased, and only the first line of trenches was in action.

The second line commanded the first, and as the

light grew the war correspondent could make out the riflemen who were fighting these monsters, crouched in knots and crowds behind the transverse banks that crossed the trenches against the eventuality of an enfilade. The trenches close to the big machines were empty save for the crumpled suggestions of dead and wounded men; the defenders had been driven right and left as soon as the prow of this land ironclad had loomed up over the front of the trench. He produced his field-glass, and was immediately a centre of inquiry from the soldiers about him.

They wanted to look, they asked questions, and after he had announced that the men across the traverses seemed unable to advance or retreat, and were crouching under cover rather than fighting, he found it advisable to loan his glasses to a burly and incredulous corporal. He heard a strident voice, and found a lean and sallow soldier at his back talking to the artist.

'There's chaps down there caught,' the man was saying. 'If they retreat they got to expose themselves, and the fire's too straight. –'

'They aren't firing much, but every shot's a hit.'

'Who?'

'The chaps in that thing. The men who're coming up –'

'Coming up where?'

'We're evacuating them trenches where we can. Our chaps are coming back up the zigzags. ... No end of 'em hit. ... But when we get clear our turn'll come. Rather! These things won't be able to cross a trench or get into it; and before they can get back our guns'll smash 'em up. Smash 'em right up. See?' A brightness came into his eyes. 'Then we'll have a go at the beggar inside,' he said. ...

The war correspondent thought for a moment, trying to realise the idea. Then he set himself to recover his field-glasses from the burly corporal. ...

The daylight was getting clearer now. The clouds were lifting, and a gleam of lemon-yellow amidst the level masses to the east portended sunrise. He looked again at the land ironclad. As he saw it in the bleak grey dawn, lying obliquely upon the slope and on the very lip of the foremost trench, the suggestion of a stranded vessel was very great indeed. It might have been from eighty to a hundred feet long – it was about two hundred and fifty yards away – its vertical side was ten feet high or so, smooth for that height, and then with a complex patterning under the eaves of its flattish turtle cover. This patterning was a close interlacing of portholes, rifle barrels, and telescope tubes – sham and real – indistinguishable one from the other. The thing had come into such a position as to enfilade the trench, which was empty now, so far as he could see, except for two or three crouching knots of men and the tumbled dead. Behind it, across the plain, it had scored the grass with a train of linked impressions, like the dotted tracings sea-things leave in sand. Left and right of that track dead men and wounded men were scattered – men it had picked off as they fled back from their advanced positions in the searchlight glare from the invader's lines. And now it lay with its head projecting a little over the trench it had won, as if it were a single sentient thing planning the next phase of its attack. ...

He lowered his glasses and took a more comprehensive view of the situation. These creatures of the night had evidently won the first line of trenches and the fight had come to a pause. In the increasing light he could make out by a stray shot or a chance exposure that the defender's marksmen were lying thick in the second and third line of trenches up towards the low crest of the position, and in such of the zigzags as gave them a chance of a converging fire. The men about him were talking of guns. 'We're in the line of the big guns at the crest but they'll soon shift one to pepper them,' the lean man said, reassuringly.

'Whup,' said the corporal.

'Bang! bang! bang! Whir-r-r-r!' It was a sort of nervous jump, and all the rifles were going off by themselves. The war correspondent found himself and the artist, two idle men crouching behind a line of preoccupied backs, of industrious men discharging magazines. The monster had moved. It continued to move regardless of the hail that splashed its skin with bright new specks of lead. It was singing a mechanical little ditty to itself, 'Tuf-tuf, tuf-tuf, tuf-tuf,' and squirting out little jets of steam behind. It had humped itself up, as a limpet does before it crawls; it had lifted its skirt and displayed along the length of it – *feet*! They were thick, stumpy feet, between knobs and buttons in shape – flat, broad things, reminding one of the feet of elephants or the legs of caterpillars; and then, as the skirt rose higher, the war correspondent, scrutinising the thing through his glasses again, saw that these feet hung, as it were, on the rims of wheels. His thoughts whirled back to Victoria Street, Westminster, and he saw himself in the piping times of peace, seeking matter for an interview.

'Mr. – Mr. Diplock,' he said; 'and he called them Pedrails ... Fancy meeting them here!'

The marksman beside him raised his head and shoulders in a speculative mood to fire more certainly – it seemed so natural to assume the attention of the monster must be distracted by this trench before it – and was suddenly knocked backwards by a bullet through his neck. His feet flew up, and he vanished out of the margin of the watcher's field of vision.

The war correspondent grovelled tighter, but after a glance behind him at a painful little confusion, he resumed his field-glass, for the thing was putting down its feet one after the other, and hoisting itself farther and farther over the trench. Only a bullet in the head could have stopped him looking just then.

The lean man with the strident voice ceased firing to turn and reiterate his point. 'They can't possibly cross,' he bawled. 'They – '

'Bang! Bang! Bang! Bang!' – drowned everything.

The lean man continued speaking for a word or so, then gave it up, shook his head to enforce the impossibility of anything crossing a trench like the one below, and resumed business once more.

And all the while that great bulk was crossing. When the war correspondent turned his glass on it again it had bridged the trench, and its queer feet were rasping away at the farther bank, in the attempt to get a hold there. It got its hold. It continued to crawl until the greater bulk of it was over the trench – until it was all over. Then it paused for a moment, adjusted its skirt a little nearer the ground, gave an unnerving 'toot, toot,' and came on abruptly at a pace of, perhaps, six miles an hour straight up the gentle slope towards our observer.

The war correspondent raised himself on his elbow and looked a natural inquiry at the artist.

For a moment the men about him stuck to their position and fired furiously. Then the lean man in a mood of precipitancy slid backwards, and the war correspondent said 'Come along' to the artist, and led the movement along the trench.

As they dropped down, the vision of a hillside of trench being rushed by a dozen vast cockroaches disappeared for a space, and instead was one of a narrow passage, crowded with men, for the most part receding, though one or two turned or halted. He never turned back to see the nose of the monster creep over the brow of the trench; he never even troubled to keep in touch with the artist. He heard the 'whit' of bullets about him soon enough, and saw a man before him stumble and drop, and then he was one of a furious crowd fighting to get into a transverse zigzag ditch that enabled the defenders to get under cover up and down the hill. It was like a theatre panic. He gathered from signs and fragmentary words that on ahead another of these monsters had also won to the second trench.

He lost his interest in the general course of the battle for a space altogether; he became simply a modest egotist, in a mood of hasty circumspection, seeking the farthest rear, amidst a dispersed multitude of disconcerted riflemen similarly employed. He scrambled down through trenches, he took his courage in both hands and sprinted across the open, he had moments of panic when it seemed madness not to be quadrupedal, and moments of shame when he stood up and faced about to see how the fight was going. And he was one of many thousand very similar men that morning. On the ridge he halted in a knot of scrub, and was for a few minutes almost minded to stop and see things out.

The day was now fully come. The grey sky had changed to blue, and of all the cloudy masses of the dawn there remained only a few patches of dissolving fleeciness. The world below was bright and singularly clear. The ridge was not, perhaps, more than a hundred feet or so above the general plain, but in this flat region it sufficed to give the effect of extensive view. Away on the north side of the ridge, little and far, were the camps, the ordered wagons, all the gear of a big army; with officers galloping about and men doing aimless things. Here and there men were falling in, however, and the cavalry was forming up on the plain beyond the tents. The bulk of men who had been in the trenches were still on the move to the rear, scattered like sheep without a shepherd over the farther slopes. Here and there were little rallies and attempts to wait and do – something vague; but the general drift was away from any concentration. There on the southern side was the elaborate lacework of trenches and defences, across which these iron turtles, fourteen of them spread out over a line of perhaps three miles, were now advancing as fast as a man could trot, and methodically shooting down and breaking up any persistent knots of resistance. Here and there stood little clumps of men, outflanked and unable to get away, showing the white flag, and the invader's cyclist-infantry was advancing now across the open, in open order but unmolested, to complete the work of the machines. Surveyed at large, the defenders already looked a beaten army. A mechanism that was effectually ironclad against bullets, that could at a pinch cross a thirty-foot trench, and that seemed able to shoot out rifle-bullets with unerring precision, was clearly an inevitable victor against anything but rivers, precipices, and guns.

He looked at his watch. 'Half-past four! Lord! What things can happen in two hours. Here's the whole blessed army being walked over, and at half-past two –

'And even now our blessed louts haven't done a thing with their guns!'

He scanned the ridge right and left of him with his glasses. He turned again to the nearest land ironclad, advancing now obliquely to him and not three hundred yards away, and then scrambled the ground over which he must retreat if he was not to be captured.

'They'll do nothing,' he said, and glanced again at the enemy.

And then from far away to the left came the thud of a gun, followed very rapidly by a rolling gunfire.

He hesitated and decided to stay.

III

The defender had relied chiefly upon his rifles in the event of an assault. His guns he kept concealed at various points upon and behind the ridge ready to bring them into action against any artillery preparations for an attack on the part of his antagonist. The situation had rushed upon him with the dawn, and by the time the gunners had their guns ready for motion, the land ironclads were already in among the foremost trenches. There is a natural reluctance to fire into one's own broken men, and many of the guns, being intended simply to fight an advance of the enemy's artillery, were not in positions to hit anything in the second line of trenches. After that the advance of the land ironclads was swift. The defender-general found himself suddenly called upon to invent a new sort of warfare, in which guns were to fight alone amidst broken and retreating infantry. He had scarcely thirty minutes in which to think it out. He did not respond to the call, and what happened that morning was that the advance of the land ironclads forced the fight, and each gun and battery made what play its circumstances dictated. For the most part it was poor play.

Some of the guns got in two or three shots, some one or two, and the percentage of misses was unusually high. The howitzers, of course, did nothing. The land ironclads in each case followed much the same tactics. As soon as a gun came into play the monster turned itself almost end on, so as to minimise the chances of a square hit, and made not for the gun, but for the nearest point on its flank from which the gunners could be shot down. Few of the hits scored were very effectual; only one of the things was disabled, and that was the one that fought the three batteries attached to the brigade on the left wing. Three that were hit when close upon the guns were clean shot through without being put out of action. Our war correspondent did not see that one momentary arrest of the tide of victory on the left; he saw only the very ineffectual fight of half-battery 96B close at hand upon his right. This he watched some time beyond the margin of safety.

Just after he heard the three batteries opening up upon his left he became aware of the thud of horses' hoofs from the sheltered side of the slope, and presently saw first one and then two other guns galloping into position along the north side of the ridge, well out of sight of the great bulk that was now creeping obliquely towards the crest and cutting up the lingering infantry beside it and below, as it came.

The half-battery swung round into line – each gun describing its curve – halted, unlimbered, and prepared for action. ...

'Bang!'

The land ironclad had become visible over the brow of the hill, and just visible as a long black back to the gunners. It halted, as though it hesitated.

The two remaining guns fired, and then their big antagonist had swung round and was in full view, end on, against the sky, coming at a rush.

The gunners became frantic in their haste to fire again. They were so near the war correspondent could see the expressions on their excited faces through his field-glass. As he looked he saw a man drop, and realised for the first time that the ironclad was shooting.

For a moment the big black monster crawled with an accelerated pace towards the furiously active gunners. Then, as if moved by a generous impulse, it turned its full broadside to their attack, and scarcely forty yards away from them. The war correspondent turned his field-glass back to the gunners and perceived it was now shooting down the men about the guns with the most deadly rapidity.

Just for a moment it seemed splendid and then it seemed horrible. The gunners were dropping in heaps about their guns. To lay a hand on a gun was death. 'Bang!' went the gun on the left, a hopeless miss, and that was the only second shot the half-battery fired. In another moment half-a-dozen surviving artillerymen were holding up their hands amidst a scattered muddle of dead and wounded men, and the fight was done.

The war correspondent hesitated between stopping in his scrub and waiting for an opportunity to surrender decently, or taking to an adjacent gully he had discovered. If he surrendered it was certain he would get no copy off; while, if he escaped, there were all sorts of chances. He decided to follow the gully, and take the first offer in the confusion beyond the camp of picking up a horse.

IV

Subsequent authorities have found fault with the first land ironclads in many particulars, but assuredly they served their purpose on the day of their appearance. They were essentially long, narrow, and very strong steel frameworks carrying the engines, and borne upon eight pairs of big pedrail wheels, each about ten feet in diameter, each a driving wheel and set upon long axles free to swivel round a common axis. This arrangement gave them the maximum of adaptability to the contours of the ground. They crawled level along the ground with one foot high upon a hillock and another deep in a depression, and they could hold themselves erect and steady sideways upon even a steep hillside. The engineers directed the engines under the command of the captain, who had look-out points at small ports all round the upper edge of the adjustable skirt of twelve-inch iron-plating which protected the whole affair, and could also raise or depress a conning-tower set about the portholes through the centre of the iron top cover. The riflemen each occupied a small cabin of peculiar construction and these cabins were slung along the sides of and before and behind the great main framework, in a manner suggestive of the slinging of the seats of an Irish jaunting-car. Their rifles, however, were very different pieces of apparatus from the simple mechanisms in the hands of their adversaries.

These were in the first place automatic, ejected their cartridges and loaded again from a magazine each time they fired, until the ammunition store was at an end, and they had the most remarkable sights imaginable, sights which threw a bright little camera-obscura picture into the light-tight box in which the rifleman sat below. This camera-obscura picture was marked with two crossed lines, and whatever was covered by the intersection of these two lines, that the rifle hit. The sighting was ingeniously contrived. The rifleman stood at the table with a thing like an elaboration of a draughtsman's dividers in his hand, and he opened and closed these dividers, so that they were always at the apparent height – if it was an ordinary-sized man – of the man he wanted to kill. A little twisted strand of wire like an electric-light wire ran from this implement up to the gun, and as the dividers opened and shut the sights went up and down. Changes in the clearness of the atmosphere, due to changes of moisture, were met by an ingenious use of that meteorologically sensitive substance, catgut, and when the land ironclad moved forward the sites got a compensatory deflection in the direction of its motion. The riflemen stood up in his pitch-dark chamber and watched the little picture before him. One hand held the dividers for judging distance, and the other grasped a big knob like a door-handle. As he pushed this knob about the rifle above swung to correspond, and the picture passed to and fro like an agitated panorama. When he saw a man he wanted to shoot he brought him up to the cross-lines, and then pressed a finger upon a little push like an electric bell-push, conveniently placed in the centre of the knob. Then the man was shot. If by any chance the rifleman missed his target he moved the knob a trifle, or readjusted his dividers, pressed the push, and got him the second time.

This rifle and its sights protruded from a porthole, exactly like a great number of other portholes that ran in a triple row under the eaves of the cover of the land ironclad. Each porthole displayed a rifle and sight in dummy, so that the real ones could only be hit by a chance shot, and if one was, then the young man below said 'Pshaw!' turned on an electric light, lowered the injured instrument into his camera, replaced the injured part, or put up a new rifle if the injury was considerable.

You must conceive these cabins as hung clear above the swing of the axles, and inside the big wheels upon which the great elephant-like feet were hung, and behind these cabins along the centre of the monster ran a central gallery into which they opened, and along which worked the big compact engines. It was like a long passage into which this throbbing machinery had been packed, and the captain stood about the middle, close to the ladder that led to his conning-tower, and directed the silent, alert engineers – for the most part by signs. The throb and noise of the engines mingled with the reports of the rifles and the intermittent clangour of the bullet hail upon the armour. Ever and again he would touch the wheel that raised his conning-tower, step up his ladder until his engineers could see nothing of him above the waist, and then come down again with orders. Two small electric lights were all the illumination of this space – they were placed to make him most clearly visible to his subordinates; the air was thick with the smell of oil and petrol, and had the war correspondent been suddenly transferred from the spacious dawn outside to the bowels of the apparatus he would have thought himself fallen into another world.

The captain, of course, saw both sides of the battle. When he raised his head into his conning-tower there were the dewy sunrise, the amazed and disordered trenches, the flying and falling soldiers, the depressed-looking groups of prisoners, the beaten guns; when he bent down again to signal 'half speed', 'quarter speed', 'half circle round towards the right', or what not, he was in the oil-smelling twilight of the ill-lit engine room. Close beside him on either side was the mouthpiece of a speaking-tube, and ever and again he would direct one side or other of his strange craft to 'Concentrate fire forward on gunners', or to 'clear out trench about a hundred yards on our right front.'

He was a young man, healthy enough but by no means sun-tanned, and of a type of feature and expression that prevails in His Majesty's Navy: alert, intelligent, quiet. He and his engineers and his riflemen all went about their work, calm and reasonable men. They had none of that flapping strenuousness of the half-wit in a hurry, that excessive strain upon the blood-vessels, that hysteria of effort which is so frequently regarded as the proper state of mind for heroic deeds.

For the enemy these young engineers were defeating they felt a certain qualified pity and a quite unqualified contempt. They regarded these big, healthy men they were shooting down precisely as these same big, healthy men might regard some inferior kind of native. They despised them for making war; despised their bawling patriotisms and their emotionality profoundly; despised them, above all, for the petty cunning and the almost brutish want of imagination their method of fighting displayed. 'If they *must* make war,' these young men thought, 'why in thunder don't they do it like sensible men?' They resented the assumption that their own side was too stupid to do anything more than play their enemy's game, that they were going to play this costly folly according to the rules of unimaginative men. They resented being forced to the trouble of making man-killing machinery; resented the alternative of having to massacre these people or endure their truculent yappings; resented the whole unfathomable imbecility of war.

Meanwhile, with something of the mechanical precision of a good clerk posting a ledger, the riflemen moved their knobs and pressed their buttons. ...

41

The captain of Land Ironclad Number Three had halted on the crest close to his captured half-battery. His lined-up prisoners stood hard by and waited for the cyclists behind to come for them. He surveyed the victorious morning through his conning-tower.

He read the general's signals. 'Five and Four are to keep among the guns to the left and prevent any attempt to recover them. Seven and Eleven and Twelve, stick to the guns you have got; Seven, get into position to command the guns taken by Three. Then, we're to do something else, are we? Six and One, quicken up to about ten miles an hour and walk round behind that camp to the levels near the river – we shall bag the whole crowd of them,' interjected the young man. 'Ah, here we are! Two and Three, Eight and Nine, Thirteen and Fourteen, space out to a thousand yards, wait for the word, and then go slowly to cover the advance of the cyclist infantry against any charge of mounted troops. That's all right. But where's Ten? Halloa! Ten to repair and get movable as soon as possible. They've broken up Ten!'

The discipline of the new war machines was business-like rather than pedantic, and the head of the captain came down out of the conning-tower to tell his men. 'I say, you chaps there. They've broken up Ten. Not badly, I think; but anyhow, he's stuck.'

But that still left thirteen of the monsters in action to finish up the broken army.

The war correspondent stealing down his gully looked back and saw them all lying along the crest and talking fluttering congratulatory flags to one another. Their iron sides were shining golden in the light of the rising sun.

V

The private adventures of the war correspondent terminated in surrender about one o'clock in the afternoon, and by that time he had stolen a horse, pitched off it, and narrowly escaped being rolled upon; found the brute had broken its leg, and shot it with his revolver. He had spent some hours in the company of a squad of dispirited riflemen, had quarrelled with them about topography at last, and gone off by himself in a direction that should have brought him to the banks of the river and didn't. Moreover, he had eaten all his chocolate and found nothing in the whole world to drink. Also, it had become extremely hot. From behind a broken, but attractive, stone wall he had seen far away in the distance the defender-horsemen trying to charge cyclists in open order, with land ironclads outflanking them on either side. He had discovered that cyclists could retreat over open turf before horsemen with a sufficient margin of speed to allow of frequent dismounts and much terribly effective sharpshooting; and he had a sufficient persuasion that those horsemen, having charged their hearts out, had halted just beyond his range of vision and surrendered. He had been urged to sudden activity by a forward movement of one of those machines that had threatened to enfilade his wall. He had discovered a fearful blister on his heel.

He was now in a scrubby gravelly place, sitting down and meditating on his pocket-handkerchief, which had in some extraordinary way become in the last twenty-four hours extremely ambiguous in hue. 'It's the whitest thing I've got,' he said.

He had known all along that the enemy was east, west, and south of him, but when he heard war ironclads Numbers One and Six talking in their measured, deadly way not half a mile to the north he decided to make his own little unconditional peace without any further risks. He was for hoisting his white flag to a bush and taking up a position of modest obscurity near it, until someone came along. He became aware of voices, clatter, and the distinctive noises of a body of horse, quite near, and he put his handkerchief in his pocket again and went to see what was going forward.

The sound of firing ceased, and then as he drew near he heard the deep sounds of many simple, coarse, but hearty and noble-hearted soldiers of the old school swearing with vigour.

He emerged from his scrub upon a big level plain, and far away a fringe of trees marked the banks of the river. In the centre of the picture was a still intact road bridge, and a big railway bridge a little to the right. Two land ironclads rested, with a general air of being long, harmless sheds, in a pose of anticipatory peacefulness right and left of the picture, completely commanding two miles and more of the river levels. Emerged and halted a few yards from the scrub was the remainder of the defender's cavalry, dusty, a little disordered and obviously annoyed, but still a very fine show of men. In the middle distance three or four men and horses were receiving medical attendance, and nearer a knot of officers regarded the distant novelties in mechanism with profound distaste. Everyone was very distinctly aware of the twelve other ironclads, and of the multitude of townsmen soldiers, on bicycles or afoot, encumbered now by prisoners and captured war-gear but otherwise thoroughly effective, who were sweeping like a great net in their rear.

'Checkmate,' said the war correspondent, walking out into the open. 'But I surrender in the best of company. Twenty-four hours ago I thought war was impossible – and these beggars have captured the whole blessed army! Well! Well!' He thought of his talk with the young lieutenant. 'If there's no end to the surprises of science, the civilised people have it, of course. As long as their science keeps going they will necessarily be ahead of open-country men. Still. ...' He wondered for a space what might have happened to the young lieutenant.

The war correspondent was one of those inconsistent people who always want the beaten side to win. When he saw all these burly, sun-tanned horsemen, disarmed and dismounted and lined up; when he saw their horses unskilfully led away by the singularly not equestrian cyclists to whom they had surrendered; when he saw these truncated Paladins watching this scandalous sight, he forgot altogether that he had called these men 'cunning louts' and wished them beaten not four-and-twenty hours ago. A month ago he had seen that regiment in its pride going forth to war, and had been told of its terrible prowess, how it could charge in open order with each man firing from his saddle, and sweep before it anything else that ever came out to battle in any sort of order, foot or horse. And it had had to fight a few score of young men in atrociously unfair machines!

'Manhood *versus* Machinery' occurred to him as a suitable headline. Journalism curdles all one's mind to phrases.

He strolled as near the lined-up prisoners as the sentinels seemed disposed to permit and surveyed them and compared their sturdy proportions with those of their lightly built captors.

'Smart degenerates,' he muttered. 'Anæmic cockneydom.'

The surrendered officers came quite close to him presently, and he could hear the colonel's high-pitched tenor. The poor gentleman had spent three years of arduous toil upon the best material in the world perfecting that shooting from the saddle charge, and he was mourning with phrases of blasphemy, natural under the circumstances what one could be expected to do against this suitably consigned ironmongery.

'Guns,' said someone.

'Big guns they can walk round. You can't shift big guns to keep pace with them and little guns in the open they rush. I saw 'em rushed. You might do a surprise now and then – assassinate the brutes, perhaps –'

'You might make things like 'em.'

'What? *More* ironmongery? Us? ...'

'I'll call my article,' meditated the war correspondent, "Mankind *versus* Ironmongery", and quote the old boy at the beginning.'

And he was much too good a journalist to spoil his contrast by remarking that the half-dozen comparatively slender young men in blue pyjamas who were standing about their victorious land ironclad, drinking coffee and eating biscuits, had also in their eyes and carriage something not altogether degraded below the level of a man.

INTRODUCTION

'No Man's Land', Susan Gates
'Christmas Truce', Robert Graves

One Christmas day during the First World War, German and British troops declared a truce, climbed out of their trenches and played a game of football. In context of the millions who were killed during this war, a moment of such ordinariness was completely *extra*ordinary.

In each of these two stories a boy learns about the football match long after the war has ended, but the authors tell their tales very differently. In Robert Graves' story an old man recounts the tale. In Susan Gates' story the boy is thrust right into the action. It might be interesting to consider which story makes it easier to imagine being there, and which does a better job of teaching us something about war.

NO MAN'S LAND

Susan Gates

Jake ripped open his last present. He'd been hoping against hope, even though it wasn't ball-shaped. When he saw it was a pair of gloves, his face scrunched into a scowl.

'Where's my football?' he said.

'What?'

Mum poked her head out of the steamy kitchen. It was only just after breakfast but she was already cooking Christmas dinner. She'd got up at six o' clock that morning to put the turkey in.

'My football,' demanded Jake. 'You said I'd definitely get one for Christmas.'

'Did I?' said Mum vaguely, fanning herself to get some cool air. 'It's like a sauna in this kitchen.'

'I said I wanted one. And you promised.'

'Did I?' repeated Mum, looking as if she had more important things on her mind.

'I told and told you,' said Jake. He felt bad temper

blooming inside him, like an evil flower. And he'd been in a great mood when he got up this morning! 'I told you loads of times.'

'I can't remember that,' said Mum. She frowned suddenly. 'I've still got those potatoes to peel.'

'What was I supposed to do? Tattoo it up here?' Jake dragged a finger across his forehead. 'Like, "BUY JAKE A FOOTBALL"? I thought you were listening.'

He made an ugly face at the gloves. They were woolly, from his great-gran. She probably knitted them herself. He wouldn't have minded a cool pair from a skateboarding shop.

'Stupid gloves.' He chucked them across the room.

He knew he was taking a big risk. Mum wasn't the patient type at the best of times. But on Christmas mornings she could go off like a firework. That's what she did now.

'Don't you start!' she exploded. 'You ungrateful brat! You've got loads of nice presents. And you're moaning about not having a football. You should be ashamed of yourself! Some poor kid in a refugee camp would give his right arm for those gloves!'

Jake opened his mouth to protest. He wanted to explain. How he'd already told his mates he was getting a football. How it was all arranged. In twenty minutes, they were meeting him at the field for a game. What were they going to say when he turned up without a ball?

'But Mum!' he said.

She gave him that killer shark glare. The one that could shrivel you up. It meant, 'You think I'm giving you a hard time now? You haven't seen nothing yet. Any second now I'm going to blow like a volcano. Then you'd better run for cover.'

Jake backed down. Better not upset her. Mum had the whole family coming for Christmas dinner. She'd probably already started on the sherry. Dad was keeping out of the way, down the shed.

Reluctantly, Jake clamped his mouth shut. Mum hung around in the doorway, still looking dangerous. But then a timer went off in the kitchen, PING!

'My sprouts!' shouted Mum, and she ducked back into the steam.

'Phew, those sprouts saved my life,' said Jake, wiping imaginary sweat off his forehead.

It was no good. He was never going to get Mum to understand his bitter disappointment.

He stomped out the house, his shoulders hunched, and headed for the park.

'It's not fair!' he hissed through gritted teeth. He'd dropped loads of hints about that football. He'd even shown her the one he wanted in a shop window.

He gave a big sigh. 'And I thought she was taking it all in,' he said. There was a Coke can on the pavement. He gave it a vicious kick.

Mum had no idea what it was like. Every time he wanted a kick about, he had to wait for someone to turn up who had their own ball. That meant Bradley, who had about two brain cells. He always got the time wrong. He arrived after you'd got fed up and gone home. Or he went to the wrong place and waited for hours, wondering, *Why am I the only one here?* Or Harry, who was dead keen and always turned up right on time. But was absolute rubbish at football.

It was frosty. Ice sparkled on the pavement. Jake cupped his cold hands and puffed hot breath into them. He should have worn those Christmas gloves after all.

'Maybe they won't turn up,' he thought, hopefully.

Fat chance. Two were waiting already. Stamping about to keep themselves warm. They had new football strips on.

They got what they wanted for Christmas, thought Jake.

Three others were straggling across the park. Lenny was using his mobile.

He's probably phoning my house, thought Jake, *to say, 'We can't start without you. You're bringing the ball. Get your lazy butt out of bed.'*

But that reminded him. He'd asked for a mobile for Christmas too. One of the latest models. But he knew he'd never get that, not in a million years.

At the last minute, he veered away from the field, dodged through some bushes. He just couldn't face his mates. It was too embarrassing.

'They'll think I was lying again,' he told himself. Sometimes he did lie, saying he'd got things his Mum and Dad couldn't afford. He'd got into big trouble with that trail bike. 'Yeah, my dad bought me it,' he'd boasted. And, of course, they'd all begged, 'Give us a ride on it!' He'd had to do even more lying, to get out of that one.

He felt sorry for himself. 'All I wanted this time was one crappy football!' It wasn't like he was asking for the world.

He didn't want to go home yet. So he knocked on Great-Gran's door. She lived in the old people's bungalows, just outside the park. She looked surprised when he walked in. She was still in her dressing gown.

'It's not that time already, is it?' she said. 'I thought your dad was picking me up at twelve.'

'He is,' said Jake, slumping into a chair. 'I'm here on my own. Got any microchips?'

After he'd glugged red sauce on his chips and slotted a few into his mouth, he felt happier.

'Hey, thanks for the gloves,' he told Great-Gran, grudgingly.

'Did you get some nice presents? Things you wanted?'

'I didn't get a football.' He just couldn't help blurting it out. 'And Mum practically promised me one.'

'That's a shame,' said Great-Gran, grieving along with him. Then her look brightened. 'Wait a minute,' she said. 'I've got a football somewhere.'

Jake stared at her, a microchip halfway to his mouth. 'Have you?'

Magic, was his first thought. Then he thought again. 'What kind of football?' he asked her, suspiciously. Great-Gran knew nothing about footballs. It was probably a little kids' blow-up beach ball. It was probably one she'd knitted.

'Oh, it's a proper one,' said Great-Gran, as if she was reading his mind. She bustled out of the room. He heard her rummaging around in the cupboard under the stairs. 'It belonged to your great-great-grandad.'

'Who?' said Jake.

'My dad,' explained Great-Gran, coming back with a dusty cardboard box. 'I haven't looked at it for donkey's years.'

She lifted it out of the box.

'It just needs pumping up a bit,' she said.

Jake groaned. Why had he got his hopes up? It was a proper football all right. It was even made of leather. But it was a joke. It was the saddest, scabbiest, most scuffed football Jake had ever seen. He couldn't help grinning.

'Gran! It's a mess. It looks like a dog's been chewing it. I can't take that down the park. My mates would fall about laughing.'

Great-Gran looked hurt. 'Is it no good then? I suppose it is a bit old.'

'How old?' asked Jake.

Great-Gran did some counting up in her head. 'About ninety years old.'

Jake burst out laughing. 'Gran! It's as old as you. It's ancient. It ought to be on the Antiques Roadshow.'

Great-Gran looked hurt again.

Just to please her, Jake pretended to be interested in the football. He took it from her.

'Ow!'

As soon as he touched it, a cold tingling feeling surged up his arms. When it reached the back of his neck, it made the hairs lift, like they do when you're scared. But what was there to be scared of? He was safe, here, in Great-Gran's bungalow. She even had an alarm, to call the warden.

Quickly, he put the ball down. He rubbed his tingling arms. He picked up his box of chips. But he couldn't shake off that strange feeling of dread. He even looked over his shoulder, as if there were someone hiding behind his chair.

'Put that ball away, Gran,' he shuddered. 'I don't want it. Put it back in the box.'

But Great-Gran had gone all misty-eyed. She was caught up in memories. She'd got something else out the box. It was a tatty yellow piece of paper.

'This was the letter his mate brought back, when he came home on leave from the Great War.'

'What war is that?' said Jake. His history was a bit hazy.

'It's the First World War I'm talking about,' said Great-Gran. 'Nineteen-fourteen to nineteen-eighteen. My dad was a soldier in that war. He fought the Germans. Except for Christmas Day, 1914. When he played football with them.'

'Played football with the German soldiers?' said Jake, confused. 'Weren't they supposed to be killing each other?'

'Not on Christmas Day,' said Gran. 'There was a truce.'

She unfolded the letter. It seemed as fragile as a cobweb. She put on her reading glasses. Jake fidgeted. He'd suddenly got itchy feet. 'Got to go now, Gran,' he said.

Great-Gran took no notice. She pursed her lips, following the lines on the letter with her finger.

'There's some bits Dad wrote about the rats and the mud and the fighting and how awful it was in the trenches. But here's the part about that football game.'

Gran read it, in a high warbly voice, sometimes stumbling over the words.

'The dawn was freezing cold and foggy at first. It was dead quiet, without the shells and the guns. My mates said, "You're barmy." I don't know what made me do it. But I just stood up on the parapet and no one shot me! So I took my football and went out into No Man's Land. I saw Fritz poking his head above his parapet so I gives the ball a kick and says, "Fancy a game, Fritz?" and blow me someone says, "OK, Tommy." And they all comes trooping out, real friendly. We even shake hands, like we hadn't been blasting each other to kingdom come the day before!'

Great-Gran stopped reading. She folded the letter up again.

Jake jumped to his feet. 'Can I borrow that ball, Gran?' He'd forgotten how even touching it had spooked him, seconds ago.

Great-Gran looked surprised, 'I thought you didn't want it.'

'Yeah, but that was before. Before I knew my great-great-grandad was a soldier. And that he had a kick about with some Germans on Christmas Day. I want to show my mates. This football is famous!'

He scooped up the ball. Again that chilly shiver ran up his arms. As if some kind of connection were being made. But he hardly noticed. He was more excited now than scared.

'Can I have the letter too?' He reached out to take it but Great-Gran drew it back.

'I think I'll keep it here,' she said.

For a second Jake was indignant. Great-Gran never said no. She always let him have anything he wanted. 'Why?' he frowned.

'Because I don't want nothing to happen to it. I told you, Dad's best mate brought it back for his family, along with this football and some of his other things. My dad never got the chance to post this letter,' said Great-Gran, her face suddenly filling with sadness. 'He got shot. Boxing Day, 1914, when I was just a baby.'

'Wow!' said Jake, excited. 'So that letter got found on his body? Are those bloodstains?' This was going to make a great story to tell his mates. They might even forget that he hadn't got a new football.

'Catch you later, Gran.'

Leaving Great-Gran still lost in her memories, he went speeding up the path. He was pleased to be outside. It was too hot and stuffy in Great-Gran's house. After about twenty minutes talking to her, he always wanted to escape.

He raced back to the park, with the football under

his arm. Were his mates still there? Some had gone home. But three or four were still hanging around, their breath making white clouds in the frosty air.

'Hey, you guys, guess what I've got?' he shouted.

The faces they turned towards him weren't welcoming.

'So you decided to turn up,' said Lenny, sarcastically. 'We've been freezing to death, waiting for you. You said ten o clock.'

Jake held out the football, 'I've got this, though.'

There was dead silence. Then someone hooted with laughter. And Lenny said, in disgust, 'You trying to be funny or what? You keep us waiting for ages. Then you turn up with that?'

'No, no,' said Jake, struggling to explain. 'You don't understand. It's not to play with. It's an antique. I just bought it to show you. It's a famous football. My great-great-grandad, he was a soldier. Right? And he played a game with the Germans, with this football, in the First World War.'

'So?' said Lenny, still in the same sarcastic voice.

And someone else said, 'Does that mean you didn't get a new football? Just like you didn't get that trail bike? So you're making up some kind of stupid lie. About a famous football or something?'

'Yeah,' added Lenny. 'Look at the state of it. He probably picked it out of a skip on the way here.'

'I didn't. I didn't,' spluttered Jake, his face turning bright red. 'And I'm not lying.'

But they were already walking away. They didn't once look back. They disappeared through the big, iron gates. There was no one else around, not even dog-walkers. He was alone, in an empty park, on a frozen football field.

Suddenly, the football felt as heavy as a boulder in his arms. Jake dropped it on to the grass. Why had he brought it to show them? He must have had a brainstorm. He should have known they'd just make fun of it.

'Stupid football.' He gave it a kick.

There was no chance of a game now. He had no one to play with. He shivered and hugged himself. It was getting colder. The kind of cold that went right through to your bones.

'Might as well go home,' he muttered to himself.

Fed up, he gave the football another boot.

There was a strange mist creeping towards him across the grass. Where had that come from? It curled and writhed like snakes. It lapped around his shoes in creamy waves.

Suddenly, he realized, he'd lost the football. The mist had swallowed it. That football was a family heirloom. Great-Gran would go mad!

But the mist was rising, getting thicker. First the

trees were fuzzy black shapes. Then they vanished altogether. Now, there were white cotton-wool walls closing in on him. Jake blundered about in the fog, his sense of direction totally scrambled.

'Aaargh!'

He was teetering on the edge of a big crater. His arms whirled like windmills. He saved himself, just in time, from slithering down the sides. What was that doing there? There should be barriers to keep kids from falling in. There should be signs saying, 'DANGER. KEEP OUT.'

The bottom was full of slushy mud. It looked like lumpy, yellow porridge.

'You could drown in there!' Jake gasped, horrified.

And, if anyone heard your cries for help, in this fog they wouldn't be able to find you. When he stretched out his arm, he couldn't even see his own fingers, waggling in front of his face.

He stumbled into a muddy rut. It had frozen, hard as iron. What had happened to their football field? It hadn't been smooth before. But now it was like a construction site.

Where am I? thought Jake. He didn't know this part of the park. He felt scared, totally disorientated.

'You've got to get out of here,' he told himself. 'Find the park gates.' Even a bench, or a litter bin would be something familiar.

Then something rolled slowly towards his foot. His toe stopped it. He looked down. It was the football, lying in an icy puddle. Someone had just kicked it back to him.

Those hairs on the back of his neck weren't just lifting now. They were wriggling about, like maggots.

'Who's there?' he shouted, trying to peer through the smoky swirls. Maybe one of his mates had come back, looking for him.

'Who's there?' he shouted again. 'Is that you, Lenny?'

His eyes screwed up. What was that? He could see twinkling lights in the fog. A row of twinkling lights, floating high up above the ground.

'What's happening?' Jake thought, panic-stricken. 'What is this place?'

Then a voice drifted through the freezing, foggy air. 'Merry Christmas, Tommy!'

My name's not Tommy, thought Jake, bewildered.

He stumbled into something. It was a bunch of tunic jackets, some khaki, some grey, piled up in a heap. There was another heap over there. He could just make it out, through the haze.

He and his mates often piled up their hoodies and jackets like that.

It looks like ... goalposts, thought Jake, frowning.

'Pass that ruddy ball, Fritz!'

Without thinking, Jake reacted. He booted the ball. Instantly the fog around him was full of running figures. The ball came back to him.

Jake started running too. But he kept the ball at his feet. He booted it again. It curved off into the mist. The figures around were keeping up with him. He was in a football game! He couldn't see faces, only shapes. But they were laughing, shouting, skidding on ice.

'Over here!' shouted Jake wildly, all flushed and excited. And someone passed him the ball. With a mighty kick, he belted it back into the fog.

'Goal!' someone yelled. 'Well done, Tommy!'

Hey, thought Jake. *I'm doing good here.*

'Look out, Jake!'

Who'd shouted that? It was an English voice. It came out of the fog and stopped him pitching head-first into another huge crater. He flung himself down, just in time, at its icy edge. But he slid forward so he was almost overhanging it, staring into its depths.

'No!' There were things floating in the mud. He didn't want to look. An arm sticking out, a boot. The back of someone's head. There were dead soldiers down there!

Jake scrambled up. He thought, *I'm gonna be sick.* His legs felt as wonky as a newborn foal's.

Then, out of the fog, Great-Great-Grandad's football trickled gently towards him. It stopped at his feet.

Suddenly, he found the strength to run. He snatched up the ball and hared off. Soon, he was on smoother ground, dodging through the fog, slamming into trees and park benches. Until he was hanging, half-hysterical, on to the park gates, gasping for breath, his heart hammering.

'You all right, son?' said someone. It was an old guy, walking his dog.

Jake could hardly speak. He pointed a shaking finger. 'Out there! Out there! Look!'

Together, they stared into the park. The fog had gone. There were only a few wispy rags left.

'What you on about, son?' the man said.

'Can't you see?' screamed Jake. 'It's No Man's Land!'

But No Man's Land had gone too. The litter bins, benches, and trees were back. The park looked just the same as it always did. Except the sun had come out over their football field. Making the ice crystals on the grass sparkle like jewels.

His brain numb, Jake trudged back to Great-Gran's, carrying the football. He couldn't think, daren't think, about what had just happened. And what he'd seen.

The ball was soggy now, heavy to carry. It made his arms ache.

Jake plodded wearily into Great-Gran's living room.

'Take those shoes off!' said Great-Gran straightaway. 'You're making a right mess of my carpets!'

Dazed, Jake looked down. His trainers were caked with thick yellow mud. There was no mud that colour round here.

'Where've you been?' fussed Great-Gran. 'In a mud bath? Look at your clothes. Your mum's going to have a fit.'

Jake slumped into a chair.

'Here's your ball back,' he said to Great-Gran. He wiped some mud off it with his sleeve. Then put it gently on the coffee table.

'You know,' said Great-Gran, 'after you'd gone, I had a proper read of Dad's letter. Would you believe it, them Germans put up trees at Christmas? On top of their trenches, all among the barbed wire? They even lit candles on the branches. They looked real pretty, Dad said, twinkling through the morning mist.'

'I saw them,' said Jake, speaking as if he was in a trance. 'And we played football. And someone knew my name, Gran. Someone called out to warn me.'

'What, my pet?' said Great-Gran, looking totally baffled.

Jake sighed. He shook himself like a wet dog.

'Never mind, Gran,' he said. 'I'm just talking rubbish.'

Had he really played football with ghosts in No Man's Land? And had his own great-great-grandad called out to him? To save him from falling into a shell hole full of corpses?

He shivered. His brain couldn't cope with that. Best not to think about it. Block it right out of his mind. Pretend it never happened. But there was one thing to say before he did.

'Put that football back in the box, Gran,' he begged. 'And don't take it out again, ever.'

'I'll buy you a brand new one, pet,' offered Great-Gran, shutting the ball away and closing the box lid. 'You can come with me. Show me which one you want.'

'Thanks, Gran,' said Jake, pleased.

'But we won't be able to get it until the shops open, after Christmas.'

'That's OK,' Jake told her. 'It's not that important. I can wait.'

CHRISTMAS TRUCE

Robert Graves

Young Stan comes around yesterday about tea-time – you know my grandson Stan? He's a Polytechnic student, just turned twenty, as smart as his dad was at the same age. Stan's all out to be a commercial artist and do them big coloured posters for the hoardings. Doesn't answer to 'Stan', though – says it's 'common'; says he's either 'Stanley' or he's nothing.

Stan's got a bagful of big, noble ideas; all schemed out carefully, with what he calls 'captions' attached.

Well, I can't say nothing against big, noble ideas. I was a red-hot Labour-man myself for a time, forty years ago now, when the Kayser's war ended and the war-profiteers began treading us ex-heroes into the mud. But that's all over long ago – in fact, Labour's got a damn sight too respectable for my taste! Worse than Tories, most of their leaders is now – especially them that used to be the loudest in rendering 'We'll Keep the

Red Flag Flying Still'. They're all Churchwardens now, or country gents, if they're not in the House of Lords.

Anyhow, yesterday Stan came around, about a big Ban-the-Bomb march all the way across England to Trafalgar Square. And couldn't I persuade a few of my old comrades to form a special squad with a banner marked 'First World War Veterans Protest Against the Bomb'? He wanted us to head the parade, ribbons, crutches, wheelchairs and all.

I put my foot down pretty hard. 'No, Mr Stanley,' I said politely, 'I regret as I can't accept your kind invitation.'

'But why?' says he. 'You don't want another war, Grandfather, do you? You don't want mankind to be annihilated? This time it won't be just a few unlucky chaps killed, like Uncle Arthur in the First War, and Dad in the Second ... It will be all mankind.'

'Listen, young 'un,' I said. 'I don't trust nobody who talks about mankind – not parsons, not politicians, not anyone else. There ain't no such thing as "mankind", not practically speaking there ain't.'

'Practically speaking, Grandfather,' says young Stan, 'there *is*. Mankind means all the different nations lumped together – us, the Russians, the Americans, the Germans, the French, and all the rest of them. If the bomb goes off, everyone's finished.'

'It's not going off,' I says.

'But it's gone off twice already – at Hiroshima and Nagasaki,' he argues, 'so why not again? The damage will be definitely final when it *does* go off.'

I wouldn't let Stan have the last word. 'In the crazy, old-fashioned war in which I lost my foot,' I said, a bit sternly, 'the Fritzes used poison gas. They thought it would help 'em to break through at Wipers. But somehow the line held, and soon our factories were churning out the same stinking stuff for us to use on them. All right, and now what about Hitler's war?'

'What about it?' Stan asks.

'Well,' I says, 'everyone in England was issued an expensive mask in a smart-looking case against poison-gas bombs dropped from the air – me, your dad, your ma, and yourself as a tiny tot. But how many poison-gas bombs were dropped on London, or on Berlin? Not a damned one! Both sides were scared stiff. Poison-gas had got too deadly. No mask in the market could keep the new sorts out. So there's not going to be no atom bombs dropped neither, I tell you, Stanley my lad; not this side of the Hereafter! Everyone's scared stiff again.'

'Then why do both sides manufacture quantities of atom bombs and pile them up?' he asks.

'Search me,' I said, 'unless it's a clever way of keeping up full employment by making believe there's a war on. What with bombs and fall-out shelters, and radar equipment, and unsinkable aircraft-carriers, and satellites, and shooting rockets at the moon, and keeping up big armies – takes two thousand quid nowadays to maintain a soldier in the field, I read the other day – what with all that play-acting, there's full employment assured for everyone, and businessmen are rubbing their hands.'

'Your argument has a bad flaw, Grandfather. The Russians don't need to worry about full employment.'

'No,' said I, 'perhaps they don't. But their politicians and commissars have to keep up the notion of a wicked Capitalist plot to wipe out the poor workers. And they have to show that they're well ahead in the Arms Race. Forget it, lad, forget it! Mankind, which is a term used by maiden ladies and bun-punchers, ain't going to be annihilated by no atom bomb.'

Stan changed his tactics. 'Nevertheless, Grandfather,' he says, 'we British want to show the Russians that we're not engaged in any such Capitalist plot. All men are brothers, and I for one have nothing against my opposite number in Moscow, Ivan. Whoever-he-may-be … This protest march is the only logical way I can show him my dislike of organized propaganda.'

'But Ivan Orfalitch ain't here to watch you march; nor the Russian telly ain't going to show him no picture of it. If Ivan thinks you're a bleeding Capitalist, then he'll go on thinking you're a bleeding Capitalist; and he won't be so far out, neither, in my opinion. No, Stan, you can't fight organized propaganda with amachoor propaganda.

'Oh, can it, Grandfather!' says Stan. 'You're a professional pessimist. And *you* didn't hate the Germans even when you were fighting them – in spite of the newspapers. What about that Christmas Truce?'

Well, I'd mentioned it to him one day, I own; but it seems he'd drawn the wrong conclusions and didn't want to be put straight. However, I'm a lucky bloke – always being saved by what other blokes call 'coincidences', but which I don't; because they always happen when I need 'em most. In the trenches we used to call that 'being in God's pocket'. So, of course, we hear a knock at the door and a shout, and in steps my old mucking-in chum Dodger Green, formerly 301691, Pte Edward Green of the 1st Batt., North Wessex Regiment – come to town by bus for a Saturday-night booze with me, every bit of twenty miles.

'You're here in the exact nick, Dodger,' says I, 'as once before.' He'd nappooed a Fritz officer one day when I was lying with one foot missing outside Delville Wood, and the Fritz was kindly putting us wounded out of our misery with an automatic pistol.

'What's new, Fiddler?' he asks.

'Tell this lad about the *two* Christmas truces,' I said. 'He's trying to enlist us for a march to Moscow, or somewhere.'

'Well,' says Dodger, 'I don't see no connexion, not yet. And marching to Moscow ain't no worse nor marching to Berlin, same as you and me did – and never got more nor a few hundred yards forward in the three years we were at it. But, all right, I'll give him the facts, since you particularly ask me.'

Stan listened quietly while Dodger told his tale. I'd heard it often enough before, but Dodger's yarns improve with the telling. You see, I missed most of that first Christmas Truce, as I'll explain later. But I came in for the second; and saw a part of it what Dodger didn't. And the moral I wanted to impress on young Stan depended on there being *two* truces, not one: them two were a lot different from one another.

I brings a quart bottle of wallop from the kitchen, along with a couple of glasses – not three, because young Stan don't drink anything so 'common' as beer – and Dodger held forth. Got a golden tongue, has Dodger – I've seen him hold an audience spellbound at The Three Feathers from opening-time to stoptap, and his glass filled every ten minutes, free.

'Well,' he says, 'the first truce was in 1914, about four months after the Kayser's war began. They say that the old Pope suggested it, and that the Kayser agreed, but that Joffre, the French C-in-C wouldn't allow it. However, the Bavarians were sweating on a short spell of peace and goodwill, being Catholics, and sent word around that the Pope was going to get his way. Consequently, though we didn't have the Bavarians in front of us, there at Boy Greneer, not a shot was fired on our sector all Christmas Eve. In those days we hadn't been issued with Mills bombs, or trench-mortars, or Very pistols, or steel helmets, or sandbags, or any of them later luxuries; and only two machine-guns to a battalion. The trenches were shallow and knee-deep in water, so that most of the time we had to crouch on the fire step. God knows how we kept alive and smiling ... It wasn't no picnic, was it, Fiddler? – and the ground half-frozen, too!

'Christmas Eve, at seven thirty p.m., the enemy trenches suddenly lit up with a row of coloured Chinese lanterns and a bonfire started in the village behind. We stood to arms, prepared for whatever happened. Ten minutes later the Fritzes began singing a Christmas carol called "Stilly Nucked". Our boys answered with "Good King Wenceslas", which they'd learned the first verse of as Waits, collecting coppers from door to door. Unfortunately no one knew more than two verses, because Waits always either get a curse or a copper before they reach the third verse.

'Then a Fritz with a megaphone shouts, "Merry Christmas, Wessex!"

'Captain Pomeroy was commanding us. Colonel Baggie had gone sick, second-in-command still on leave, and most of the other officers were young second-lieutenants straight from Sandhurst – we'd taken such a knock, end of October. The Captain was a real gentleman: father, grandfather and greatgrandfather all served in the Wessex. He shouts back: "Who are you?" And they say that they're Saxons, same as us, from a town called Hully in West Saxony.

'"Will your commanding officer meet me in no man's land to arrange a Christmas truce?" the Captain shouts again. "We'll respect a white flag," he says.

'That was arranged, so Captain Pomeroy and the Fritz officer, whose name was Lieutenant Coburg, climbed out from their trenches and met half-way. They didn't shake hands, but they saluted, and each gave the other word of honour that his troops wouldn't fire a shot for another twenty-four hours. Lieutenant Coburg explained that his Colonel and all the senior officers were back taking it easy at Regimental HQ. It seems they liked to keep their boots clean, and their hands warm: not like our officers.

'Captain Pomeroy came back pleased as Punch, and said: "The truce starts at dawn, Wessex; but meanwhile we stay in trenches. And if any man of you dares break the truce tomorrow," he says, "I'll shoot him myself, because I've given that German officer my word. All the same, watch out, and don't let go of your bundooks."

'That suited us; we'd be glad to get up from them damned fire steps and stretch our legs. So that night we serenaded the Fritzes with all manner of songs, such as "I want to go Home!" and "The Top of the Dixie Lid", and the one about "Old Von Kluck, He Had a Lot of Men"; and they serenaded us with "*Deutschland Über Alles*", and songs to the concertina.

'We scraped the mud off our puttees and shined our brasses, to look a bit more regimental next morning. Captain Pomeroy, meanwhile, goes out again with a flashlight and arranges a Christmas football match – kick-off at ten thirty – to be followed at two o'clock by a burial service for all the corpses what hadn't been taken in because of lying too close to the other side's trenches.

'"Over the top with the best of luck!" shouts the Captain at eight a.m., the same as if he was leading an attack. And over we went, a bit shy of course, and stood there waiting for the Fritzes. They advanced to meet us, shouting, and five minutes later, there we were …

'Christmas was a peculiar sort of day, if ever I spent one. Hobnobbing with the Hun, so to speak: swapping fags and rum and buttons and badges for brandy, cigars and souvenirs. Lieutenant Coburg and several of the Fritzes talked English, but none of our blokes could sling a word of their bat.

'No man's land had seemed ten miles across when we were crawling out on a night patrol; but now we found it no wider than the width of two football pitches. We provided the football, and set up stretchers as goalposts; and the Reverend Jolly, our Padre, acted as ref. They beat us three–two, but the Padre had showed a bit too much Christian charity – their outside-left shot the deciding goal, but he was miles offside and admitted it soon as the whistle went. And we spectators were spread nearly two deep along the touch-lines with loaded rifles slung on our shoulders.

'We had Christmas dinner in our own trenches, and a German bugler obliged with the mess call – same tune as ours. Captain Pomeroy was invited across, but didn't think it proper to accept. Then one of our sentries, a farmer's son, sees a hare loping down the line between us. He gives a view halloo, and everyone rushes to the parapet and clambers out and runs forward to cut it off. So do the Fritzes. There ain't no such thing as harriers in Germany; they always use shot-guns on hares. But they weren't allowed to shoot this one, not with the truce; so they turned harriers same as us.

'Young Totty Fahy and a Saxon corporal both made a grab for the hare as it doubled back in their direction. Totty catches it by the forelegs and the Corporal catches it by the hindlegs, and they fall on top of it simultaneous.

'Captain Pomeroy looked a bit worried for fear of a shindy about who caught that hare; but you'd have laughed your head off to see young Totty and the Fritz both politely trying to force the carcase on each other! So the Lieutenant and the Captain gets together, and the Captain says: "Let them toss a coin for it." But the Lieutenant says: "I regret that our men will not perhaps understand. With us, we draw straws." So they picked some withered stems of grass, and Totty drew the long one. He was in our section, and we cooked the hare with spuds that night in a big iron pot borrowed from Duck Farm; but Totty gave the Fritz a couple of bully-beef tins, and the skin. Best stoo I ever ate!

'We called 'em "Fritzes" at that time. Afterwards they were "Jerries", on account of their tin hats. Them helmets with spikes called *Pickelhaubes* was still the issue in 1914, but only for parade use. In the trenches caps were worn; like ours, but grey, and no stiffening in the top. Our blokes wanted *pickelhaubes* badly to take their fiancées when they went home on leave; but Lieutenant Coburg says, sorry, all *pickelhaubes* was in store behind the lines. They had to be content with belt-buckles.

'General French commanded the BEF at the time – decent old stick. Said afterwards that if he'd been consulted about the truce, he'd have agreed for chivalrous reasons. He must have reckoned that whichever side beat, us or the Germans, a Christmas truce would help considerably in signing a decent peace at the finish. But the Kayser's High Command were mostly Prussians, and Lieutenant Coburg told us that the Prussians were against the truce, which didn't agree with their "frightfulness" notions; and though other battalions were fraternizing with the Fritzes up and down the line that day – but we didn't know it – the Prussians weren't having any. Nor were some English regiments: such as the East Lanes on our right flank and the Sherwood Foresters on the left – when the Fritzes came out with white flags, they fired over their heads and waved 'em back. But they didn't interfere with our party. It was worse in the French line: them Frogs machine-gunned all the "Merry Christmas" parties … Of course, the French go in for New Year celebrations more than Christmas.

'One surprise was the two barrels of beer that the Fritzes rolled over to us from the brewery just behind their lines. I don't fancy French beer; but at least this wasn't watered like what they sold us English troops in the *estaminets*. We broached them out in the open, and the Fritzes broached another two of their own.

'When it came to the toasts, the Captain said he wanted to keep politics out of it. So he offered them "Wives and Sweethearts!" which the Lieutenant accepted. Then the Lieutenant proposed "The King!" which the Captain accepted. There was a King of Saxony too, you see, in them days, besides a King of England; and no names were mentioned. The third toast was "A Speedy Peace!" and each side could take it to mean victory for themselves.

'After dinner came the burial service – the Fritzes buried their corpses on their side of the line; we buried ours on ours. But we dug the pits so close together that one service did for both. The Saxons had no Padre with them; but they were Protestants, so the Reverend Jolly read the service, and a German divinity student translated for them. Captain Pomeroy sent for the drummers and put us through that parade in proper regimental fashion: slow march, arms reversed, muffled drums, a Union Jack and all.

'An hour before dark, a funny-faced Fritz called Putzi came up with a trestle table. He talked English like a Yank. Said he'd been in Ringling's Circus over in the United States. Called us "youse guys", and put on a hell of a good gaff with conjuring tricks and juggling

– had his face made up like a proper clown. Never heard such applause as we gave Herr Putzi!

'Then, of course, our bastard of a Brigadier, full of turkey and plum pudding and mince pies, decides to come and visit the trenches to wish us Merry Christmas! Captain Pomeroy got the warning from Fiddler here, who was away down on light duty at Battalion HQ. Fiddler arrived in the nick, running split-arse across the open, and gasping out: "Captain, sir, the Brigadier's here; but none of us hasn't let on about the truce."

'Captain Pomeroy recalled us at once. "*Imshi*, Wessex!" he shouted. Five minutes later the Brigadier came sloshing up the communication trench, keeping his head well down. The Captain tried to let Lieutenant Coburg know what was happening; but the Lieutenant had gone back to fetch him some warm gloves as a souvenir. The Captain couldn't speak German; what's more, the Fritzes were so busy watching Putzi that they wouldn't listen. So Captain Pomeroy shouts to me: "Private Green, run along the line and order the platoon commanders from me to fire three rounds rapid over the enemies' heads." Which I did; and by the time the Brigadier turns up, there wasn't a Fritz in sight.

'The Brigadier, whom we called "Old Horseflesh", shows a lot of Christmas jollity. "I was very glad," he says, "to hear that Wessex fusillade, Pomeroy. Rumours have come in of fraternization elsewhere along the line. Bad show! Disgraceful! Can't interrupt a war for freedom just because of Christmas! Have you anything to report?"

'Captain Pomeroy kept a straight face. He says: "Our sentries report that the enemy have put up a trestle table in no man's land, sir. A bit of a puzzle, sir. Seems to have a bowl of goldfish on it." He kicked the Padre, and the Padre kept his mouth shut.

'Old Horseflesh removes his brass hat, takes his binoculars, and cautiously peeps over the parapet. "They *are* goldfish, by Gad!" he shouts. "I wonder what new devilish trick the Hun will invent next. Send out a patrol tonight to investigate." "Very good, sir," says the Captain.

'Then Old Horseflesh spots something else: it's Lieutenant Coburg strolling across the open between his reserve and front lines; and he's carrying the warm gloves. "What impudence! Look at that swaggering German officer! Quick, here's your rifle, my lad! Shoot him down point-blank!" It seems Lieutenant Coburg must have thought that the fusillade came from the Foresters on our flank; but now he suddenly stopped short and looked at no man's land, and wondered where everyone was gone.

'Old Horseflesh shoves the rifle into my hand.

"Take a steady aim," he says. "Squeeze the trigger, don't pull!" I aimed well above the Lieutenant's head and fired three rounds rapid. He staggered and dived head-first into a handy shell-hole.

"'Congratulations," said Old Horseflesh, belching brandy in my face. "You can cut another notch in your rifle butt. But what effrontery! Thought himself safe on Christmas Day, I suppose! Ha, ha!" He hadn't brought Captain Pomeroy no gift of whisky or cigars, nor nothing else; stingy bastard, he was. At any rate, the Fritzes caught on, and their machine-guns began traversing tock-tock-tock, about three feet above our trenches. That sent the Brigadier hurrying home in such a hurry that he caught his foot in a loop of telephone wire and went face forward into the mud. It was his first and last visit to the front line.

'Half an hour later we put up an ALL CLEAR board. This time us and the Fritzes became a good deal chummier than before. But Lieutenant Coburg suggests it would be wise to keep quiet about the lark. The General Staff might get wind of it and kick up a row, he says. Captain Pomeroy agrees. Then the Lieutenant warns us that the Prussian Guards are due to relieve his Saxons the day after Boxing Day. "I suggest that we continue the truce until then, but with no more fraternization," he says. Captain Pomeroy agrees again. He accepts the warm gloves and in return gives the Lieutenant a

Shetland wool scarf. Then he asks whether, as a great favour, the Wessex might be permitted to capture the bowl of goldfish, for the Brigadier's sake. Herr Putzi wasn't too pleased, but Captain Pomeroy paid him for it with a gold sovereign and Putzi says: "Please, for Chrissake, don't forget to change their water!"

'God knows what the Intelligence made of them goldfish when they were sent back to Corps HQ, which was a French luxury *shadow* ... I expect someone decided the goldfish have some sort of use in trenches, like the canaries we take down the coal pits.

'Then Captain Pomeroy says to the Lieutenant: "From what I can see, Coburg, there'll be a stalemate on this front for a year or more. You can't crack our line, even with massed machine-guns; and we can't crack yours. Mark my words: our Wessex and your West Saxons will still be rotting here next Christmas – what's left of them."

'The Lieutenant didn't agree, but he didn't argue. He answered: "In that case, Pomeroy, I hope we both survive to meet again on that festive occasion; and that our troops show the same gentlemanly spirit as today."

'"I'll be very glad to do so," says the Captain, "if I'm not scuppered meanwhile." They shook hands on that, and the truce continued all Boxing Day. But nobody went out into no man's land, except at night to strengthen the wire where it had got trampled by the festivities. And of course we couldn't prevent our gunners from shooting; and neither could the Saxons prevent theirs. When the Prussian Guards moved in, the war started again; fifty casualties we had in three days, including young Totty who lost an arm.

'In the meantime a funny thing had happened: the sparrows got wind of the truce and came flying into our trenches for biscuit crumbs. I counted more than fifty in a flock on Boxing Day.

'The only people who objected strongly to the truce, apart from the Brigadier and a few more like him, was the French girls. Wouldn't have nothing more to do with us for a time when we got back to billets. Said we were *no bon* and *boko camarade* with the *Allemans*.'

Stan had been listening to this tale with eyes like stars. 'Exactly,' he said. 'There wasn't any feeling of hate between the individuals composing the opposite armies. The hate was all whipped up by the newspapers. Last year, you remember, I attended the Nürnberg Youth Rally. Two other fellows whose fathers had been killed in the last war, like mine, shared the same tent with four German war-orphans. They weren't at all bad fellows.'

'Well, lad,' I said, taking up the yarn where Dodger

left off, 'I didn't see much of that first Christmas Truce owing to a spent bullet what went into my shoulder and lodged under the skin: the Medico cut it out and kept me off duty until the wound healed. I couldn't wear a pack for a month, so, as Dodger told you, I got Light Duty down at Battalion HQ, and missed the fun. But the second Christmas Truce, now that was another matter. By then I was Platoon Sergeant to about twenty men signed on for the Duration of the War – some of them good, some of 'em His Majesty's bad bargains.

'We'd learned a lot about trench life that year; such as how to drain trenches and build dugouts. We had barbed wire entanglements in front of us, five yards thick, and periscopes, and listening-posts out at sap-heads; also trench-mortars and rifle-grenades, and bombs, and steel-plates with loop-holes for sniping through.

'Now I'll tell you what happened, and Dodger here will tell you the same. Battalion orders went round to Company HQ every night in trenches, and the CO was now Lieutenant-Colonel Pomeroy – DSO with bar. He'd won brevet rank for the job he did rallying the battalion when the big German mine blew C Company to bits and the Fritzes followed up with bombs and bayonets. However, when he sent round Orders two days before Christmas 1915, Colonel Pomeroy (accidentally on purpose) didn't tell the Adjutant to include the "Official Warning to All Troops" from General Sir Douglas Haig. Haig was our new Commander-in-Chief. You hear about him on Poppy Day – the poppies he sowed himself, most of 'em! He'd used his influence with King George, to get General French booted out and himself shoved into the job. His "Warning" was to the effect that any man attempting to fraternize with His Majesty's enemies on the poor excuse of Christmas would be court-martialled and shot. But Colonel Pomeroy never broke his word not even if he swung for it; and here he was alongside the La Bassée Canal, and opposite us were none other than the same West Saxons from Hully!

'The Colonel knew who they were because we'd coshed and caught a prisoner in a patrol scrap two nights before, and after the Medico plastered his head, the bloke was brought to Battalion HQ under escort (which was me and another man). The Colonel questioned him through an interpreter about the geography of the German trenches: where they kept that damned minny-werfer, how and when the ration parties came up, and so on. But this Fritz wouldn't give away a thing; said he'd lost his memory when he'd got coshed. So at last the Colonel remarked in English: "Very well that's all. By the way, is Lieutenant Coburg still alive?"

'"Oh, yeah," says the Fritz, surprised into talking English. "He's back again after a coupla wounds. He's a Major now, commanding our outfit."

'Then a sudden thought struck him. "For Chrissake," he says, "ain't you the Wessex officer who played Santa Claus last year and fixed that truce?"

'"I am," says the Colonel, "and you're Putzi Cohen the Conjurer, from whom I once bought a bowl of goldfish! It's a small war!"

'That's why, you see, the Colonel hadn't issued Haig's warning. About eighty or so of us old hands were still left, mostly snobs, bobbajers, drummers, transport men or wounded blokes rejoined. The news went the rounds, and they all rushed Putzi and shook his hand and asked couldn't he put on another conjuring gaff for them? He says: "Ask Colonel Santa Claus! He's still feeding my goldfish."

'I was Putzi's escort, before I happened to have coshed him and brought him in; but I never recognized him without his greasepaint – not until he started talking his funny Yank English.

'The Colonel sends for Putzi again, and says: "I don't think you're quite well enough to travel. I'm keeping you here as a hospital case until after Christmas."

'Putzi lived like a prize pig the next two days, and put on a show every evening – card tricks mostly, because he hadn't his accessories. Then came

Christmas Eve, and a sergeant of the Holy Boys who lay on our right flank again, remarked to me it was a pity that "Stern-Endeavour" Haig had washed out our Christmas fun. "First I've heard about it," says I, "and what's more, chum, I don't want to hear about it, see? Not officially, I don't."

'I'd hardly shut my mouth before them Saxons put out Chinese lanterns again and started singing "Stilly Nucked". They hadn't fired a shot, neither, all day.

'Soon word comes down the trench: "Colonel's orders: no firing as from now, without officer's permission."

'After stand-to next morning, soon as it was light, Colonel Pomeroy he climbed out of the trench with a white handkerchief in his hand, picked his way through our wire entanglements and stopped half-way across no man's land. "Merry Christmas, Saxons!" he shouted. But Major Coburg had already advanced towards him. They saluted each other and shook hands. The cheers that went up! "Keep in your trenches, Wessex!" the Colonel shouted over his shoulder. And the Major gave the same orders to his lot.

'After jabbering a bit they agreed that any bloke who'd attended the 1914 party would be allowed out of trenches, but not the rest – they could trust only us regular soldiers. Regulars, you see, know the rules of war and don't worry their heads about politics nor propaganda; them Duration blokes sickened us sometimes with their patriotism and their lofty skiting, and their hatred of "the Teuton foe" as one of 'em called the Fritzes.

'Twice more Saxons than Wessex came trooping out. We'd strict orders to discuss no military matters – not that any of our blokes had been studying German since the last party. Football was off, because of the overlapping shell holes and the barbed wire, but we got along again with signs and a bit of café French, and swapped fags and booze and buttons. But the Colonel wouldn't have us give away no badges. Can't say we were so chummy as before. Too many of ours and theirs had gone west that year and, besides, the trenches weren't flooded like the first time.

'We put on three boxing bouts: middle, welter and light; won the welter and light with KOs, lost the middle on points. Colonel Pomeroy took Putzi up on parole, and Putzi gave an even prettier show than before, because Major Coburg had sent back for his greasepaints and accessories. He used a parrakeet this time instead of goldfish.

'After dinner we found we hadn't much more to tell the Fritzes or swap with them, and the officers decided to pack up before we all got into trouble. The Holy Boys had promised not to shoot, and the left flank was screened by the Canal bank. As them two was busy discussing how long the no-shooting truce should last, all of a sudden the Christmas spirit flared up again. We and the Fritzes found ourselves grabbing hands and forming a ring around the pair of them – Wessex and West Saxons all mixed anyhow and dancing from right to left to the tune of "Here We Go Round the Mulberry Bush", in and out of shell holes. Then our RSM pointed to Major Coburg, and some of our blokes hoisted him on their shoulders and we all sang "For He's a Jolly Good Fellow". And the Fritzs hoisted our Colonel up on their shoulders too, and sang "*Hock Solla Leeben*", or something … Our Provost-sergeant took a photo of that; pity he got his before it was developed.

'Now here's something I heard from Lightning Collins, an old soldier in my platoon. He'd come close enough to overhear the Colonel and the Major's conversation during the middle-weight fight when they thought nobody was listening. The Colonel says: "I prophesied last year, Major, that we'd still be here this Christmas, what was left of us. And now I tell you again that we'll still be here *next* Christmas, *and* the Christmas after. If we're not scuppered; and that's a ten to one chance. What's more, next Christmas there won't be any more fun and games and fraternization. I'm doubtful whether I'll get away with this present act of insubordination; but I'm a man of my word, as you are, and we've both kept our engagement."

'"Oh, yes, Colonel," says the Major. "I too will be lucky if I am not court-martialled. Our orders were as severe as yours." So they laughed like crows together.

'Putzi was the most envied man in France that day: going back under safe escort to a prison camp in Blighty. And the Colonel told the Major: "I congratulate you on that soldier. He wouldn't give away a thing!"

'At four o'clock sharp we broke it off; but the two officers waited a bit longer to see that everyone got back. But no, young Stan that's not the end of the story! I had a bloke in my platoon called Gipsy Smith, a dark-faced, dirty soldier, and a killer. He'd been watching the fun from the nearest sap-head, and no sooner had the Major turned his back than Gipsy aimed at his head and tumbled him over.

'The first I knew of it was a yell of rage from everyone all round me. I see Colonel Pomeroy run up to the Major, shouting for stretcher-bearers. Them Fritzes must have thought the job was premeditated, because when our stretcher-bearers popped out of the trench, they let 'em have it and hit one bloke in the leg. His pal popped back again.

'That left the Colonel alone in no man's land. He strolled calmly towards the German trenches, his hands in his pockets – being too proud to raise them over his head. A couple of Fritzes fired at him, but both missed. He stopped at their wire and shouted: "West Saxons, my men had strict orders not to fire. Some coward has disobeyed. Please help me carry the Major's body back to your trenches! Then you can shoot me, if you like; because I pledged my word that there'd be no fighting."

'The Fritzes understood, and sent stretcher-bearers out. They took the Major's body back through a crooked lane in their wire and Colonel Pomeroy followed them. A German officer bandaged the Colonel's eyes as soon as he got into the trench, and we waited without firing a shot to see what would happen next. That was about four o'clock, and nothing did happen until second watch. Then we see a flashlight signalling, and presently the Colonel comes back, quite his usual self.

'He tells us that, much to his relief, Gipsy's shot hadn't killed the Major but only furrowed his scalp and knocked him senseless. He'd come to after six hours, and when he saw the Colonel waiting there, he'd ordered his immediate release. They'd shaken hands again, and said: "Until after the war!", and the Major gives the Colonel his flashlight.

'Now the yarn's nearly over, Stan, but not quite. News of the truce got round, and General Haig ordered first an Inquiry and then a Court Martial on

Colonel Pomeroy. He wasn't shot, of course; but he got a severe reprimand and lost five years' seniority. Not that it mattered, because he got shot between the eyes in the 1916 Delville Wood show where I lost my foot.

'As for Gipsy Smith, he said he'd been obeying Haig's strict orders not to fraternize, and also he'd felt bound to avenge a brother killed at Loos. "Blood for blood," he said "is our gipsy motto." So we couldn't do nothing but show what we thought by treating him like the dirt he was. And he didn't last long. I sent Gipsy back with the ration party on Boxing Night. We were still keeping up our armed truce with the Saxons, but again their gunners weren't a party to it, and outside the Quartermaster's hut Gipsy got his backside removed by a piece of howitzer shell. Died on the hospital train, he did.

'Oh, I was forgetting to tell you that no sparrows came for biscuit crumbs that Christmas. The birds had all cleared off months before.

'Every year that war got worse and worse. Before it ended, nearly three years later, we'd have ten thousand officers and men pass through that one battalion, which was never at more than the strength of five hundred rifles. I'd had three wounds by 1916; some fellows got up to six before it finished. Only Dodger here came through without a scratch. That's how he got his name, dodging the bullet that had his name and number on it. The Armistice found us at Mons, where we started. There was talk of "Hanging the Kayser"; but they left him to chop wood in Holland instead. The rest of the Fritzes had their noses properly rubbed in the dirt by the Peace Treaty. But we let them rearm in time for a second war, Hitler's war, which is how your dad got killed. And after Hitler's war there'd have been a third war, just about now, which would have caught you, Stanley my lad, if it weren't for that blessed bomb you're asking me to march against.

'Now, listen, lad: if two real old-fashioned gentlemen like Colonel Pomeroy and Major Coburg – never heard of him again, but I doubt if he survived, having the guts he had – if two real men like them two couldn't hope for a third Christmas Truce in the days when "mankind", as you call 'em, was still a little bit civilized, tell me, what can you hope for now?

'Only fear can keep the peace,' I said. 'The United Nations are a laugh, and you know it. So thank your lucky stars that the Russians have H-bombs and that the Yanks have H-bombs, stacks of 'em, enough to blow your "mankind" up a thousand times over; and that everyone's equally respectful of everyone else, though not on regular visiting terms.'

I stopped, out of breath, and Dodger takes Stan by

the hand. 'You know what's right for *you*, lad?' he says, 'So don't listen to your granddad. Don't be talked out of your beliefs! He's one of the Old and Bold, but maybe he's no wiser nor you and I.'

INTRODUCTION

'Zakky', Robert Westall
'The Destructors', Graham Greene

Not all war stories show us the whites of enemy soldiers' eyes. War can affect people who are never on the front line. In Robert Westall's story, the narrator observes with growing concern the damage that war has wreaked on his Polish friend, Zakky. Although it is a bleak portrayal, the actions of the wider community provide some notes of hope.

'The Destructors' by Graham Greene has no explicit links to war. A group of teenagers execute a plan to destroy an old man's house – a house that survived the Blitz during the Second World War. The story was written less than 10 years after the end of the war and it is implicit that the teenagers and their behaviour are products of war. Looking to these boys' futures you could also read the story as a prediction of future war.

What do the violent acts in these two stories tell us about the impact of war, and what different predictions do they hold for the future?

ZAKKY

Robert Westall

Dad's Army?

I'll bet it made you laugh. But none of it was true, not round where I lived.

That rubbish about drilling with pitchforks and broom handles. Every lad in our village had his own shotgun by sixteen; been using one since he was ten. They could drop a half-grown rabbit at a hundred yards. What else d'you think they lived on? Farm-labourers' wages? All the government had to do was issue shot-gun cartridges containing one big solid shot, which would have blown a hole in Jerry big enough to put your hand through.

We had five gamekeepers in our lot; knew every spinney and gap in the hedge for miles. And twice as many poachers, fly enough to swipe the Lady Amherst pheasants off the terrace of Birleigh Manor, while his lordship sat there drinking afternoon tea. Brutal men, all of them. I've known some stagger home needing sixteen stitches in their head after some little encounter in the dark. They made peace while they were on Home Guard duty, and went back to their private war afterwards.

Yes, we did have a poet. Laurie Tomlinson. Professor somewhere now. But then he'd just got back from the Spanish Civil War. Showed us how to garrotte a man with a piece of piano wire so he died without a sigh. Showed the village blacksmith how to make a two-inch mortar from a yard of steel gas-piping. The army took those off us later, saying they were too dangerous to use. But they fired mortar-bombs all right; the ones Pincher Morton pinched from the Polish camp down the road.

And we never drilled in pinstripe suits or cricket shirts. We never wasted time drilling at all. We went on patrol in the washed-out browns and greys that poachers wore, which blend with the woodland at five paces. Laurie taught us how to put boot-polish on our faces so that it didn't crack and drop off like mud. Our village poachers still use boot-polish ...

And, poachers or not, they were all old *soldiers*. From the Last Lot. Hard-bodied farmhands of forty, who'd been snipers in the mud of the Somme, or bomb-throwers in the Ypres Salient. When we finally got our old Canadian rifles, dating from 1912, they nursed them like grim mothers. Very anxious to get their hands on the bayonets. First they sharpened them on their own whetstones, then they blackened them so no glint would give away their position.

All the young lads were mad to join. The veterans wouldn't have 'em. War wasn't for kids, they said. Forgetting they'd been little more than kids themselves in the Last Lot. We only ever had two young 'uns in our platoon. I was one.

I'd tried for a commission in our county regiment. Then for the RAF as anything. Even the navy, though I was seasick crossing to the Isle of Wight. But I had flat feet. When I put any weight on my feet, my toes pointed up in the air like ac-ac guns. Didn't count that I played rugger, and ran cross-country. I was *out.*

Went to see Major Newsam; asked if he'd pull a few strings for me with his old mates. He shook his head and told me the best thing I could do was to farm the land my father had left me as well as I damned well could. Damned U-boats would try to starve the country out, just like the Last Lot.

As a sop, he let me join his Home Guard. As second-in-command, with a pip on my shoulder.

'Old soldiers need someone to look up to,' he said. 'Someone to look after. Leave all the organizing to your platoon-sergeant. Never ask a man to do what you can't do yourself.'

It was a rule he kept himself, even though he'd lost half an arm in Iraq in 1924.

When they asked for Draggett's Mill as their HQ, I couldn't refuse. Right in the middle of my land; on the highest hill for miles, to make the best of the wind. But Draggett had been gone a long time, and the mill was just an empty stone shell, like a squat, blackened milk-bottle. They fitted it out with new floors and ladders, and with a parapet of sandbags and a corrugated iron roof, it made an ideal look-out for German paratroopers dropping in.

It was there, as we stood-to one lovely soft summer evening in 1940, that they dragged Zakky in. They'd caught him following them, and they thought he was a German spy. He'd put up a hell of a fight; three of them were bleeding. They'd had to knock him senseless with a rifle-butt. They poured water over him from our brew-up milk-churn, and he opened one swollen eye a green slit and said,

'*English!* If you had been Germans, I would have killed you all.'

'Nasty little sod, sir,' said Curly Millbank. 'He had this hidden under his shirt, at the back of his neck.' He passed me a simple flat knife, honed to a needle point.

'Give me my knife!' The thin wet figure on the floor

came at me so fast he knocked me clean across the trestle table that served as our office. All knees and elbows he was, and they felt as sharp as needles too. It took four of them to drag him off me, and somebody else got bitten.

'Who are you?' I asked, when I'd got my breath back.

'I am *soldier.*' He drew himself up to his full five foot three. 'Zbigniew Zakrewski, Polish Army.' He gabbled some long number. 'They give me a number. They had no rifles.'

'I think I've seen him hanging round the Polish camp, sir,' said Pincher Morton. 'The soldiers feed him. But he's not one of them.'

Zakky pulled a horrible face. 'I go to them. Tell them how to kill Nazis. They make me peel spuds.' He spat on our highly polished floor. 'That is why I follow your men. I will show *you* how to kill Nazis.'

He drew his hand across his throat.

Major Newsam came in then, and took over. I was still feeling a bit shaken.

'Checked up on him with the Poles,' Newsam told me at stand-to next evening. 'He's Polish all right. Thirteen years old. Joined the Polish Army in their retreat last September. Never had a rifle, never had a uniform. Marched five days, then met the Russkis coming the other way. Got away when the rest surrendered. Seems to have sneaked out through the Balkans and stowed away on a ship from Piraeus. Lot of Poles came that way. The Polish Government in exile tried putting him in a children's home, but he just kept running away. Apparently he eats at the Polish camp and sleeps in the woods. Keeps trying to nick weapons from their armoury. They're terrified he'll end up doing somebody an injury. I mean, all the Poles are fighting-mad, but he's got even them scared *silly*. They asked if I could get somebody to adopt him ...' He looked at me queryingly. 'Think your mother could take him on?'

Old Newsam was a bit sweet on my mother; thought she was wonder-woman.

I looked him straight in the eye. 'You'll have to bribe him. Let him join the Home Guard ...'

He grinned and said, 'Pity about your flat feet, Keith. You wouldn't have made a bad officer, given time.'

So I drove him home in my old farm van, the scruffy little tick. He ponged out the van to high heaven. When we got home, I heard my mother playing the piano. Chopin. She used to work like hell all day: the farm, evacuees, WVS, the lot. But when she was finally done for the day, she still liked to get dressed up a bit, and have a drink, and light the tall thin brass candles that stood on the piano, and play Chopin. Said it convinced her there'd be a better world again, some day.

I was going to march straight in and interrupt her, because I wanted to get back to the mill in case anything had happened while I'd been gone. But, in the half-open doorway, a small, steely hand caught my wrist. And Zakky just stood there till she had finished, the tears running down his cheek in the candle-light. It was the Chopin, I suppose.

When she had finished, and turned and smiled at us, he went straight up to her, clicked his heels together, and gave a funny little bow of his head. He was such an odd little scruff, I wondered how even a woman as wise as my mother would take it. But she took it all in her stride, shook him by the hand, and asked him if he'd care for a bath?

So I left her to get on with it. The next morning he came down to breakfast in one of my old grey school suits, white shirt and tie, long dark hair slicked down with tap water. Apparently she'd laid out the suit and shirt next to his pathetic rags on his bed, while he had a bath, and he'd chosen freely to wear them. Only he'd asked her to wash the rags for him, because they were Polish and precious. (And she spent hours mending them, as well.) And he'd showed her a solid gold locket, with a photo of a fierce, moustached military man on one side, and a rather lovely dark-haired woman on the other.

'My father. My mother.' He had clicked his heels again.

'Where are they now, Zakky?'

'Dead,' he said and took the locket back, and he never showed it to anybody else, ever. She said it was the only thing he had, except for the throwing knife that he still wore at the back of his neck, under the grey English suit.

I studied him over the bacon and eggs. I think his family must have been pretty well off, back in Poland, because he had exquisite table manners, only a little strange and foreign. And though he had the body of a half-starved kid, his face was ... ageless. Beaky nose, strong Polish cheekbones and a strong Polish jawbone, the sort you never see in an Englishman. His eyes were deep-sunken. They were either blazing with excitement, or too sad to look at direct.

They only blazed when he talked about Poland; or killing Nazis. Or when he was talking direct to my mother. In his eyes, my mother could do no wrong. He always called her Madam Bosworth, whether she was there or not. I think he would have done anything for her, even died.

I think she could even have got him to go to our village school, when it reopened in September.

But she hadn't the heart. She soon found he spoke excellent French, and they would prattle away for hours, faster than I could follow. She found he knew quite a lot of German too, but he would never speak it, even for her.

'German is language for pigs.' He also said 'Russian is language for pigs', so I suppose he had Russian as well. Neither of us could imagine him sitting at a desk among the village children.

Anyway, all his heart was set on killing Nazis. He was at the mill every spare hour. When he wasn't cleaning rifles (which he learnt quickly and did with incredible thoroughness), he was our look-out, following every vapour-trail in the sky, like a cat following the flight of birds. We found him some Home Guard overalls, nearly small enough. My mother took three inches off the leg. And we ordered him to stay at his post of duty on top of the mill, whatever happened. I think old Newsam was afraid of something nasty happening. It was the height of the Battle of Britain, and there were a lot of parachutes coming down during the daytime air-battles, and, thank God, the majority were Jerries. The farmhands of our platoon worked in the fields with their rifles at the ready. But any Jerries they rounded up, they always took straight down to the police-station in the next village. By tacit agreement, nobody ever brought a Jerry to the mill.

But Zakky certainly earned his keep. As he learnt to trust us, he would bring in the weapons from his hidden caches in the woods. Two Bren guns we returned to the Poles; Newsam gave their CO a right rocket about the security of their armoury. But the rifles we kept, and the Mills bombs and mortar-bombs. With Jerry waiting just across the Channel, we weren't inclined to be over-generous.

And at stand-to and stand-down, we would gather in amazement to hear his impromptu lectures on how to kill Nazis. He had some incredible idea about electrocuting tank-crews with the fallen electric cables from tram-cars, but as the nearest trams were fifty miles away, in Piccadilly Circus, that wasn't much good. But we liked his idea about stretching a steel cable between two tree-trunks, to decapitate Nazi despatch riders. And he showed us how to make a Molotov cocktail that really worked. And explained how to feed petrol-soaked blankets into the tracks of tanks, and how to leap on tanks from behind and block up their periscopes with a handful of mud. From the way he explained it, I thought he'd really done that. So did old Newsam.

Zakky was good for us. Half our men saw war as charging with fixed bayonets across the sea of mud and shell-holes that was no man's land. The other

107

half saw it as slinking through the bushes, taking pot-shots at Jerries as if they were pheasants.

Zakky had seen tanks. In action.

But the men never loved him; he never belonged. He accepted being called 'Old Zakky' with good grace. But he would never laugh, never take part in their jokes and horseplay. Jokes were a serious waste of time. And he could never bear to be touched. Once Curly Millbank grabbed him from behind in fun and ended up on his back with a sprained wrist, which put him off work for a week.

Then came 'Cromwell'. The codeword for 'Invasion Imminent'. We shouldn't have been told, but Newsam had mates at Southern Command.

At stand-to, the men took it silently, very silently. Only Pincher Morton said, 'So it's come, then.' Some asked permission to go and say goodbye to their wives, but Newsam said no. He didn't want a panic like in France, with refugees blocking the roads. There was no argument; they were old soldiers. They got on with it.

We half blocked the London road, rolling out the great cylinders of concrete. Then all we had to do was wait, and inspect the passes of any car or lorry that passed. And watch from the top of the mill, for Jerry paratroopers landing.

I was up there with Newsam and Zakky. Below, the men who weren't manning the road-block were huddled round our transport: two private cars and a farmer's motorized haycart. The men were smoking, but cupping their hands round the glowing ends. The night was moonlit through wispy cloud. A good night for spotting parachutes. Behind our backs, London was burning again, a pulsating pink glow in the sky.

'Think we can hold them, sir?' I only said it for something to say. It felt like the start of a rugger-match against a big rugger school: not much hope of winning, but wanting to put up a good show.

'If the army can hold them on the beaches, I think we can mop up any paratroops.'

'If?' I squeaked. 'Montgomery's Third Division's down there.'

'They've got no heavy stuff; they had to leave all their heavy stuff behind at Dunkirk. Hardly an anti-tank gun to bless themselves with, poor bastards. Hardly a heavy machine-gun ...'

'So what are *we* supposed to do?'

'I expect we'd last about five minutes against tanks. But some of the men should get away into the woods. After that, it's up to them. Might as well go back to their wives; sniping won't stop an armoured column ...'

'Oh,' I said again. Was 'oh' all I could find to say?

I nodded down towards the hands cupped round cigarettes. 'Do *they* know that?'

'They know. Sorry to be a pessimist, Keith, on your first show. But I don't want you having any illusions.'

'We will kill Nazis!' said Zakky harshly, from across the observation platform. 'We will kill *many* Nazis!'

We both jumped; I think we had forgotten he was there. He came across and glared at us. I could see, in the moonlight, that he was trembling. Not with fear, I think. More like a whippet just before you unleash it against a rabbit.

'Many, many Nazis,' he said again, then went back on watch, turning his back on us. As if in disgust.

'That boy worries me,' muttered Newsam. 'Keep a tight rein on him. He's going to kill somebody before the night's out, if we're not careful. I wish we could send him home. But he'll just bugger off into the woods. Best here, where we can keep an eye on him.'

The waiting was appalling. The night was so still, except for the odd rumble or series of sharp cracks, ghosting down the warm night wind from London. The countryside I loved lay on peacefully, under the dim moon. The black bulk of the church tower. Silver light gleaming on the huddled thatch of the village. The stooks of corn in my own top field, standing neat as guards on parade. We were too far west to be in the direct path of the Jerry bombers heading for London.

Then the phone rang. A man seen climbing through the window of Elm Cottage ... Newsam shot off in his old Morris, four riflemen jammed in with him.

They were back in ten minutes. Newsam settled again, elbows on the sandbags of the parapet.

'Well?' I asked, after a long silence. I saw his shoulders heave, and thought for a wild second that he was crying. Then he said with a snort,

'Bobby Finlayson in bed with Len Taylor's missis. We dragged them both out mother-naked. There'll be hell to pay in the morning.' He couldn't stop laughing.

We were busy after that. Impounded a lorry of black market meat on its way up to London. Caught a vicar with six rover-scouts, all looking for a place to die for their country. Two courting couples in lay-bys, tanks full of black-market petrol. One enterprising burglar, with a mixed bag of silver from Mottersdon Court.

'Had no idea there was so much night-life in the country!' snorted Newsam.

'*English!*' muttered Zakky darkly to himself. But all this dashing about did everyone a bit of good. It was better than hanging around. Every time they came back they were laughing over something.

And then, just before dawn, we had three phone-calls in rapid succession, and I was left alone on top of the mill with Zakky.

Why was it then that we heard the sound of planes above the hazy moonlit clouds? And saw two parachutes sloping gently down, towards the wooded crest of Burrow's Hill, across our little valley.

While I was still dithering with shock, Zakky said 'Nazis' and was gone down the top ladder.

I suppose I should've done something intelligent, like phone for help. But I couldn't think of who to phone. Perhaps I should have run to the men manning the road-block, but they were a hundred yards away. So I stupidly left my post of duty and ran after him.

As I said before, I'd been a cross-country runner. But pound along in my hobnailed boots as I might, I couldn't catch up with Zakky. I had him in sight as far as the village, but in the cornfields beyond I lost him. I knew where the parachutes had fallen, roughly. I knew the short-cuts through the wood. But Zakky knew them even better than me ...

Yet it seemed as though I had got to a parachute first. No sign of Zakky. The chute was caught up in a tree, like a great white rustling ghost. A dark figure dangled below, about four feet off the ground, helpless, silent. I ran up to it, pulling out my dad's old Webley revolver from its First World War leather holster. I didn't know what to expect. They told us that in Holland and Belgium the German paratroops came down disguised as policemen, vicars and nuns.

But this one ... as the body swung and turned in the breeze, I saw the round top of a flying helmet and the glint on goggles. The bulk of a sheepskin flying-jacket.

'Christ,' said the body suddenly, 'cut me down, for God's sake. This crotch-strap's nearly got me cut in half.' He did sound like he was in agony. And he had a very Welsh accent.

I got out my clasp-knife and climbed the tree and cut him down somehow. I suppose it never occurred to me that a Nazi might have a Welsh accent. Anyway, once he was free, he just fell in a heap on the ground.

The next thing he said was, 'You'd better go and find Stan – Stanislav – my gunner. His English isn't much cop – he's a Pole. I don't want some yokel lynching him for a Nazi.'

'Where'd he come down?'

'Over there, somewhere.' He pointed vaguely towards the edge of the wood.

I've never run so fast in all my life. But I was too late: I found Zakky crouching over a body.

'Is dead,' said Zakky, with a lot of satisfaction.

'He's one of ours,' I said numbly, staring down at the dim white face beneath the flying-helmet. 'He was called Stanislav. He was a Pole.'

There was a long and terrifying silence. It just went on and on and on. When I couldn't stand it any longer I said,

'There's another one down the hill. He's Welsh. I think they bailed out of their night-fighter. You'd better give me a hand getting him back to the mill.'

It helped, getting the pilot down off the hill. He was quite badly hurt, and we had to carry him between us, making a chair of our hands. It gave me something to do, instead of thinking about Zakky and the dead gunner. Then I had to get the ambulance out to us.

The Welshman asked about his gunner, and I told him the gunner was dead. He just closed his eyes and nodded; I suppose they were used to losing their mates. He was a Defiant pilot, and Defiants didn't have much luck in the Battle of Britain.

Then some daft bugger over Malbury way rang the church bells, meaning the Invasion had really started, and all hell broke loose, with civilians taking to the roads, trying to get away from the coast. And then suddenly it was dawn, and word slowly trickled through that bugger-all had happened anywhere, except an extra-big raid on London.

'Ah, well,' said Newsam, 'we live to fight again.'

'Nearly time to get the cows milked,' said Pincher Morton. 'No point goin' to bed now. Just makes you feel dopey.'

I drove Zakky home. Neither of us said a word. I didn't ask him how the gunner died; I couldn't bear to know. Maybe he just found him dead. I preferred to think that. Nothing I could do would bring the gunner back to life.

They came with a hearse and took the gunner's body away, later that morning. We never heard any more about it.

Then came October, with the equinoctial gales lashing up the Channel, and news that Hitler was dispersing his flat-bottomed barges at Boulogne. We were safe for the winter.

Newsam still drove us hard. He talked endlessly about *when* Hitler came in the spring. We trained more men; we were a full company now, four platoons, and I was a platoon-commander. They built us pill-boxes of foot-thick concrete, and we trained with something called a Blacker Bombard that threw thermite-bombs at fake tanks made of corrugated iron which ran down a little railway outside Eastbourne. But somehow we couldn't *quite* believe in it; there was a feeling that Hitler had missed the boat.

All except Zakky, who grew grimmer than ever. He made this huge plywood cut-out of a Nazi storm-trooper, advancing with a hideous grimace and a sub-machine-gun. Spent hours throwing his knife at it. I'd never believed in throwing-knives, couldn't see how they could even go through the cloth of a uniform. They were something you saw in the movies. But

Zakky could throw from all angles and never missed, and I once tried levering his knife out of the thick plywood. It was embedded two inches, and I had a hell of a time getting it out. One or two of the platoon had narrow squeaks, coming across Zakky without warning when he was practising. It didn't make him any more loved. But he was something to talk about in the dull times, when we were out all night in the rain, and had nothing to show for it but the crew of some Jerry night-bomber, well soaked and ready to surrender for a mug of tea.

But we had to find him something to do, besides endlessly oiling rifles and throwing his knife at plywood. My mother got more and more worried about him. And the rabbits he brought back from the woods, always killed by his knife, did nothing to lessen her worries, though they helped out the rations.

Then came the blessed day that my new Fordson tractor broke down, only a week out of the factory. Furious, I rang Tom Hands the blacksmith, who fiddled with cars as a sideline.

That evening, when I got back from ploughing with our two old horses, the tractor was mended, and Tom and Zakky were in the kitchen with my mother, drinking tea from white enamel mugs, smirched with oily fingerprints. They were all as thick as thieves.

Tom announced that Zakky had a gift with engines. My mother announced that Tom was taking on Zakky as an apprentice. As spring broadened into summer, Tom and Zakky became inseparable. Worn-out farm machinery kept breaking down all over the place; they never had an idle moment.

And then Hitler invaded Russia, and we knew the threat from across the Channel was gone. To celebrate, Pincher Morton bought himself a plot in the village churchyard. Said he felt happier, knowing where he was going to end up.

We all felt happier; except Zakky. The further away the threat of invasion got, the blacker he became. You could feel the pressure building up in him. He was always wanting to *wrestle* with me. I took him on once or twice, in fun. Going gently, not wanting to hurt him, for I was a big lad by then, nearly fourteen stone.

He had me on my face in about ten seconds; somebody had taught him unarmed combat along the way. He never hurt me, but it was bloody humiliating. In the end I refused to do it any more, so he began jumping out on me from dark corners. Said I had to learn, for when the Nazis came.

But it wasn't the Nazis who came; it was the Canadians, whole divisions of them, armed to the teeth with American tanks and guns and lorries.

We had to pretend to defend the villages, while the Canadians pretended to attack them. Quite realistic, it was. Blank ammunition, thunderflashes, wired explosions, smoke-grenades. The trouble was, we were pretty good by then, and we knew the countryside. And they were so *green*; lousy soldiers who bunched up too close together, and stuck to the metalled roads. We ambushed and slaughtered them over and over again. Then they gave us fags and chewing-gum, grinning sheepishly. The battle-umpires kept running up and telling us *we* were dead, without giving any reasons. I don't think they wanted the Canadians to get too discouraged. Our old hands weren't too surprised when the Canadians finally got a bloody nose from real Germans, in the Dieppe Raid.

It was from one of these exercises that Zakky didn't come home. My mother and I were just setting out to look for him, in the van, when word came that Zakky was being held by the military. It seemed he had gone berserk and seriously injured a Canadian ...

Major Newsam drove up to London, with my mother and the vicar. They must have talked bloody hard, because they brought Zakky back with them, paler and more silent, and blacker in his moods than ever.

Some weeks later, as we were getting ready for Christmas, the Japs attacked Pearl Harbor. In the New

Year, we settled down to teaching the first American troops a thing or two.

All except Zakky.

The Americans were even more generous and clumsy than the Canadians had been. But, as Major Newsam said sadly, when we got our first issue of American tommy-guns, us Home Guard were all dressed up with nowhere to go. We were just actors now; the invasion threat had gone for ever. Still, we enjoyed the Camels and Hershey Bars.

Zakky was sixteen by then; as tall as he ever got, five feet seven. He shaved earlier than me, had a fine black moustache, whereas I could still get away with shaving twice a week. I suppose he was handsome in a thin, peaky, tragic sort of way. A lot of the local girls eyed him, even with the Americans about. Rosemary Thomas, whose dad ran the White Lion, especially, though she was older than he was. I suppose the girls sensed the darkness in him; wanted to rescue him from it. But he had little time for them ...

He was well in with the local farmers too. A natural mechanic, which was quite something in those days when we had to hold tractors together with tin cans and wire. I know he brought my mother's car back from the grave more than once, though he always insisted afterwards that she crawl underneath it, to be shown exactly what he'd done. He'd still do anything for her.

He even talked German now. Because she'd hit on a way of holding him steady. Soon, she told him, a great army would be invading Europe to fight the Nazis. They would need people who could speak French and German fluently ... I think Major Newsam had something to do with that. He and my mother were as thick as thieves by that time. But I wasn't jealous. It was just nice to see two people I liked being happy.

They got married after harvest. October 1943. The whole village nearly went mad over it. We'd had a lot of wartime weddings, with blokes going off to the war, and people thinking they wouldn't come back. Desperate weddings, a kind of laughter on the edge of the grave. But my mother's wedding was different. It was, in a way, the first of our post-war weddings. People knew *they* were going to stay around and be married for the rest of their natural lives. There was no desperation in the laughter. We held the reception in the village hall, and the whole neighbourhood made a festival of it. They were both pretty popular with the locals and everyone chipped in with the eats, so we had a good spread in spite of the rationing. I gave my mother away in church and made a speech afterwards, which got a lot of laughs, Major Newsam being older than me, and my commanding officer in the Home Guard, which gave me plenty of openings for funny cracks.

I still have a photo of Zakky taken at the reception. My mother had asked him to be a groomsman, and he looked very dashing in hired morning-dress, holding his glass and laughing. He was willing to be happy for my mother, when he would never be happy for himself. And behind him in the photo is Rosemary Thomas, looking at him as if she wanted to eat him. Even now, when I look at it, it makes me shudder.

That Christmas Zakky got his chance. Major Newsam took him up for an interview at the War Office, and apparently he chattered French and English and German and Polish like a bird, and they grabbed him like he was the best thing since sliced bread.

He came back for a fortnight's leave in May 1944, in the uniform of the Intelligence Corps. He was truly happy, I think, for that fortnight. Southern England was, by that time, as packed with allied soldiers as an egg is full of meat, and he knew at last he was going to have his feast of death. He wasn't even eighteen, but he'd have passed for twenty-five with his hair cropped.

We went for a last walk before he left. My bottom field was full of Shermans under camouflage, and the

Yank tank-crews bivouacked. He was quickly among them, shaking hands and laughing and talking about killing Nazis. It was pretty crazy and pretty painful, because the Yanks kept looking at each other and tapping their heads with their fingers, once he'd passed. I was bloody terrified he'd see them, because the little bulge at the back of his battle-dress collar told me the deadly knife was still there.

Walking home, we met Rosemary Thomas in the lane outside our house. I think she'd come looking for him. They went off together, his arm around her waist, natural as any young couple, laughing.

But I shuddered. He could afford to laugh, because he was going to kill. He could afford to love, because he was going to die. He was like a dragonfly that only lives a few days of summer; a dragonfly that is a gaudy killer.

I thought of him on D-Day. D-Day was a strange time for us Home Guard. Endless streams of allied planes flying east, where once there had been endless streams of Germans flying west. Endless streams of American armour pouring through our village, where once we'd stood expecting streams of German panzers.

In one day we became pointless. No one left to fight; no one even left to train. Our hands full of the very latest, useless guns. Newsam told me an order was coming out, to disband us, with thanks. We'd never fired a shot in anger; only blanks at friends.

Still, there was the harvest to get in. The hay was early that year. And that night I first met Shirley Harris, as we gathered round the radio in the pub to listen to the news from Normandy.

He never wrote.

There was one snippet about him in the local paper. BIRSBY MAN WINS MILITARY MEDAL.

Major Newsam tried to find out more from his mates at the War Office. He got very little, except that Zakky had been promoted to sergeant. And a hint of cloak-and-dagger. Raids behind enemy lines, co-operation with the French Maquis, throats cut and no questions asked. A very dirty war indeed.

'Not my kind of war,' said Newsam. 'Not my kind of war at all.'

And then, nothing. VE day passed with great rejoicing, our village green packed with trestle tables, hung with red, white and blue bunting left over from the Coronation, the Silver Jubilee, Queen Victoria's birthday, for all I knew. We choked with the dust as we hung it up. A little band played for dancing, and women danced with women and children. Then VJ day, and the men began coming home, and still nothing. Six weeks later I married Shirley Harris. There was nothing to stop us. My mother had gone to live with the Major, in a country club he was trying to haul back to life further along the south coast.

And then, towards the back-end of 1945, I got home from a cattle auction, and Shirley met me in the yard and said,

'You've got a visitor.'

She looked scared to death, and she's not the nervous sort. So I went in feeling very proprietorial, and rather angry.

He was sitting at the kitchen table. Shirley had given him a cup of tea and a piece of home-made cake, as she did with everybody who called. He'd let the tea go cold, and rolled her good cake into tiny dark balls on the plate. Our kitchen was full of ... the smell of him? The *vibes* of him? The only thing I can compare it to was the atmosphere at the funeral of a friend who had committed suicide. It was that black.

I made myself shake hands. His hand was very bony and cold. His hair was cropped like a convict's; you could see the white scalp showing through the black stubble. His flamboyant moustache was gone. So was any glint of life in his eyes; they were like two holes burnt in a grey blanket.

I said I was glad to see him, but I wasn't. I asked him whether he'd been demobbed. He said,

'They have stopped killing Nazis. Germany is full of Nazis but they are making them into burgomasters now. Because they are the only ones left who can run that country.' I noticed he was wearing one of those awful demob suits; it hung on him as it might have hung on a rail.

I tried to tell him about this and that; country gossip. But he cut me short, he didn't want to know.

I told myself he was still only a kid, not yet nineteen. But he wasn't. I even began to wish he had died, like the dragonfly, that gaudy killer. So that he didn't have to come back here and plague us. I began to worry he might ask after my mother ...

In the end I said, straight out,

'What can I do for you, Zakky?'

'I wish to rent the mill. I will pay you fair rent.'

Should I have said no? So he might have drifted off and plagued somebody else? But all I wanted was him out of my kitchen, and the mill seemed a cheap price to pay. It still had its floors and roof, as the Home Guard had left it. I had no use for it.

We agreed a rent. I wasn't such a fool as to offer it to him for nothing, but I threw in some old furniture. Anything to get him out of my kitchen. He was death, walking. They had glutted him with killing, then turned him loose on a world at peace.

And yet, it might still have worked for him. Lost in the world as he was, the mill became his fortress, the one place where his life had meaning. He kept it spotless, I was told. He even filled the little walled enclosure full of flowers. Only all the colours were those of the old Polish flag. A Polish flag now flew from the little flagpole we'd left on the roof. Inside, there was another Polish flag, draped round a photograph of the late General Sikorski. And there was a large radio, permanently tuned to Radio Warsaw.

But Poland was Communist now; full of Russians talking the language of pigs. We all knew he could never go home.

He scratched a living, mending machinery. Tom Hands offered him a partnership, but he refused. You never saw him talking to anybody round the village. But when he met any member of the old Home Guard, he would give a curt, abrupt nod of the head.

Only Rosemary Thomas did not despair. She beat against the walls of that mill, like a moth beating against a lamp. But, it seemed, in vain.

Yet she found fresh-killed rabbits on the pub doorstep some mornings. Killed by a knife-throw.

And then PC Morris from the next village came to

see me. He'd heard rumours that Zakky had guns hung on the wall. Not shotguns, either. Guns from the war, people said ...

I told him it was rubbish. They *must* be shotguns. I said I would be responsible for Zakky; see he didn't cause any trouble. Frankly, I told him anything I could think of, to get him to go away.

To tell the truth, I feared for his life, if he tried to interfere.

And then, God help us, came the start of the post-war housing boom. Homes fit for heroes. Town vied with town. And our blessed district council decided to double the size of our village. On my land. By compulsory purchase order.

Mind you, they offered a fair price, and I had my eye on a bigger farm. I had no cause to grumble.

Till I heard the mill had to go, too.

I *pleaded* with the clerk to the council. I spent four hours trying to explain about Zakky. Didn't make a ha'p'orth of difference. Even ex-servicemen with valiant war-records must learn to make way for progress. Why, this whole scheme was *designed* for ex-servicemen. Mr Zakrewski might apply for one of the houses, if he was a married man with at least two children. But if he insisted on being awkward, that was surely a matter for the police ...

Truly, I felt the ground open up beneath me.

I was still moving in that dark nightmare the following morning when I drove my tractor on to a too-steep bit of hillside, and it turned over on me. I was in a coma for six weeks, and my life was despaired of.

The morning Shirley finally drove me home from hospital, we came in on the road past Draggett's Mill.

It was gone; flat. All around, workmen were digging foundations for houses.

'Zakky ...' I said. Full of dread, loss, a terrible feeling of letting people down.

'Gone,' said Shirley. 'Safe gone.'

'HOW?'

'Birsby Home Guard's last and best manoeuvre ...'

'What *sort* of manoeuvre?'

'Old Comrades' Reunion. At Rosemary's pub. Zakky was formally requested to attend, or his old comrades would be *deeply* insulted. Given that Polish sense of honour, could Zakky refuse? Just for half an hour of course ...'

'And then ...?'

'Well, people began to drink toasts, with vodka bought off a Polish ship in Southampton. Oh, so *many* toasts. The late General Sikorski, and every member of his late government. Major Newsam had all their names off by heart, and nearly cracked his jaw pronouncing them. Zakky kept correcting him.

Then Mr Churchill, President Roosevelt, President Truman, Chang Kai-Shek, General de Gaulle, the RAF, the Home Guard, the Royal Navy. You name it, we had it. And Zakky couldn't refuse to drink to a single one, could he? On his Polish honour. And he was drinking neat vodka, and the rest were drinking vodka and water. Half the pub's glasses ended up smashed at the back of the pub fireplace. And every time a vodka glass was smashed, the flames would leap up nearly to the pub ceiling. A right little fire risk. Zakky loved every moment of it. Till he passed out cold.'

'Then?'

'Well, they had to carry him home to the mill, didn't they? And they took the rest of the vodka with them. And he'd left a fire burning at the mill. And ... or so they said ... they started drinking again, and smashing more glasses in the fireplace in true Polish fashion, and a full bottle of vodka somehow got broken in the fireplace, and ... well, the whole mill went up in flames, and they only just got Zakky out in time. The mill was alight from top to bottom by the time the fire brigade got there. Weapons, bullets, hand-grenades, the lot went up. Quite a little fireworks display. There wasn't a lot left of the mill by the time they were finished. Even the stone walls fell in.'

'How did Zakky take it?'

'Well, they'd carried him back to the pub, overnight.

And Rosemary was fluttering about him, tending to his hangover. And they all looked very sheepish, and told him what they'd done, and how sorry they were. And that they felt honour-bound to make amends for his loss.

And he could hardly blame them for going on in such a Polish way, could he? Nor refuse their honourable desire to make amends. He went off with five hundred quid in his pocket. I think Major Newsam gave half ...'

'What good is *money* to him?' I asked desperately.

'Oh, I wouldn't worry too much about him. Rosemary went with him.'

'Where, for God's sake?'

'Marbury, in Cheshire, according to Rosemary's letters. Hundreds of ex-Polish army up there. Starting to marry local girls, thinking of building their own church. She still has hopes he'll do the honourable thing, and marry her. Of course, she had a hand in the whole thing from the start ...'

'*Women*,' I said.

'Women,' she agreed, smiling. 'What would you all do without us? Welcome home, Keith.'

THE DESTRUCTORS

Graham Greene

1

It was on the eve of August Bank Holiday that the latest recruit became the leader of the Wormsley Common Gang. No one was surprised except Mike, but Mike at the age of nine was surprised by everything. 'If you don't shut your mouth,' somebody once said to him, 'you'll get a frog down it.' After that Mike kept his teeth tightly clamped except when the surprise was too great.

The new recruit had been with the gang since the beginning of the summer holidays, and there were possibilities about his brooding silence that all recognized. He never wasted a word even to tell his name until that was required of him by the rules. When he said 'Trevor' it was a statement of fact, not as it would have been with the others a statement of shame or defiance. Nor did anyone laugh except Mike, who finding himself without support and meeting the dark gaze of the newcomer opened his mouth and was quiet again. There was every reason why T., as he was afterwards referred to, should have been an object of mockery – there was his name (and they substituted the initial because otherwise they had no excuse not to laugh at it), the fact that his father, a former architect and present clerk, had 'come down in the world' and that his mother considered herself better than the neighbours. What but an odd quality of danger, of the unpredictable, established him in the gang without any ignoble ceremony of initiation?

The gang met every morning in an impromptu car-park, the site of the last bomb of the first blitz. The leader, who was known as Blackie, claimed to have heard it fall, and no one was precise enough in his dates to point out that he would have been one year old and fast asleep on the down platform of Wormsley Common Underground Station. On one side of the car-park leant the first occupied house, No. 3, of the shattered Northwood Terrace – literally leant, for it had suffered from the blast of the bomb and the side walls were supported on wooden struts. A smaller bomb and incendiaries had fallen beyond, so that the house stuck up like a jagged tooth and carried on the further wall relics of its neighbour, a dado, the remains of a fireplace. T., whose words were almost confined to voting 'Yes' or 'No' to the plan of operations proposed each day by Blackie, once startled the whole gang by saying broodingly, 'Wren built that house, father says.'

'Who's Wren?'

'The man who built St Paul's.'

'Who cares?' Blackie said. 'It's only Old Misery's.'

Old Misery – whose real name was Thomas – had once been a builder and decorator. He lived alone in the crippled house, doing for himself: once a week you could see him coming back across the common with bread and vegetables, and once as the boys played in the car-park he put his head over the smashed wall of his garden and looked at them.

'Been to the lav,' one of the boys said, for it was common knowledge that since the bombs fell something had gone wrong with the pipes of the house and Old Misery was too mean to spend money on the property. He could do the redecorating himself at cost price, but he had never learnt plumbing. The lav was a wooden shed at the bottom of the narrow garden with a star-shaped hole in the door: it had escaped the blast which had smashed the house next door and sucked out the window-frames of No. 3.

The next time the gang became aware of Mr Thomas was more surprising. Blackie, Mike and a thin yellow boy, who for some reason was called by his surname Summers, met him on the common coming back from the market. Mr Thomas stopped them. He said glumly, 'You belong to the lot that play in the car-park?'

Mike was about to answer when Blackie stopped him. As the leader he had responsibilities. 'Suppose we are?' he said ambiguously.

'I got some chocolates,' Mr Thomas said. 'Don't like 'em myself. Here you are. Not enough to go round, I don't suppose.

'There never is,' he added with sombre conviction. He handed over three packets of Smarties.

The gang was puzzled and perturbed by this action and tried to explain it away. 'Bet someone dropped them and he picked 'em up,' somebody suggested.

'Pinched 'em and then got in a bleeding funk,' another thought aloud.

'It's a bribe,' Summers said. 'He wants us to stop bouncing balls on his wall.'

'We'll show him we don't take bribes,' Blackie said, and they sacrificed the whole morning to the game of bouncing that only Mike was young enough to enjoy. There was no sign from Mr Thomas.

Next day T. astonished them all. He was late at the rendezvous, and the voting for that day's exploit took place without him. At Blackie's suggestion the gang was to disperse in pairs, take buses at random and see how many free rides could be snatched from unwary conductors (the operation was to be carried out in pairs to avoid cheating). They were drawing lots for their companions when T. arrived.

'Where you been, T.?' Blackie asked. 'You can't vote now. You know the rules.'

'I've been *there*,' T. said. He looked at the ground, as though he had thoughts to hide.

'Where?'

'At Old Misery's.' Mike's mouth opened and then hurriedly closed again with a click. He had remembered the frog.

'At Old Misery's?' Blackie said. There was nothing in the rules against it, but he had a sensation that T. was treading on dangerous ground. He asked hopefully, 'Did you break in?'

'No. I rang the bell.'

'And what did you say?'

'I said I wanted to see his house.'

'What did he do?'

'He showed it me.'

'Pinch anything?'

'No.'

'What did you do it for then?'

The gang had gathered round: it was as though an impromptu court were about to form and try some case of deviation. T. said, 'It's a beautiful house,' and still watching the ground, meeting no one's eyes, he licked his lips first one way, then the other.

'What do you mean, a beautiful house?' Blackie asked with scorn.

'It's got a staircase two hundred years old like a corkscrew. Nothing holds it up.'

'What do you mean, nothing holds it up. Does it float?'

'It's to do with opposite forces, Old Misery said.'

'What else?'

'There's panelling.'

'Like in the Blue Boar?'

'Two hundred years old.'

'Is Old Misery two hundred years old?'

Mike laughed suddenly and then was quiet again. The meeting was in a serious mood. For the first time since T. had strolled into the car-park on the first day of the holidays his position was in danger. It only needed a single use of his real name and the gang would be at his heels.

'What did you do it for?' Blackie asked. He was just, he had no jealousy, he was anxious to retain T. in the gang if he could. It was the word 'beautiful' that worried him – that belonged to a class world that you could still see parodied at the Wormsley Common Empire by a man wearing a top hat and a monocle, with a haw-haw accent. He was tempted to say, 'My dear Trevor, old chap,' and unleash his hell hounds. 'If you'd broken in,' he said sadly – that indeed would have been an exploit worthy of the gang.

'This was better,' T. said. 'I found out things.' He continued to stare at his feet, not meeting anybody's eye, as though he were absorbed in some dream he was unwilling – or ashamed – to share.

'What things?'

'Old Misery's going to be away all tomorrow and Bank Holiday.'

Blackie said with relief, 'You mean we could break in?'

'And pinch things?' somebody asked.

Blackie said, 'Nobody's going to pinch things. Breaking in – that's good enough, isn't it? We don't want any court stuff.'

'I don't want to pinch anything,' T. said. 'I've got a better idea.'

'What is it?'

T. raised eyes, as grey and disturbed as the drab August day. 'We'll pull it down,' he said. 'We'll destroy it.'

Blackie gave a single hoot of laughter and then, like Mike, fell quiet, daunted by the serious implacable gaze. 'What'd the police be doing all the time?' he said.

'They'd never know. We'd do it from inside. I've found a way in.' He said with a sort of intensity, 'We'd be like worms, don't you see, in an apple. When we came out again there'd be nothing there, no staircase, no panels, nothing but just walls, and then we'd make the walls fall down – somehow.'

'We'd go to jug,' Blackie said.

'Who's to prove? and anyway we wouldn't have pinched anything.' He added without the smallest flicker of glee, 'There wouldn't be anything to pinch after we'd finished.'

'I've never heard of going to prison for breaking things,' Summers said.

'There wouldn't be time,' Blackie said. 'I've seen housebreakers at work.'

'There are twelve of us,' T. said. 'We'd organize.'

'None of us know how …'

'I know,' T. said. He looked across at Blackie. 'Have you got a better plan?'

'Today,' Mike said tactlessly, 'we're pinching free rides …'

'Free rides,' T. said. 'Kid stuff. You can stand down, Blackie, if you'd rather …'

'The gang's got to vote.'

'Put it up then.'

Blackie said uneasily, 'It's proposed that tomorrow and Monday we destroy Old Misery's house.'

'Here, here,' said a fat boy called Joe.

'Who's in favour?'

T. said, 'It's carried.'

'How do we start?' Summers asked.

'He'll tell you,' Blackie said. It was the end of his leadership. He went away to the back of the car-park and began to kick a stone, dribbling it this way and that. There was only one old Morris in the park, for few cars were left there except lorries: without an attendant there was no safety. He took a flying kick at the car and scraped a little paint off the rear mudguard. Beyond, paying no more attention to him than to a stranger, the gang had gathered round T.; Blackie was dimly aware of the fickleness of favour. He thought of going home, of never returning, of letting them all discover the hollowness of T.'s leadership, but suppose after all what T. proposed was possible – nothing like it had ever been done before. The fame of the Wormsley Common car-park gang would surely reach around London. There would be headlines in the papers. Even the grown-up gangs who ran the betting at the all-in wrestling and the barrow-boys would hear with respect of how Old Misery's house had been destroyed. Driven by the pure, simple and altruistic ambition of fame for the gang, Blackie came back to where T. stood in the shadow of Old Misery's wall.

T. was giving his orders with decision: it was as though this plan had been with him all his life, pondered through the seasons, now in his fifteenth year crystallized with the pain of puberty. 'You,' he said to Mike, 'bring some big nails, the biggest you can find, and a hammer. Anybody who can, better bring a hammer and a screwdriver. We'll need plenty of them. Chisels too. We can't have too many chisels. Can anybody bring a saw?'

'I can,' Mike said.

'Not a child's saw,' T. said. 'A real saw.'

Blackie realized he had raised his hand like any ordinary member of the gang.

'Right, you bring one, Blackie. But now there's a difficulty. We want a hacksaw.'

'What's a hacksaw?' someone asked.

'You can get 'em at Woolworth's,' Summers said.

The fat boy called Joe said gloomily, 'I knew it would end in a collection.'

'I'll get one myself,' T. said. 'I don't want your money. But I can't buy a sledge-hammer.'

Blackie said, 'They are working on No. 15. I know where they'll leave their stuff for Bank Holiday.'

'Then that's all,' T. said. 'We meet here at nine sharp.'

'I've got to go to church,' Mike said.

'Come over the wall and whistle. We'll let you in.'

2

On Sunday morning all were punctual except Blackie, even Mike. Mike had a stroke of luck. His mother felt ill, his father was tired after Saturday night, and he was told to go to church alone with many warnings of what would happen if he strayed. Blackie had difficulty in smuggling out the saw, and then in finding the sledge-hammer at the back of No. 15. He approached the house from a lane at the rear of the garden, for fear of the policeman's beat along the main road. The tired evergreens kept off a stormy sun: another wet Bank Holiday was being prepared over the Atlantic, beginning in swirls of dust under the trees. Blackie climbed the wall into Misery's garden.

There was no sign of anybody anywhere. The lav stood like a tomb in a neglected graveyard. The curtains were drawn. The house slept. Blackie lumbered nearer with the saw and the sledge-hammer. Perhaps after all nobody had turned up: the plan had been a wild invention: they had woken wiser. But when he came close to the back door he could hear a confusion of sound hardly louder than a hive in swarm: a clickety-clack, a bang bang, a scraping, a creaking, a sudden painful crack. He thought: it's true, and whistled.

They opened the back door to him and he came in. He had at once the impression of organization, very different from the old happy-go-lucky ways under his leadership. For a while he wandered up and down stairs looking for T. Nobody addressed him: he had a sense of great urgency, and already he could begin to see the plan. The interior of the house was being carefully demolished without touching the walls. Summers with hammer and chisel was ripping out the skirting-boards in the ground floor dining-room: he had already smashed the panels of the door. In the same room Joe was heaving up the parquet blocks, exposing the soft wood floorboards over the cellar. Coils of wire came out of the damaged skirting and Mike sat happily on the floor clipping the wires.

On the curved stairs two of the gang were working hard with an inadequate child's saw on the banisters – when they saw Blackie's big saw they signalled for it wordlessly. When he next saw them a quarter of the banisters had been dropped into the hall. He found T. at last in the bathroom – he sat moodily in the least cared-for room in the house, listening to the sounds coming up from below.

'You've really done it,' Blackie said with awe. 'What's going to happen?'

'We've only just begun,' T. said. He looked at the sledge-hammer and gave his instructions. 'You stay here and break the bath and the wash-basin. Don't bother about the pipes. They come later.'

Mike appeared at the door. 'I've finished the wires, T.,' he said.

'Good. You've just got to go wandering round now. The kitchen's in the basement. Smash all the china and glass and bottles you can lay hold of. Don't turn on the taps – we don't want a flood – yet. Then go into all the rooms and turn out the drawers. If they are locked get one of the others to break them open. Tear up any papers you find and smash all the ornaments. Better take a carving knife with you from the kitchen. The bedroom's opposite here. Open the pillows and tear up the sheets. That's enough for the moment. And you, Blackie, when you've finished in here crack the plaster in the passage up with your sledge-hammer.'

'What are you going to do?' Blackie asked.

'I'm looking for something special,' T. said.

It was nearly lunch-time before Blackie had finished and went in search of T. Chaos had advanced. The kitchen was a shambles of broken glass and china. The dining-room was stripped of parquet, the skirting was up, the door had been taken off its hinges, and the destroyers had moved up a floor. Streaks of light came in through the closed shutters where they worked with the seriousness of creators - and destruction after all is a form of creation. A kind of imagination had seen this house as it has now become.

Mike said, 'I've got to go home for dinner.'

'Who else?' T. asked, but all the others on one excuse or another had brought provisions with them.

They squatted in the ruins of the room and swapped unwanted sandwiches. Half an hour for lunch and they were at work again. By the time Mike returned they were on the top floor, and by six the superficial damage was completed. The doors were all off, all the skirtings raised, the furniture pillaged and ripped and smashed – no one could have slept in the house except on a bed of broken plaster. T. gave his orders – eight o'clock next morning, and to escape notice they climbed singly over the garden wall, into the car-park. Only Blackie and T. were left: the light had nearly gone, and when they touched a switch, nothing worked – Mike had done his job thoroughly.

'Did you find anything special?' Blackie asked.

T. nodded. 'Come over here,' he said, 'and look.' Out of both pockets he drew bundles of pound notes. 'Old Misery's savings,' he said. 'Mike ripped out the mattress, but he missed them.'

'What are you going to do? Share them?'

'We aren't thieves,' T. said. 'Nobody's going to steal anything from this house. I kept these for you and me – a celebration.' He knelt down on the floor and counted them out – there were seventy in all. 'We'll burn them,' he said, 'one by one,' and taking it in turns they held a note upwards and lit the top corner, so that the flame burnt slowly towards their fingers. The grey ash floated above them and fell on their heads like age. 'I'd like to see Old Misery's face when we are through,' T. said.

'You hate him a lot?' Blackie asked.

'Of course I don't hate him,' T. said. 'There'd be no fun if I hated him.' The last burning note illuminated his brooding face. 'All this hate and love,' he said, 'it's soft, it's hooey. There's only things, Blackie,' and he looked round the room crowded with the unfamiliar shadows of half things, broken things, former things. 'I'll race you home, Blackie,' he said.

3

Next morning the serious destruction started. Two were missing – Mike and another boy whose parents were off to Southend and Brighton in spite of the slow warm drops that had begun to fall and the rumble of thunder in the estuary like the first guns of the old blitz. 'We've got to hurry,' T. said.

Summers was restive. 'Haven't we done enough?' he asked. 'I've been given a bob for slot machines. This is like work.'

'We've hardly started,' T. said. 'Why, there's all the floors left, and the stairs. We haven't taken out a single window. You voted like the others. We are going to *destroy* this house. There won't be anything left when we've finished.'

They began again on the first floor picking up the

top floorboards next to the outer wall, leaving the joists exposed. Then they sawed through the joists and retreated into the hall, as what was left of the floor heeled and sank. They had learnt with practice, and the second floor collapsed more easily. By the evening an odd exhilaration seized them as they looked down the great hollow of the house. They ran risks and made mistakes: when they thought of the windows it was too late to reach them. 'Cor,' Joe said, and dropped a penny down into the dry rubble-filled well. It cracked and span amongst the broken glass.

'Why did we start this?' Summers asked with astonishment; T. was already on the ground, digging at the rubble, clearing a space along the outer wall. 'Turn on the taps,' he said. 'It's too dark for anyone to see now, and in the morning it won't matter.' The water overtook them on the stairs and fell through the floorless rooms.

It was then they heard Mike's whistle at the back. 'Something's wrong,' Blackie said. They could hear his urgent breathing as they unlocked the door.

'The bogies?' Summers asked.

'Old Misery,' Mike said. 'He's on his way,' he said with pride.

'But why?' T. said. 'He told me ...' He protested with the fury of the child he had never been, 'It isn't fair.'

'He was down at Southend,' Mike said, 'and he was on the train coming back. Said it was too cold and wet.' He paused and gazed at the water. 'My, you've had a storm here. Is the roof leaking?'

'How long will he be?'

'Five minutes. I gave Ma the slip and ran.'

'We better clear,' Summers said. 'We've done enough, anyway.'

'Oh no, we haven't. Anybody could do this –' 'this' was the shattered hollowed house with nothing left but the walls. Yet walls could be preserved. Façades were valuable. They could build inside again more beautifully than before. This could again be a home. He said angrily, 'We've got to finish. Don't move. Let me think.'

'There's no time,' a boy said.

'There's got to be a way,' T. said. 'We couldn't have got this far …'

'We've done a lot,' Blackie said.

'No. No, we haven't. Somebody watch the front.'

'We can't do any more.'

'He may come in at the back.'

'Watch the back too.' T. began to plead. 'Just give me a minute and I'll fix it. I swear I'll fix it.' But his authority had gone with his ambiguity. He was only one of the gang. 'Please,' he said.

'Please,' Summers mimicked him, and then suddenly

struck home with the fatal name. 'Run along home, Trevor.'

T. stood with his back to the rubble like a boxer knocked groggy against the ropes. He had no words as his dreams shook and slid. Then Blackie acted before the gang had time to laugh, pushing Summers backward. 'I'll watch the front, T.,' he said, and cautiously he opened the shutters of the hall. The grey wet common stretched ahead, and the lamps gleamed in the puddles. 'Someone's coming, T. No, it's not him. What's your plan, T.?'

'Tell Mike to go out to the lav and hide close beside it. When he hears me whistle he's got to count ten and start to shout.'

'Shout what?'

'Oh, "Help", anything.'

'You hear, Mike,' Blackie said. He was the leader again. He took a quick look between the shutters. 'He's coming, T.'

'Quick, Mike. The lav. Stay here, Blackie, all of you, till I yell.'

'Where are you going, T.?'

'Don't worry. I'll see to this. I said I would, didn't I?'

Old Misery came limping off the common. He had mud on his shoes and he stopped to scrape them on the pavement's edge. He didn't want to soil his house, which stood jagged and dark between the bomb-sites, saved so narrowly, as he believed, from destruction. Even the fan-light had been left unbroken by the bomb's blast. Somewhere somebody whistled. Old Misery looked sharply round. He didn't trust whistles. A child was shouting: it seemed to come from his own garden. Then a boy ran into the road from the car-park. 'Mr Thomas,' he called, 'Mr Thomas.'

'What is it?'

'I'm terribly sorry, Mr Thomas. One of us got taken short, and we thought you wouldn't mind, and now he can't get out.'

'What do you mean, boy?'

'He's got stuck in your lav.'

'He'd no business ... Haven't I seen you before?'

'You showed me your house.'

'So I did. So I did. That doesn't give you the right to ...'

'Do hurry, Mr Thomas. He'll suffocate.'

'Nonsense. He can't suffocate. Wait till I put my bag in.'

'I'll carry your bag.'

'Oh no, you don't. I carry my own.'

'This way, Mr Thomas.'

'I can't get in the garden that way. I've got to go through the house.'

'But you *can* get in the garden this way, Mr Thomas. We often do.'

'You often do?' He followed the boy with a scandalized fascination.

'When? What right ... ?'

'Do you see ... ? the wall's low.'

'I'm not going to climb walls into my own garden. It's absurd.'

'This is how we do it. One foot here, one foot there, and over.' The boy's face peered down, an arm shot out, and Mr Thomas found his bag taken and deposited on the other side of the wall.

'Give me back my bag,' Mr Thomas said. From the loo a boy yelled and yelled. 'I'll call the police.'

'Your bag's all right, Mr Thomas. Look. One foot there. On your right. Now just above. To your left.' Mr Thomas climbed over his own garden wall. 'Here's your bag, Mr Thomas.'

'I'll have the wall built up,' Mr Thomas said, 'I'll not have you boys coming over here, using my loo.' He stumbled on the path, but the boy caught his elbow and supported him. 'Thank you, thank you, my boy,' he murmured automatically. Somebody shouted again through the dark. 'I'm coming, I'm coming,' Mr Thomas called. He said to the boy beside him, 'I'm not unreasonable. Been a boy myself. As long as things are done regular. I don't mind you playing round the place Saturday mornings. Sometimes I like company. Only it's got to be regular. One of you asks leave and I say Yes.

Sometimes I'll say No. Won't feel like it. And you come in at the front door and out at the back. No garden walls.'

'Do get him out, Mr Thomas.'

'He won't come to any harm in my loo,' Mr Thomas said, stumbling slowly down the garden. 'Oh, my rheumatics,' he said. 'Always get 'em on Bank Holiday. I've got to be careful. There's loose stones here. Give me your hand. Do you know what my horoscope said yesterday? "Abstain from any dealings in first half of week. Danger of serious crash." That might be on this path,' Mr Thomas said. 'They speak in parables and double meanings.' He paused at the door of the loo. 'What's the matter in there?' he called. There was no reply.

'Perhaps he's fainted,' the boy said.

'Not in my loo. Here, you, come out,' Mr Thomas said, and giving a great jerk at the door he nearly fell on his back when it swung easily open. A hand first supported him and then pushed him hard. His head hit the opposite wall and he sat heavily down. His bag hit his feet. A hand whipped the key out of the lock and the door slammed. 'Let me out,' he called, and heard the key turn in the lock. 'A serious crash,' he thought, and felt dithery and confused and old.

A voice spoke to him softly through the star-shaped hole in the door. 'Don't worry, Mr Thomas,' it said, 'we won't hurt you, not if you stay quiet.'

Mr Thomas put his head between his hands and pondered. He had noticed that there was only one lorry in the car-park, and he felt certain that the driver would not come for it before the morning. Nobody could hear him from the road in front, and the lane at the back was seldom used. Anyone who passed there would be hurrying home and would not pause for what they would certainly take to be drunken cries. And if he did call 'Help', who, on a lonely Bank Holiday evening, would have the courage to investigate? Mr Thomas sat on the loo and pondered with the wisdom of age.

After a while it seemed to him that there were sounds in the silence – they were faint and came from the direction of his house. He stood up and peered through the ventilation-hole – between the cracks in one of the shutters he saw a light, not the light of a lamp, but the wavering light that a candle might give. Then he thought he heard the sound of hammering and scraping and chipping. He thought of burglars – perhaps they had employed the boy as a scout, but why should burglars engage in what sounded more and more like a stealthy form of carpentry? Mr Thomas let out an experimental yell, but nobody answered. The noise could not even have reached his enemies.

4

Mike had gone home to bed, but the rest stayed. The question of leadership no longer concerned the gang. With nails, chisels, screwdrivers, anything that was sharp and penetrating, they moved around the inner walls worrying at the mortar between the bricks. They started too high, and it was Blackie who hit on the damp course and realized the work could be halved if they weakened the joints immediately above. It was a long, tiring, unamusing job, but at last it was finished. The gutted house stood there balanced on a few inches of mortar between the damp course and the bricks.

There remained the most dangerous task of all, out in the open at the edge of the bomb-site. Summers was sent to watch the road for passers-by, and Mr Thomas, sitting on the loo, heard clearly now the sound of sawing. It no longer came from the house, and that a little reassured him. He felt less concerned. Perhaps the other noises too had no significance.

A voice spoke to him through the hole. 'Mr Thomas.'

'Let me out,' Mr Thomas said sternly.

'Here's a blanket,' the voice said, and a long grey sausage was worked through the hole and fell in swathes over Mr Thomas's head.

'There's nothing personal,' the voice said. 'We want you to be comfortable tonight.'

'Tonight,' Mr Thomas repeated incredulously.

'Catch,' the voice said. 'Penny buns – we've buttered them, and sausage-rolls. We don't want you to starve, Mr Thomas.'

Mr Thomas pleaded desperately. 'A joke's a joke, boy. Let me out and I won't say a thing. I've got rheumatics. I got to sleep comfortable.'

'You wouldn't be comfortable, not in your house, you wouldn't. Not now.'

'What do you mean, boy?' But the footsteps receded. There was only the silence of night: no sound of sawing. Mr Thomas tried one more yell, but he was daunted and rebuked by the silence – a long way off an owl hooted and made away again on its muffled flight through the soundless world.

At seven next morning the driver came to fetch his lorry. He climbed into the seat and tried to start the engine. He was vaguely aware of a voice shouting, but it didn't concern him. At last the engine responded and he backed the lorry until it touched the great wooden shore that supported Mr Thomas's house. That way he could drive right out and down the street without reversing. The lorry moved forward, was momentarily checked as though something were pulling it from behind, and then went on to the sound of a long rumbling crash. The driver was astonished to see bricks bouncing ahead of him, while stones hit the roof of his cab. He put on his brakes. When he climbed out the whole landscape had suddenly altered. There was no house beside the car-park, only a hill of rubble. He went round and examined the back of his lorry for damage, and found a rope tied there that was still twisted at the other end round part of a wooden strut.

The driver again became aware of somebody shouting. It came from the wooden erection which was the nearest thing to a house in that desolation of broken brick. The driver climbed the smashed wall and unlocked the door. Mr Thomas came out of the loo. He was wearing a grey blanket to which flakes of pastry adhered. He gave a sobbing cry. 'My house,' he said. 'Where's my house?'

'Search me,' the driver said. His eye lit on the remains of a bath and what had once been a dresser and he began to laugh. There wasn't anything left anywhere.

'How dare you laugh,' Mr Thomas said. 'It was my house. My house.'

'I'm sorry,' the driver said, making heroic efforts, but when he remembered the sudden check of his lorry, the crash of bricks falling, he became convulsed again. One moment the house had stood there with such dignity between the bomb-sites like a man in a top hat, and then, bang, crash, there wasn't anything left – not anything. He said, 'I'm sorry. I can't help it, Mr Thomas. There's nothing personal, but you got to admit it's funny.'

1954

INTRODUCTION

'Ex Voto', Geraldine McCaughrean
'The War Prayer', Mark Twain

Mark Twain's 'The War Prayer' is a brilliant, scathing attack on militant patriotism. An old man interrupts a sermon in which the priest is praying for victory to add a prayer of his own and illuminate the inevitable consequences of one army's success.

Geraldine McCaughrean offers up a more sinister man of God – one whose black heart people have long ago seen right through. Both stories present characters who believe in their just wars. Both authors confront that belief and suggest that victory in war is meaningless.

Who do you think the authors believe to be the victims in war?

EX VOTO

Geraldine McCaughrean

As his sword hit the plaster, a spark flew, then the blade's tip snapped off. Hugh's breath escaped him in a heavy sob halfway to a laugh. That it should break now – this blade that had travelled so far with him! Having weathered the blazing desert heat, the freezing desert nights, having struck limbs from bodies, heads from shoulders, having driven chain-mail links into flesh like currants into dough, it chose now to snap, inside the chapel of this peaceful English monastery. Plaster fell on to his face, like quicklime on to a corpse.

Sir Hugh shrugged – well, would have shrugged but for the wound in his shoulder. The flesh had healed but not the joint beneath, which never would. He could already foresee the nicknames they would dub him: 'Lapwing', 'Hunchback', 'the Tilt' ... What name would his mother call him, he wondered, if she proved still to be alive? He went back to gouging away at the wall of the nave. His bad shoulder ached. The pain no longer troubled Hugh; he had endured so much that it had lost the power even to annoy him.

Morning sunbeams, shining in over the rim of the high windows, also drove long blades of light into the plastered wall. Perhaps the sun too was carving its *ex-voto*, in thanks at having survived another night. How quiet it was, this place he had chanced upon. Unusually quiet, even for a monastery chapel.

'Devil toss you on his pitchfork, you thieving dog!' said a voice behind him and a blow across his back felled him to his knees. As he fell, he assessed the degree of pain, the likelihood of death. He also began counting seconds: he had learned precisely how long an enemy took to deliver a second blow. Before his attacker could hit him again, he had rolled over and up and lunged with his sword. If the tip had not been broken, it would have pierced the abbot's belly.

The abbot was holding the candle sconce like a quarter-staff, and his lips were drawn back off his teeth in a ferocious snarl.

'An *ex-voto*! I was carving an *ex-voto*!' cried Hugh in self-defence and the abbot, recognizing a cultured voice, stood the large candlestick back on its base.

'I thought you were prising the chains out of the wall,' he said (though he did not apologize). And now that Hugh looked, he could see that the beautiful wooden font had indeed been chained to the chapel wall. 'They pilfer. All the time, they pilfer, God rot them,' said the abbot. He examined the hole Hugh had made in the plaster. 'Poor effort.'

'Not for want of gratitude to my maker,' said Hugh. 'Only for want of a fit tool.'

The abbot promptly disappeared out of a side door and returned a minute later with a mason's awl that he tossed to the knight. 'I fine you one crown for scarring church fabric … Here. You'll make a better job with this.' As Hugh paid, the abbot tried his hardest to see into the purse.

Hugh gladly laid aside his sword. It was much easier using the awl. He was able to scrape out the shape of a fluked cross around the dent he had already made. He worked on steadily, tongue creeping out of the corner of his mouth as he concentrated on his *ex-voto* – his note of thanks to God for bringing him safe home from the war.

He was not the first returning Crusader to carve on the chapel wall. Several 'fines' must have been paid to the abbot. Two dozen crosses were cut in the plaster – even into the marble floor around the font – some as deep as arrow slits, some as shallow as hastily dug graves. Hugh's heart filled with gratitude that these men, too, had survived the bloodbath of the Holy Wars – had dragged themselves home across desert, through hostile countries, escaped diseases, avoided capture or slavery or shipwreck or bandits or open wounds festering or rotten food ... Each carved cross represented a miracle really.

His head also filled with the faces of those who had not survived – friends, comrades, yeomen of his own levy, his brother Luke ...

'You use the devil's hand to work, I see,' said the abbot sourly.

'I took a hurt in my shoulder,' said Sir Hugh. 'I have to use my left hand.'

One question had rolled around inside Hugh all the way home, like a stone in his boot. Suddenly – he did not know why – it found its way out of his mouth. 'Why did God not grant us the victory, Father Abbot? I know, I know – serving the Lord is a privilege ... But you would suppose – given that He called us to go on Crusade – that God would grant us the victory. Or why –'

The question gave the abbot no difficulty at all. 'Too many sinners among you,' he said. 'The feet of the army stumbled upon their own trespasses and they were mired in sin.' It sounded like a quotation from the Bible, though Sir Hugh could not place it. He tried to picture the great army of the Second Crusade, and behind it its siege engines, forges and field kitchens, and behind them – biggest of all – a vast bundle holding all the sins of the marching men, gradually dragging them to a standstill.

'But we went on the Crusade to be forgiven, Father! The priests told us it was our duty to go and our reward to be forgiven! One thousand years less in purgatory! Our accounts wiped clean! Our souls washed in the blood of the Heathen! Why did the victory go to the heathen, Father?'

'The ways of God are not our ways,' snapped the abbot glibly. 'You brought home other rewards, I dare swear. Loot? Plunder?'

Sir Hugh thought of the contents of his saddlebag. 'Something for my sweetheart,' he admitted.

The abbot shuddered with distaste at the mention of a sweetheart but still wanted to see what loot the knight had brought. So Hugh went outside to his horse, tethered in the monastery garden. He stayed to stroke her – the winded, galled, ringwormed nag that had once been the finest in the county. Hardship had made them the best of friends. He told her about the *ex-voto* he had carved and the horse nodded her head in approval. Then Hugh got the pomegranate out of his saddle-wallet and took it back into the chapel. He had picked it in the Holy Land. The hard rind was browner now, but still as hard as eggshell.

The abbot took hold of it with a look of disgust. 'Is this all?'

'We had to travel light. It was bad. At the end. Chaos. We were lucky to get away with our skins. The ones who did.' In the back of Hugh's head familiar monsters squirmed into view – the ones he tried so hard to block out: the pomegranate hanging on its tree; the men lying under that tree as though resting in its shade; its roots soaking up their blood. Perhaps the fruit of the pomegranate tree grew red from drinking the blood of the Crusades.

A cord ran down inside the abbot's skirts. He pulled out a bunch of keys and useful implements. With a knife he ringed the pomegranate and twisted it open. Some of the seeds fell out on to his foot. The juice stained his hands. Those hands will be sticky all day now, thought Hugh absently.

He did not trouble to grieve for the loss of the pomegranate. Such things are not important in comparison with being alive. And now that it was open, the fruit reminded him too much of things he had seen after a sword stroke cut through a helmet, a limb, a horse's flank.

'How many did you kill?' asked the abbot, sniffing the fruit dubiously and giving both halves back to Hugh.

'Sorry, Father?'

'How many heathens did you kill?'

Hugh shook his head. The colourful monsters

writhed in the back of his brain: black, blood-red, tripe-white, chestnut, sallow, bay ... 'Fifty. Sixty, maybe.'

The abbot raised his hands, so that the sunlight fell on his fat white fingers. Hugh bent one knee, thinking to be blessed. But the abbot was simply doing his sums. 'Eight hundred crowns should void it,' he said.

'Father?'

'Well? Did you think to break the Sixth Commandment and not pay the price? *Thou shalt not kill.* The fine has been fixed at twelve crowns per head. Best pay me as much as you can here and now and receive forgiveness. You could wait until you reach your own estates, but the roads are rife with thieves, and if you were to die unshriven ...'

Hunger and sickness had kept Hugh company all the way from Palestine. Now they gave him a push and he reeled with dizziness. 'I'm sorry. I fear I do not understand you, Father.'

The abbot pursed his lips impatiently. His face seemed to ask how such a stupid knight had managed to find his way home at all. 'Blood weighs heavy, young man. I counsel you earnestly to wash away your sins! Ransom your soul. Some piece of carving on a wall won't do.'

Hysteria, somewhere between laughter and tears, caught in Hugh's throat.

When the call to arms had come, his parents had dug deep to furnish him and his brother with horse, weaponry and armour, so that they might serve the holy cause – recapture Jerusalem for Christ and Christendom! Now Hugh alone was home again, penniless, his only wealth oozing from the broken rind of a pomegranate. And was his surcoat too soaked, his soul too sodden, his scabbard too brimful of blood for him to enter heaven?

'Let me be sure I understand you,' Hugh said slowly and deliberately. 'The Church sends us to war, telling us that fighting for Christ will save our souls. Then, when we come home, you tell us we are sinners for taking lives? And must buy back our innocence with twelve pieces of silver?' Rage flashed behind his eyes as red as blood.

What hatred had he ever felt for the dark-faced strangers who had confronted him over the rim of his shield, who had crossed swords with him, whose thighs had touched his as their horses collided? What wrong had he ever felt he was righting? How holy had it ever felt to wipe the sweat from his lip and taste blood on his glove?

Now this fat abbot, smug and supercilious, was telling him it had been for nothing – for less than nothing – had fitted him for nothing but damnation, had earned him nothing but the tortures of hell. And was his brother even now roasting in hell, for killing Moors at the Holy Church's command?

A red fog clouded Hugh's eyes. The same fog had helped him face a charging horde of Arab horsemen without turning tail, had let him torch a village and trample the dead under his horse's hoofs. Now it blinded him to the sacredness of his surroundings, the light-pierced beauty of the nave, the reverent respect owed to a minister of God. Hugh went for his sword. But of course he had laid it aside. His scabbard was empty.

All of a sudden, something flew through the sun-filled slit of the window above him and landed on the floor of the nave with a crack. It was a rock. Hugh stared at it, bewildered. More rocks hit the outside of the wall, with a noise like hoofs clipping flint. The abbot moved with remarkable speed to push shut the open door, shooting the bolt just as someone tried to enter.

Fuddled by hunger and fatigue, Hugh was slow to grasp what was going on. 'Are we under attack?'

The abbot was running full tilt from font to vestry to transept, bolting doors, shouting as he did so, 'Three thousand years in hell to you all! Devil gripe you, you godless Gadarene swine!'

As more rocks rattled down round and about him, Hugh recovered himself. The red fog cleared.

He slipped back into the role of Christian knight defending the True Faith. Who but the wicked would attack a monastery chapel? He only wished he could have brought his poor mare indoors.

Cakes of dung and half a rusty ploughshare came through the lancet windows. He retreated to the centre of the nave. Fists were beating on all the doors now, filling the nave with a clamour that reverberated through the choir stalls and up the yawning emptiness of the bell-tower. Birds and bats swooped in terror through the nave. Hugh's sword still lay by the font.

'Scum! Vermin! Devil slit you, you heathen plague rats!' bawled the abbot, his voice cracking like an old stirrup leather. 'By bell, book and candle I cut you off from all hope of heaven!' He ran to the vestry and fetched out a richly embroidered surplice.

At least the man means to die in the robes of his calling! thought Hugh. And he resolved to do his Christian duty as a knight and defend the abbot with his life's blood against whatever godless fiends were outside.

The fiends outside seemed to care nothing about damnation, but redoubled their efforts to break in. A tree branch hit the window and fell back on to the person who had thrown it, who cursed.

'Who *are* *they*?' Hugh asked. In his weary bewilderment he had begun to imagine Moorish faces, Moorish swords, Moorish pavilions massing outside this English monastery.

'The devil's brood, that's who!' panted the abbot, kneeling beside a gigantic coffer by the door, rattling a key in its lock. It was an intricate lock, its workings a maze of rods and junctions and curlicues filling the lid of the chest. But at last the mechanism grated and clanked, and the hasp was free. The abbot threw open the lid and began pulling out various leather bags, jute sacks and church plate. 'They'd sooner buy cheese and ale than pay their tithes to me!' His spittle spattered the plates and chalices as he wrapped them in the embroidered surplice. As he worked, he shouted at the top of his voice: 'Sons of Gomorrah! Worshippers of Mammon!'

(Daughters of Gomorrah too, to judge by the shrill taunts coming through the lepers' window.) Who could they be, these witches and demons who felt no fear of God or His ministers?

'Thankless serpents and vipers!' hissed the abbot, knotting together the corners of the surplice and dragging it to the side door. 'You must hold them off, knight, while I ... while I ... save the treasures of St Ivo!' Suddenly remembering the saintly relic kept under the altar in a lead-lined casket, he dragged it out and shunted it down the choir, like a child trying to toboggan on thin snow. 'Want to kiss it?' he grunted.

Sir Hugh knelt and kissed the casket as it skidded past him, its hasp catching him a blow across the nose. The heart of St Ivo encased in lead made a screaming noise as the nails in its base scraped the marble floor.

'Why does no one come to our aid?' Hugh asked, realizing, for the first time, that he had seen no monks other than the abbot since riding up to the chapel door an hour before.

'Gone already – like rats from a leaky ship. Judgement fall on them! Fire and brimstone scorch their dirty hides!'

Hugh had the nightmarish impression that he must have brought war home with him, along with the lice in his hair, the fleas in his blanket, the ringworm in his horse. It was as if the ghostly spectre of war had ridden home behind him, sharing his saddle, resting its sharp chin on his shoulder. Now chaos would engulf the rolling green English countryside – and it would all be his fault!

'In the name of Christ, I charge you to defend this place!' commanded the abbot, thrusting Hugh's sword at him so that he dropped the pomegranate. 'I must save the relic of St Ivo! Defend this place, knight, and God will reward you!' And, dragging the heavy casket across the brass effigies in the aisle, the abbot disappeared into the shadowy transept.

And Hugh did wait, sword in hand.

A lifetime of obedience to the commands of Mother Church is not easily dislodged. Since childhood, the words 'Church' and 'Goodness' had been tangled tight in his breast: he was far too weary to wrench them apart now. Stones rattled down around him, and smoke began to crawl in under the doors. From time to time some kind of battering ram jarred the lock. Glancing down, Hugh saw that St Ivo's heart had crushed one half of the pomegranate and smeared it like blood and gristle across the brass faces of the dead.

The booming of the battering ram shook all logic out of his head. Once they broke in, how long could he last before they killed him? And even if he could kill every last one of them, how many more years would he have to suffer for it in purgatory before the sin was flayed from his soul?

He began to see demons clambering down the bell-ropes hand over hand, leering, jeering and cackling: *Got you! Tricked you! Fooled you! Caught you! Thou shalt not kill! Thou shalt not kill! We'll take you where we took your brother! Thou shalt not escape us now!* Hugh stood stock still, muscles so rigid, breath so pent, that he felt he was turning to stone like the effigies who lay along their tombs staring up into the vaulted roof. At last, with a splintering of wood, the door lurched open ...

***

After a moment, a flock of farm boys, reddlemen, shepherds, quarrymen, housewives, weavers, hedgers and children nosed their way nervously into the church. Not Moors, then, not savage, murderous heathens, thirsty for blood. Locals. The coloured light of the chapel washed over their faces and softened their scowls.

"Ems gone at last, then, them fat leeches?' called a tinsmith to the knight standing halfway up the aisle.

'Good riddance,' said a widow, devoutly crossing herself and curtseying to the altar. 'Helping themselves to anything they fancied. Breaking their vows. Dipping their hands in our pockets. Fleecing us these twenty years! Got no more conscience than dead ferrets, them beggars.'

They gathered glumly around the empty coffer until someone dragged it away as loot. The widow took the altar cloth, folding it four times and placing it on her head. There was little else left; the deserting monks had taken all they could carry.

Hugh watched them as he might people in a dream. He saw a miller step on the other half of the pomegranate and bend to study the mess, flummoxed by the oddness of what he had trodden in.

'Leeches, bleeding us white they were,' remarked a weaver, eyeing the knight's sword nervously as it twitched in his grasp. 'Had a bad harvest last year, but did they care 'bout our sorrows? Did they ask less? Did they tighten their belts? Not them! The religious life, they called it. We called it living off our backs. What's a monk anyway, but a man with a shaved head? Look at me.' And he showed the crown of his head where baldness had given him the look of a monk without the greedy, grasping nature of one. 'Do that give me the right to help myself to a slice of my neighbour's dinner?'

The widow came and peered at Hugh, her eyes straying over his features, and she absently licked a fingerful of apron and began to clean his face for him. 'Blessings on the Virgin Mary for bringing you safe home to your mother – whoever you are. I lost my men at Damascus. If you knows where in God's earth that is, you knows more than I do. These monks – they thinks up wars to take our husbands and sons from us, but they stays home themselves, living off the widows' sweat and toil!'

'No! Surely it was God above who ...' began Hugh but had to stop; the woman was busy folding back his lips to polish his teeth.

'Do not you believe it, lad! War's always the idea of men! God's just the excuse. Afterwards, men keeps the loot. All God gets is the blame.'

'Might be different, other places,' said the

reddleman, pursuing his own train of thought. 'Monks might be saints, some of 'em, for all I know. But here … We've had all of them we can stomach. Been like our own private war 'twixt them and us these two months past,' he explained to the knight. 'A nest of wasps is less of a curse than a nest of godless monks.'

A ploughboy armed with a mattock took a swing at the chain securing the font to the wall. He dislodged a cloud of plaster, and cracks spread out from the hole, crazing the *ex-votos* of a dozen Crusaders.

Then a stir of excitement fetched everyone to the side door of the chapel to see a thing of interest. The boy with the mattock prised open the casket and laid bare the heart of St Ivo. It had never meant as much to the abbot as saving his hide.

And to do that, he had helped himself to Hugh's mare and made good his escape.

THE WAR PRAYER

Mark Twain

It was a time of great and exalting excitement. The country was up in arms, the war was on, in every breast burned the holy fire of patriotism; the drums were beating, the bands playing, the toy pistols popping, the bunched firecrackers hissing and spluttering; on every hand and far down the receding and fading spread of roofs and balconies a fluttering wilderness of flags flashed in the sun; daily the young volunteers marched down the wide avenue gay and fine in their new uniforms, the proud fathers and mothers and sisters and sweethearts cheering them with voices choked with happy emotion as they swung by; nightly the packed mass meetings listened, panting, to patriot oratory which stirred the deepest deeps of their hearts, and which they interrupted at briefest intervals with cyclones of applause, the tears running down their cheeks the while; in the churches the pastors preached devotion to flag and country, and invoked the

God of Battles beseeching His aid in our good cause in outpourings of fervid eloquence which moved every listener. It was indeed a glad and gracious time, and the half dozen rash spirits that ventured to disapprove of the war and cast a doubt upon its righteousness straightway got such a stern and angry warning that for their personal safety's sake they quickly shrank out of sight and offended no more in that way.

Sunday morning came – next day the battalions would leave for the front; the church was filled; the volunteers were there, their young faces alight with martial dreams – visions of the stern advance, the gathering momentum, the rushing charge, the flashing sabres, the flight of the foe, the tumult, the enveloping smoke, the fierce pursuit, the surrender! Then home from the war, bronzed heroes, welcomed, adored, submerged in golden seas of glory! With the volunteers sat their dear ones, proud, happy, and envied by the neighbours and friends who had no sons and brothers to send forth to the field of honour, there to win for the flag, or, failing, die the noblest of noble deaths. The service proceeded; a war chapter from the Old Testament was read; the first prayer was said; it was followed by an organ burst that shook the building, and with one impulse the house rose, with glowing eyes and beating hearts, and poured out that tremendous invocation:

'God the all-terrible! Thou who ordainest! Thunder thy clarion and lightning thy sword!'

Then came the 'long' prayer. None could remember the like of it for passionate pleading and moving and beautiful language. The burden of its supplication was, that an ever-merciful and benignant Father of us all would watch over our noble young soldiers, and aid, comfort, and encourage them in their patriotic work; bless them, shield them in the day of battle and the hour of peril, bear them in His mighty hand, make them strong and confident, invincible in the bloody onset; help them to crush the foe, grant to them and to their flag and country imperishable honour and glory –

An aged stranger entered and moved with slow and noiseless step up the main aisle, his eyes fixed upon the minister, his long body clothed in a robe that reached to his feet, his head bare, his white hair descending in a frothy cataract to his shoulders, his seamy face unnaturally pale, pale even to ghastliness. With all eyes following him and wondering, he made his silent way; without pausing, he ascended to the preacher's side and stood there waiting. With shut lids the preacher, unconscious of his presence, continued with his moving prayer, and at last finished it with the words, uttered in fervent appeal, 'Bless our arms, grant us the victory, O Lord our God, Father and Protector of our land and flag!'

The stranger touched his arm, motioned him to step aside – which the startled minister did – and took his place. During some moments he surveyed the spellbound audience with solemn eyes, in which burned an uncanny light; then in a deep voice he said:

'I come from the Throne – bearing a message from Almighty God!' The words smote the house with a shock; if the stranger perceived it he gave no attention. 'He has heard the prayer of His servant your shepherd, and will grant it if such shall be your desire after I, His messenger, shall have explained to you its import – that is to say, its full import. For it is like unto many of the prayers of men, in that it asks for more than he who utters it is aware of – except he pause and think.

'God's servant and yours has prayed his prayer. Has he paused and taken thought? Is it one prayer? No, it is two – one uttered, the other not. Both have reached the ear of Him Who heareth all supplications, the spoken and the unspoken. Ponder this – keep it in mind. If you would beseech a blessing upon yourself, beware! lest without intent you invoke a curse upon a neighbour at the same time. If you pray for the blessing of rain upon your crop which needs it, by that act you are possibly praying for a curse upon some neighbour's crop which may not need rain and can be injured by it.

'You have heard your servant's prayer – the uttered part of it. I am commissioned of God to put into words the other part of it – that part which the pastor – and also you in your hearts – fervently prayed silently. And ignorantly and unthinkingly? God grant that it was so! You heard these words: "Grant us the victory, O Lord our God!" That is sufficient. The whole of the uttered prayer is compact into those pregnant words. Elaborations were not necessary. When you have prayed for victory you have prayed for many unmentioned results which follow victory – must follow it, cannot help but follow it. Upon the listening spirit of God fell also the unspoken part of the prayer. He commandeth me to put it into words. Listen!

'O Lord our Father, our young patriots, idols of our hearts, go forth to battle – be Thou near them! With them – in spirit – we also go forth from the sweet peace of our beloved firesides to smite the foe. O Lord our God, help us to tear their soldiers to bloody shreds with our shells; help us to cover their smiling fields with the pale forms of their patriot dead; help us to drown the thunder of the guns with the shrieks of their wounded, writhing in pain; help us to lay waste their humble homes with a hurricane of fire; help us to wring the hearts of their unoffending widows with unavailing grief; help us to turn them out roofless with little children to wander unfriended the wastes of their desolated land in rags and hunger and thirst, sports of the sun flames of summer and the icy winds of winter, broken in spirit, worn with travail, imploring Thee for the refuge of the grave and denied it – for our sakes who adore Thee, Lord, blast their hopes, blight their lives, protract their bitter pilgrimage, make heavy their steps, water their way with their tears, stain the white snow with the blood of their wounded feet! We ask it, in the spirit of love, of Him Who is the Source of Love, and Who is the ever-faithful refuge and friend of all that are sore beset and seek His aid with humble and contrite hearts. Amen.'

(After a pause)

'Ye have prayed it; if ye still desire it, speak! The messenger of the Most High waits!'

It was believed afterward that the man was a lunatic, because there was no sense in what he said.

INTRODUCTION

'The Princess Spy', Jamila Gavin
'His Last Bow', Arthur Conan Doyle

Few functions in war are quite so mysterious, so instinctively exciting, as that of the spy. On secret missions, undercover, behind enemy lines, they fight wars all on their own.

Sherlock Holmes is brought out of retirement in 'His Last Bow' to conduct a mission for the British during the First World War. Being Sherlock Holmes, of course, he is in possession of an instinct for brilliant disguises and a superhuman brain – the perfect spy!

Jamila Gavin's story about an eager young British agent captured by the Nazis in Paris is more brutal. Noor is not superhuman. She is mistrusted by her superiors, abandoned by her colleagues and tortured by her captors.

It would be interesting to consider the following two questions applied to each story:

Who is the spy ultimately loyal to?

In what way does the spy defeat the enemy?

THE PRINCESS SPY

Code Name: Madeleine

Jamila Gavin

Others think they know me
But I am mine; what I am, I am.

In the darkness I see no light. But there is a light in my soul which shines out and illumines my prison cell.

What can the tiger catch in the dark corners of his own lair?

In the darkness I hear no sound, but in my head I hear music, of course! Music.

Only sweet-voiced birds are imprisoned.

In my mouth I would taste only bitterness if I didn't have the memory of sweet almonds and lover's kisses.

They keep me chained to the wall like a savage dog, but I am a swallow, soaring, circling high on the air currents. Whatever they do to me, I will not let myself down. I have not betrayed my country, I have not betrayed my masters. I am a princess. The blood of the great Rajah, Tipoo Sultan, runs in my veins. I am of the warrior class. They can interrogate me all they want and torture me too, but I will not betray myself.

Her name was Noor.

Her father was an Indian prince, Hazrat Inayat Khan, a Muslim, a musician and a Sufi mystic. His reputation spread far and wide for his wise counselling – even as far as Moscow. There, the strange, powerful Russian Orthodox mystic monk, Rasputin, asked him to come to the Kremlin palace and bring his Sufi philosophy of peace and love to comfort the Tsar of All Russias, Tsar Nicholas, in his time of trouble. Russia was in turmoil. Nicholas didn't understand why. How could he, closed away in his palaces, as far removed from his people as the sun is from the earth?

So, along with his young American wife, Nora, Hazrat arrived in Moscow. Their first child, Noor, was born in the Kremlin palace on 2 January 1914; when Europe was bristling with quarrels, intrigues and assassinations, leading up to the outbreak of the First World War that August. Russia, too, was seething with unrest and things were leading inexorably towards revolution.

The stone walls surround me, yet the chains fall from my limbs and I am an infant again, crawling up the long scarlet-carpeted staircase in the Russian palace. There is an outburst of girlish laughter, and a flurry of princesses surround me like swans, gathering me up, pinching my cheeks and passing me round like a parcel: Olga, Tatiana, Maria and Anastasia. 'Let me hold her! Let me!' Their voices tinkle like bells.

'Darling Alexis!' The princesses draw in their little brother – their precious boy who, one day, will be Tsar of All Russias. 'Here. Careful now, don't drop her!' and I am passed into the arms of a boy who looks at me with sad, solemn eyes.

Their eyes gleam at me through the years of darkness. 'They came for us,' they seem to say. 'Now they have come for you.'

Look! There I am again, bundled up in furs, crammed in among the Russian princesses on the back of a sleigh, pulled by jingling horses, flying across the flat, white, rigid landscape, and plunging into birch forests, their branches drooping with snow. 'Baba Yaga, the witch, is after us,' they whispered in my ear, making me shriek with joyful terror.

They are all dead now. The tsar and his queen, my lovely swan princesses, all captured – not by Baba Yaga, but by the Bolshevik revolutionaries, who shot them all those years ago; Alexis too – my little tsaravitch.

My father's face bends over me so tenderly. His

beard is like a cloud and his dark eyes are deep pools of mystery. 'Go to sleep, my little hare,' he murmurs.

A hare? Am I the hare? Lord Buddha came as a hare, and was willing to allow himself to be eaten to feed a hungry person.

'Tell me another story,' she whimpers in the dark.

How she loved stories and made them tell her more, more, and when there were no more to tell, Noor made up her own.

Princess Noor was born to enchant. She was beautiful and talented. A child of the Muses – full of poetry, stories, dance and music. A child of rhythm – but a rhythm of her own – shy, soaring, circling among the ideas and philosophies that her father taught her.

How could her stiff English masters understand that?

When she stood before them – this dark, gleaming young woman who looked more suited to the bohemian cafes of Paris than the tight-lipped, English-public-school discipline of the War Office – they must have asked themselves, 'What on earth has she to offer?'

'Like the hare, my little princess, you can offer yourself.' My father's voice counselled me in my head.

Oh, why did you have to die, dear father?

He is the only one I weep for. My torturers have made me scream and cry as they have tried in vain to make me talk, but those tears are different; they are because of my physical pain. The pain which makes me truly weep is deeper; it is the pain of betrayal and because I no longer know who is my friend and who my enemy. It is the pain of loss because you are dead and gone. Oh, Papa! We were all thrown into such agony when we heard of your death in India while we were so far away from you in Paris. Mama locked herself away in her room and would not come out. We couldn't bear to think that never again would we hear your music, never again hear your deep, silken voice and listen to your wise words. Yet now, in this empty silence, you speak to me. You are here after all, to give me courage.

'Death is just stepping into the light, dear daughter. Remember the hare? As he entered the fire to give his body so that others could eat, the fairy of light came and made the flames as cool as water.'

We are waves whose stillness is non-being.

It was 1940. The Nazis had overrun almost the whole of Europe and were now at the gates of Paris. 'We have to leave immediately,' Noor begged her mother, who had shunned the world for twelve years, leaving Noor to be the responsible one. 'We must get out now.' With great difficulty, she persuaded her mother to flee. They all joined a long train of refugees and headed for the coast, and managed to get on to the last boat leaving for England. There, Noor and her brother wanted to help the war effort. He joined the Royal Air Force and she the Women's Auxiliary Air Force – the WAAF – and was assigned to its transport section. She was keen and dedicated. But surely she could do more?

Pinstripe-suited men discussed her, sitting on one side of a long, polished table. 'She asks to do more? We need more people in Paris. We could use her, perhaps.'

They summoned her before them.

Here in the darkness, Paris gleams out in my mind. Beautiful Paris. The boulevards are scattered with sunlight. I walk gaily, composing tunes in my head on my way to school, sniffing the honey-roasted peanuts they sell in the Luxembourg Gardens, as I cut through to St-Germain-des-Prés. I wriggle my fingers, remembering the exercises I have been practising. Paris is my home; it's where my friends are. It's where I feel alive and truly myself.

'If you send me to France, you are sending me home,' I told them.

***

'Let's see,' said Pinstripe, looking at the notes and files in front of him. 'You have been living in Paris with your mother, brother and sisters for the last seventeen years. Music student, writer of stories –' he glanced down at his notes – 'for children? You've broadcast on Paris radio – so your French is fluent – and you know the city well.'

'It's my home,' she repeated. 'I want to help.'

'Yes, well ...' They conferred while she waited outside. 'Perhaps she would be of use,' said one.

'It will be dangerous,' said another with some compassion. 'If they catch her, she'll be shot.'

'It's war. Sacrifices have to be made.'

To the men of the War Office she looked so unsuited to this work – too otherworldly, too innocent, too much of a butterfly. Not British. Most were sceptical. After all, they had never sent in a woman radio operative before. What's more, she was an Indian. India was already in conflict with the British – trying to kick them out of India. Could they be sure that she could be trusted?

'If she can't be trusted,' a cold, dark voice spoke, 'all the better for playing a game with, my dear.'

The game. What game? Everyone knew there was a game, but so few knew who the players were and what the rules of the game were.

'Send her into France as one of our operatives. Give her a radio. Ask her to send and receive messages. We'll send her information – false information. She's sure to be caught and sure to be interrogated. At first, she won't speak, but – I know these sorts of people – she'll crack. She'll spill the beans. But they'll be our beans, and they'll swallow them whole.'

So she received her instructions. 'We want you to go to France. Meet up with the Resistance; be a radio operative. You will be given a transmitter and will learn the radio game,' they told her.

She was registered in her mother's name – Norah Baker – and her training began. For long weeks, she learned how to operate the radio, how to use the codes and ciphers they would give her. They told her about the Resistance cells all over France, full of people working to free France and the rest of Europe from the Nazis.

She would have to be flown in at night, landing in a field. She would have to connect with other agents and sympathizers, and be part of a group. She must learn how to collect information and radio it back to them, to live a double life. Her cover name was to be Jeanne-Marie Regnier, her code name, 'Madeleine'.

I am flying, flying! How beautiful. The darkness of my cell is illumined by the moon. I felt close to heaven, then, as we flew; and close to you, Papa, with the stars all around and the sea glistening below. How small I felt too. Infinitesimal. How could I make any difference?

Yes, daughter, you are but a drop of water in an illimitable sea, but each drop is there to make up the consciousness of the whole ocean.

The world looked marvellously tranquil in the cloudy moonshine that June night, when the Lysander took off from England. So peaceful. Impossible to think of the terrors and dangers that awaited her.

Suddenly, from far below, a shower of sparks from a fire sprayed upwards into the air like fireflies. 'That's them!' muttered the pilot, and the little plane circled and dropped lower and lower. It hadn't seemed real till then. Just one of her stories in which she was a character – a heroine: brave, unafraid, ready to die for the good of the world. Suddenly, she felt terror.

Here in my dark silent cell, my heart is thumping. I am afraid again. They will come for me soon.

The wheels struck the ground. There was a fierce bumping as the Lysander hurtled over the rough field. The dark shadows of trees whipped by like a smear from a paintbrush. Would they ever stop? They stopped, but the propellers kept spinning. The engine noise sounded dangerously loud.

'Out, out!' they yelled, pushing Noor through the door.

She was already dressed to look like a nursemaid. She was to pretend to be on her way to Paris to look after an old lady. So she was wearing a war-worn but well-tailored suit, a beret over her black short hair and black walking shoes. She would look as if she was on her way back from leave. They tossed her suitcase out to her; shabby and scratched, but hidden within its false lining, under her nurse's apron and cap, were her transmitter and her instructions.

'You will meet Garry,' they had told her. 'Your network is called Prospero. He will take you to them.'

No sooner had she leaped to the ground than the Lysander was already moving again and was skyborne – before she'd even turned to meet the man standing in the shadows.

He grasped her hand in the darkness. '*Viens. Vite!*' He snatched her suitcase with his other hand and began to run, tugging her along. They must get away from the field. Someone may have heard the plane. The Germans could be on their way. Already Noor had a stitch in her side; she was bent double, gasping – but kept running, allowing him to drag her along, pushing her through hedges and over stiles. At last they reached a small clearing. A car was waiting. Someone opened the door. 'Get in.' The case was thrown into the boot, then they were off – driving without lights – and hit the road to Paris.

'Garry!' My heart is thumping again. I call out his name. It has a hollow ring in this dark stone cell. 'Where are you now?'

Where are any of them? Gilbert, Antoine, Marguerite, Valentin. Some are dead. She had only been in Paris a week when the Nazis rounded up nearly all of the cell called Prospero. There was treachery everywhere, but the Gestapo didn't know her yet, so she slipped away and kept up radio contact with London.

She moved from one dreary apartment to another, hanging her aerial out of the windows to pick up signals from London, while trying to evade the direction-finding trucks which roamed the streets listening out for illegal transmissions.

I can still laugh – a croaking, gulping, last-gasp laugh – when I remember one fool of a Nazi coming in on me as I tried to fix up my aerial. He thought it was a washing line and helped me.

She lived like this for three months, the only British radio operative in Paris still free, still transmitting to London – staying on air a few minutes at a time, then moving on. A man called 'B' arrived from England to check out what was left of the Resistance.

'Come home with me,' he advised. 'You know you'll be shot if they catch you?'

She refused. 'They don't know me. I can still go on working for you. There's no one else left. You need me.' So 'B' returned without her.

But the Nazis were after her. Somehow they got to know her code name – Madeleine. Someone had betrayed her. She arrived back to her apartment one day to find a Gestapo officer in her room.

'She was like a wild cat,' he had reported later. She fought and bit and tried to get out. 'I had to pull a gun on her.' He phoned for help and other officers arrived. They ransacked her room and found her transmitter, notebooks, codes and ciphers. They took her to their headquarters at the Avenue Foch for interrogation.

'Just tell us all you know. Give us names, contacts. Tell us what the British are planning to do.'

'My name is Norah Baker. My number is 9901 – assistant section officer for the Women's Auxiliary Air Force Transport Service,' was all she would tell them.

'You're a fool.' They shook their heads with false

pity. 'You'll soon speak. Take her away.'

She made another desperate attempt to escape by climbing through a window and slithering across the rooftops. But they caught her and dragged her back.

She was now classified as a 'dangerous prisoner'.

They hurt me, Papa. They hurt me so much.

'We already know everything,' sneered the Gestapo. 'Your colleague broke. We know all about the plans. You might as well give in and save yourself more pain.'

'My name is Norah Baker, number 9901 …' She refused to give more than her name, rank and number.

Her masters thought she would break in the end. It was part of the plan. She would pass on false information; would tell them there was a plan to invade, that the Allies would land in Calais – not Normandy. But after five weeks of fierce interrogation, she stayed silent.

Love is action; action is knowledge; knowledge is truth; truth is love.

She was put on a train to Karlsruhe in Germany. There she stayed for ten months, in solitary confinement, shackled in chains. In September 1944 she was put on another train.

So this is where I am, Papa; Dachau. Not many people walk out alive from here. There are three other women from my section. We will meet for the first time in a few moments. I can hear the first birdsong of dawn. Yes – even in my cell, their song reaches me. I hear footsteps. They are coming.

'Awake! For morning in the bowl of night has flung the stone that put the stars to flight.'

Four women were taken out at dawn to a place all strewn with sand.

The sand is stained with blood.
I am a hare.

They were told to kneel. Four women – strangers to each other till then – held hands like sisters and knelt down together. An SS man came up behind them and, one by one, shot them dead.

Postscript: Princess Noor Inayat Khan was posthumously awarded the George Cross by the British and the Croix de Guerre by the French.

HIS LAST BOW

An Epilogue of Sherlock Holmes

Arthur Conan Doyle

It was nine o'clock at night upon the second of August – the most terrible August in the history of the world. One might have thought already that God's curse hung heavy over a degenerate world, for there was an awesome hush and a feeling of vague expectancy in the sultry and stagnant air. The sun had long set, but one blood-red gash like an open wound lay low in the distant west. Above, the stars were shining brightly, and below, the lights of the shipping glimmered in the bay. The two famous Germans stood beside the stone parapet of the garden walk, with the long, low, heavily gabled house behind them, and they looked down upon the broad sweep of the beach at the foot of the great chalk cliff in which Von Bork, like some wandering eagle, had perched himself four years before. They stood with their heads close together, talking in low, confidential tones. From below the two glowing ends of their cigars might have been the smouldering eyes of some malignant fiend looking down in the darkness.

A remarkable man this Von Bork – a man who could hardly be matched among all the devoted agents of the Kaiser. It was his talents which had first recommended him for the English mission, the most important mission of all, but since he had taken it over those talents had become more and more manifest to the half-dozen people in the world who were really in touch with the truth. One of these was his present companion, Baron Von Herling, the chief secretary of the legation, whose huge 100-horse-power Benz car was blocking the country lane as it waited to waft its owner back to London.

'So far as I can judge the trend of events, you will probably be back in Berlin within the week,' the secretary was saying. 'When you get there, my dear Von Bork, I think you will be surprised at the welcome you will receive. I happen to know what is thought in the highest quarters of your work in this country.' He was a huge man, the secretary, deep, broad and tall, with a slow, heavy fashion of speech which had been his main asset in his political career.

Von Bork laughed.

'They are not very hard to deceive,' he remarked. 'A more docile, simple folk could not be imagined.'

'I don't know about that,' said the other

thoughtfully. 'They have strange limits and one must learn to observe them. It is that surface simplicity of theirs which makes a trap for the stranger. One's first impression is that they are entirely soft. Then one comes suddenly upon something very hard, and you know that you have reached the limit and must adapt yourself to the fact. They have, for example, their insular conventions which simply MUST be observed.'

'Meaning "good form" and that sort of thing?' Von Bork sighed as one who had suffered much.

'Meaning British prejudice in all its queer manifestations. As an example I may quote one of my own worst blunders – I can afford to talk of my blunders, for you know my work well enough to be aware of my successes. It was on my first arrival. I was invited to a weekend gathering at the country house of a cabinet minister. The conversation was amazingly indiscreet.'

Von Bork nodded. 'I've been there,' said he dryly.

'Exactly. Well, I naturally sent a resumé of the information to Berlin. Unfortunately our good chancellor is a little heavy-handed in these matters, and he transmitted a remark which showed that he was aware of what had been said. This, of course, took the trail straight up to me. You've no idea the harm that it did me. There was nothing soft about our

British hosts on that occasion, I can assure you. I was two years living it down. Now you, with this sporting pose of yours – '

'No, no, don't call it a pose. A pose is an artificial thing. This is quite natural. I am a born sportsman. I enjoy it.'

'Well, that makes it the more effective. You yacht against them, you hunt with them, you play polo, you match them in every game, your four-in-hand takes the prize at Olympia. I have even heard that you go the length of boxing with the young officers. What is the result? Nobody takes you seriously. You are a "good old sport", "quite a decent fellow for a German", a hard-drinking, night-club, knock-about-town, devil-may-care young fellow. And all the time this quiet country house of yours is the centre of half the mischief in England, and the sporting squire the most astute secret-service man in Europe. Genius, my dear Von Bork – genius!'

'You flatter me, Baron. But certainly I may claim my four years in this country have not been unproductive. I've never shown you my little store. Would you mind stepping in for a moment?'

The door of the study opened straight on to the terrace. Von Bork pushed it back, and, leading the way, he clicked the switch of the electric light. He then closed the door behind the bulky form which followed him and carefully adjusted the heavy curtain over the latticed window. Only when all these precautions had been taken and tested did he turn his sunburned aquiline face to his guest.

'Some of my papers have gone,' said he. 'When my wife and the household left yesterday for Flushing they took the less important with them. I must, of course, claim the protection of the embassy for the others.'

'Your name has already been filed as one of the personal suite. There will be no difficulties for you or your baggage. Of course, it is just possible that we may not have to go. England may leave France to her fate. We are sure that there is no binding treaty between them.'

'And Belgium?'

'Yes, and Belgium, too.'

Von Bork shook his head. 'I don't see how that could be. There is a definite treaty there. She could never recover from such a humiliation.'

'She would at least have peace for the moment.'

'But her honour?'

'Tut, my dear sir, we live in a utilitarian age. Honour is a medieval conception. Besides England is not ready. It is an inconceivable thing, but even our special war tax of fifty million, which one would think made our purpose as clear as if we had advertised it on the front page of the Times, has not roused these people from their slumbers. Here and there one hears a question. It is my business to find an answer. Here and there also there is an irritation. It is my business to soothe it. But I can assure you that so far as the essentials go – the storage of munitions, the preparation for submarine attack, the arrangements for making high explosives – nothing is prepared. How, then, can England come in, especially when we have stirred her up such a devil's brew of Irish civil war, window-breaking Furies, and God knows what to keep her thoughts at home.'

'She must think of her future.'

'Ah, that is another matter. I fancy that in the future we have our own very definite plans about England, and that your information will be very vital to us. It is today or tomorrow with Mr. John Bull. If he prefers today we are perfectly ready. If it is tomorrow we shall be more ready still. I should think they would be wiser to fight with allies than without them, but that is their own affair. This week is their week of destiny. But you were speaking of your papers.' He sat in the armchair with the light shining upon his broad bald head, while he puffed sedately at his cigar.

The large oak-panelled, book-lined room had a curtain hung in the further corner. When this was drawn it disclosed a large, brass-bound safe. Von

Bork detached a small key from his watch chain, and after some considerable manipulation of the lock he swung open the heavy door.

'Look!' said he, standing clear, with a wave of his hand.

The light shone vividly into the opened safe, and the secretary of the embassy gazed with an absorbed interest at the rows of stuffed pigeon-holes with which it was furnished. Each pigeon-hole had its label, and his eyes as he glanced along them read a long series of such titles as 'Fords', 'Harbour-defences', 'Aeroplanes', 'Ireland', 'Egypt', 'Portsmouth forts', 'The Channel', 'Rosythe' and a score of others. Each compartment was bristling with papers and plans.

'Colossal!' said the secretary. Putting down his cigar he softly clapped his fat hands.

'And all in four years, Baron. Not such a bad show for the hard-drinking, hard-riding country squire. But the gem of my collection is coming and there is the setting all ready for it.' He pointed to a space over which 'Naval Signals' was printed.

'But you have a good dossier there already.'

'Out of date and waste paper. The Admiralty in some way got the alarm and every code has been changed. It was a blow, Baron – the worst setback in my whole campaign. But thanks to my cheque-book and the good Altamont all will be well tonight.'

The Baron looked at his watch and gave a guttural exclamation of disappointment.

'Well, I really can wait no longer. You can imagine that things are moving at present in Carlton Terrace and that we have all to be at our posts. I had hoped to be able to bring news of your great coup. Did Altamont name no hour?'

Von Bork pushed over a telegram.

> Will come without fail to-night and bring new sparking plugs. Altamont.

'Sparking plugs, eh?'

'You see he poses as a motor expert and I keep a full garage. In our code everything likely to come up is named after some spare part. If he talks of a radiator it is a battleship, of an oil pump a cruiser, and so on. Sparking plugs are naval signals.'

'From Portsmouth at midday,' said the secretary, examining the superscription. 'By the way, what do you give him?'

'Five hundred pounds for this particular job. Of course he has a salary as well.'

'The greedy rogue. They are useful, these traitors, but I grudge them their blood money.'

'I grudge Altamont nothing. He is a wonderful worker. If I pay him well, at least he delivers the goods, to use his own phrase. Besides he is not a traitor. I assure you that our most pan-Germanic Junker is a sucking dove in his feelings towards England as compared with a real bitter Irish-American.'

'Oh, an Irish-American?'

'If you heard him talk you would not doubt it. Sometimes I assure you I can hardly understand him. He seems to have declared war on the King's English as well as on the English king. Must you really go? He may be here any moment.'

'No. I'm sorry, but I have already overstayed my time. We shall expect you early tomorrow, and when you get that signal book through the little door on the Duke of York's steps you can put a triumphant Finis to your record in England. What! Tokay!' He indicated a heavily sealed dust-covered bottle which stood with two high glasses upon a salver.

'May I offer you a glass before your journey?'

'No, thanks. But it looks like revelry.'

'Altamont has a nice taste in wines, and he took a fancy to my Tokay. He is a touchy fellow and needs humouring in small things. I have to study him, I assure you.' They had strolled out on to the terrace again, and along it to the further end where at a touch from the Baron's chauffeur the great car shivered and chuckled. 'Those are the lights of Harwich, I suppose,' said the secretary, pulling on his dust coat. 'How still and peaceful it all seems. There may be other lights within the week, and the English coast a less tranquil place! The heavens, too, may not be quite so peaceful if all that the good Zeppelin promises us comes true. By the way, who is that?'

Only one window showed a light behind them; in it there stood a lamp, and beside it, seated at a table, was a dear old ruddy-faced woman in a country cap. She was bending over her knitting and stopping occasionally to stroke a large black cat upon a stool beside her.

'That is Martha, the only servant I have left.'

The secretary chuckled.

'She might almost personify Britannia,' said he, 'with her complete self-absorption and general air of comfortable somnolence. Well, au revoir, Von Bork!' With a final wave of his hand he sprang into the car, and a moment later the two golden cones from the headlights shot through the darkness. The secretary lay back in the cushions of the luxurious limousine, with his thoughts so full of the impending European tragedy that he hardly observed that as his car swung round the village street it nearly passed over a little Ford coming in the opposite direction.

Von Bork walked slowly back to the study when the last gleams of the motor lamps had faded into the distance. As he passed he observed that his old housekeeper had put out her lamp and retired. It was a new experience to him, the silence and darkness of his widespread house, for his family and household had been a large one. It was a relief to him, however, to think that they were all in safety and that, but for that one old woman who had lingered in the kitchen, he had the whole place to himself. There was a good deal of tidying up to do inside his study and he set himself to do it until his keen, handsome face was flushed with the heat of the burning papers. A leather valise stood beside his table, and into this he began to pack very neatly and systematically the precious contents of his safe. He had hardly got started with the work, however, when his quick ears caught the sounds of a distant car. Instantly he gave an exclamation of satisfaction, strapped up the valise, shut the safe, locked it, and hurried out on to the terrace. He was just in time to see the lights of a small car come to a halt at the gate. A passenger sprang out of it and advanced swiftly towards him, while the chauffeur, a heavily built, elderly man with a grey moustache, settled down like one who resigns himself to a long vigil.

'Well?' asked Von Bork eagerly, running forward to meet his visitor.

For answer the man waved a small brown-paper parcel triumphantly above his head.

'You can give me the glad hand tonight, mister,' he cried. 'I'm bringing home the bacon at last.'

'The signals?'

'Same as I said in my cable. Every last one of them, semaphore, lamp code, Marconi – a copy, mind you, not the original. That was too dangerous. But it's the real goods, and you can lay to that.' He slapped the German upon the shoulder with a rough familiarity from which the other winced.

'Come in,' he said. 'I'm all alone in the house. I was only waiting for this. Of course a copy is better than the original. If an original were missing they would change the whole thing. You think it's all safe about the copy?'

The Irish-American had entered the study and stretched his long limbs from the armchair. He was a tall, gaunt man of sixty, with clear-cut features and a small goatee beard which gave him a general resemblance to the caricatures of Uncle Sam. A half-smoked, sodden cigar hung from the corner of his mouth, and as he sat down he struck a match and relit it. 'Making ready for a move?' he remarked as he looked round him. 'Say, mister,' he added, as his eyes fell upon the safe from which the curtain was now removed, 'you don't tell me you keep your papers in that?'

'Why not?'

'Gosh, in a wide-open contraption like that! And they reckon you to be some spy. Why, a Yankee crook would be into that with a can-opener. If I'd known that any letter of mine was goin' to lie loose in a thing like that I'd have been a mug to write to you at all.'

'It would puzzle any crook to force that safe,' Von Bork answered. 'You won't cut that metal with any tool.'

'But the lock?'

'No, it's a double combination lock. You know what that is?'

'Search me,' said the American.

'Well, you need a word as well as a set of figures before you can get the lock to work.' He rose and showed a double-radiating disc round the keyhole. 'This outer one is for the letters, the inner one for the figures.'

'Well, well, that's fine.'

'So it's not quite as simple as you thought. It was four years ago that I had it made, and what do you think I chose for the word and figures?'

'It's beyond me.'

'Well, I chose August for the word, and 1914 for the figures, and here we are.'

The American's face showed his surprise and admiration.

'My, but that was smart! You had it down to a fine thing.'

'Yes, a few of us even then could have guessed the date. Here it is, and I'm shutting down tomorrow morning.'

'Well, I guess you'll have to fix me up also. I'm not staying in this goldarned country all on my lonesome. In a week or less, from what I see, John Bull will be on his hind legs and fair ramping. I'd rather watch him from over the water.'

'But you're an American citizen?'

'Well, so was Jack James an American citizen, but he's doing time in Portland all the same. It cuts no ice with a British copper to tell him you're an American citizen. "It's British law and order over here," says he. By the way, mister, talking of Jack James, it seems to me you don't do much to cover your men.'

'What do you mean?' Von Bork asked sharply.

'Well, you are their employer, ain't you? It's up to you to see that they don't fall down. But they do fall down, and when did you ever pick them up? There's James – '

'It was James's own fault. You know that yourself. He was too self-willed for the job.'

'James was a bonehead – I give you that. Then there was Hollis.'

'The man was mad.'

'Well, he went a bit woozy towards the end. It's enough to make a man bug-house when he has to play a part from morning to night with a hundred guys all ready to set the coppers wise to him. But now there is Steiner – '

Von Bork started violently, and his ruddy face turned a shade paler.

'What about Steiner?'

'Well, they've got him, that's all. They raided his store last night, and he and his papers are all in Portsmouth jail. You'll go off and he, poor devil, will have to stand the racket, and lucky if he gets off with his life. That's why I want to get over the water as soon as you do.'

Von Bork was a strong, self-contained man, but it was easy to see that the news had shaken him.

'How could they have got on to Steiner?' he muttered. 'That's the worst blow yet.'

'Well, you nearly had a worse one, for I believe they are not far off me.'

'You don't mean that!'

'Sure thing. My landlady down Fratton way had some inquiries, and when I heard of it I guessed it was time for me to hustle. But what I want to know, mister, is how the coppers know these things? Steiner is the fifth man you've lost since I signed on with you, and I know the name of the sixth if I don't get a move on. How do you explain it, and ain't you ashamed to see your men go down like this?'

Von Bork flushed crimson.

'How dare you speak in such a way!'

'If I didn't dare things, mister, I wouldn't be in your service. But I'll tell you straight what is in my mind. I've heard that with you German politicians when an agent has done his work you are not sorry to see him put away.'

Von Bork sprang to his feet.

'Do you dare to suggest that I have given away my own agents!'

'I don't stand for that, mister, but there's a stool pigeon or a cross somewhere, and it's up to you to find out where it is. Anyhow I am taking no more chances. It's me for little Holland, and the sooner the better.'

Von Bork had mastered his anger.

'We have been allies too long to quarrel now at the very hour of victory,' he said. 'You've done splendid work and taken risks, and I can't forget it. By all means go to Holland, and you can get a boat from Rotterdam to New York. No other line will be safe a week from now. I'll take that book and pack it with the rest.'

The American held the small parcel in his hand, but made no motion to give it up.

'What about the dough?' he asked.

'The what?'

'The boodle. The reward. The 500 pounds. The

gunner turned damned nasty at the last, and I had to square him with an extra hundred dollars or it would have been nitsky for you and me. "Nothin' doin'!" says he, and he meant it, too, but the last hundred did it. It's cost me two hundred pound from first to last, so it isn't likely I'd give it up without gettin' my wad.'

Von Bork smiled with some bitterness. 'You don't seem to have a very high opinion of my honour,' said he, 'you want the money before you give up the book.'

'Well, mister, it is a business proposition.'

'All right. Have your way.' He sat down at the table and scribbled a cheque, which he tore from the book, but he refrained from handing it to his companion. 'After all, since we are to be on such terms, Mr. Altamont,' said he, 'I don't see why I should trust you any more than you trust me. Do you understand?' he added, looking back over his shoulder at the American. 'There's the cheque upon the table. I claim the right to examine that parcel before you pick the money up.'

The American passed it over without a word. Von Bork undid a winding of string and two wrappers of paper. Then he sat gazing for a moment in silent amazement at a small blue book which lay before him. Across the cover was printed in golden letters Practical Handbook of Bee Culture. Only for one instant did the master spy glare at this strangely irrelevant inscription. The next he was gripped at the back of his neck by a grasp of iron, and a chloroformed sponge was held in front of his writhing face.

'Another glass, Watson!' said Mr. Sherlock Holmes as he extended the bottle of Imperial Tokay.

The thickset chauffeur, who had seated himself by the table, pushed forward his glass with some eagerness.

'It is a good wine, Holmes.'

'A remarkable wine, Watson. Our friend upon the sofa has assured me that it is from Franz Josef's special cellar at the Schoenbrunn Palace. Might I trouble you to open the window, for chloroform vapour does not help the palate.'

The safe was ajar, and Holmes standing in front of it was removing dossier after dossier, swiftly examining each, and then packing it neatly in Von Bork's valise. The German lay upon the sofa sleeping stertorously with a strap round his upper arms and another round his legs.

'We need not hurry ourselves, Watson. We are safe from interruption. Would you mind touching the bell? There is no one in the house except old Martha, who has played her part to admiration. I got her the situation here when first I took the matter up. Ah, Martha, you will be glad to hear that all is well.'

The pleasant old lady had appeared in the doorway.

She curtseyed with a smile to Mr. Holmes, but glanced with some apprehension at the figure upon the sofa.

'It is all right, Martha. He has not been hurt at all.'

'I am glad of that, Mr. Holmes. According to his lights he has been a kind master. He wanted me to go with his wife to Germany yesterday, but that would hardly have suited your plans, would it, sir?'

'No, indeed, Martha. So long as you were here I was easy in my mind. We waited some time for your signal tonight.'

'It was the secretary, sir.'

'I know. His car passed ours.'

'I thought he would never go. I knew that it would not suit your plans, sir, to find him here.'

'No, indeed. Well, it only meant that we waited half an hour or so until I saw your lamp go out and knew that the coast was clear. You can report to me tomorrow in London, Martha, at Claridge's Hotel.'

'Very good, sir.'

'I suppose you have everything ready to leave.'

'Yes, sir. He posted seven letters today. I have the addresses as usual.'

'Very good, Martha. I will look into them tomorrow. Goodnight. These papers,' he continued as the old lady vanished, 'are not of very great importance, for, of course, the information which they represent has been sent off long ago to the German government.

These are the originals which could not safely be got out of the country.'

'Then they are of no use.'

'I should not go so far as to say that, Watson. They will at least show our people what is known and what is not. I may say that a good many of these papers have come through me, and I need not add are thoroughly untrustworthy. It would brighten my declining years to see a German cruiser navigating the Solent according to the mine-field plans which I have furnished. But you, Watson' – he stopped his work and took his old friend by the shoulders – 'I've hardly seen you in the light yet. How have the years used you? You look the same blithe boy as ever.'

'I feel twenty years younger, Holmes. I have seldom felt so happy as when I got your wire asking me to meet you at Harwich with the car. But you, Holmes – you have changed very little – save for that horrible goatee.'

'These are the sacrifices one makes for one's country, Watson,' said Holmes, pulling at his little tuft. 'Tomorrow it will be but a dreadful memory. With my hair cut and a few other superficial changes I shall no doubt reappear at Claridge's tomorrow as I was before this American stunt – I beg your pardon, Watson, my well of English seems to be permanently defiled – before this American job came my way.'

'But you have retired, Holmes. We heard of you as living the life of a hermit among your bees and your books in a small farm upon the South Downs.'

'Exactly, Watson. Here is the fruit of my leisured ease, the magnum opus of my latter years!' He picked up the volume from the table and read out the whole title, Practical Handbook of Bee Culture, with Some Observations upon the Segregation of the Queen. 'Alone I did it. Behold the fruit of pensive nights and laborious days when I watched the little working gangs as once I watched the criminal world of London.'

'But how did you get to work again?'

'Ah, I have often marvelled at it myself. The Foreign Minister alone I could have withstood, but when the Premier also deigned to visit my humble roof – ! The fact is, Watson, that this gentleman upon the sofa was a bit too good for our people. He was in a class by himself. Things were going wrong, and no one could understand why they were going wrong. Agents were suspected or even caught, but there was evidence of some strong and secret central force. It was absolutely necessary to expose it. Strong pressure was brought upon me to look into the matter. It has cost me two years, Watson, but they have not been devoid of excitement. When I say that I started my pilgrimage at Chicago, graduated in an Irish secret society at Buffalo, gave serious trouble to the constabulary at

Skibbareen, and so eventually caught the eye of a subordinate agent of Von Bork, who recommended me as a likely man, you will realise that the matter was complex. Since then I have been honoured by his confidence, which has not prevented most of his plans going subtly wrong and five of his best agents being in prison. I watched them, Watson, and I picked them as they ripened. Well, sir, I hope that you are none the worse!'

The last remark was addressed to Von Bork himself, who after much gasping and blinking had lain quietly listening to Holmes's statement. He broke out now into a furious stream of German invective, his face convulsed with passion. Holmes continued his swift investigation of documents while his prisoner cursed and swore.

'Though unmusical, German is the most expressive of all languages,' he observed when Von Bork had stopped from pure exhaustion. 'Hullo! Hullo!' he added as he looked hard at the corner of a tracing before putting it in the box. 'This should put another bird in the cage. I had no idea that the paymaster was such a rascal, though I have long had an eye upon him. Mister Von Bork, you have a great deal to answer for.'

The prisoner had raised himself with some difficulty upon the sofa and was staring with a strange mixture of amazement and hatred at his captor.

'I shall get level with you, Altamont,' he said, speaking with slow deliberation. 'If it takes me all my life I shall get level with you!'

'The old sweet song,' said Holmes. 'How often have I heard it in days gone by. It was a favourite ditty of the late lamented Professor Moriarty. Colonel Sebastian Moran has also been known to warble it. And yet I live and keep bees upon the South Downs.'

'Curse you, you double traitor!' cried the German, straining against his bonds and glaring murder from his furious eyes.

'No, no, it is not so bad as that,' said Holmes, smiling. 'As my speech surely shows you, Mr. Altamont of Chicago had no existence in fact. I used him and he is gone.'

'Then who are you?'

'It is really immaterial who I am, but since the matter seems to interest you, Mr. Von Bork, I may say that this is not my first acquaintance with the members of your family. I have done a good deal of business in Germany in the past and my name is probably familiar to you.'

'I would wish to know it,' said the Prussian grimly.

'It was I who brought about the separation between Irene Adler and the late King of Bohemia when your cousin Heinrich was the Imperial Envoy. It was I also who saved from murder, by the Nihilist Klopman,

Count Von und Zu Grafenstein, who was your mother's elder brother. It was I – '

Von Bork sat up in amazement.

'There is only one man,' he cried.

'Exactly,' said Holmes.

Von Bork groaned and sank back on the sofa. 'And most of that information came through you,' he cried. 'What is it worth? What have I done? It is my ruin forever!'

'It is certainly a little untrustworthy,' said Holmes. 'It will require some checking and you have little time to check it. Your admiral may find the new guns rather larger than he expects, and the cruisers perhaps a trifle faster.'

Von Bork clutched at his own throat in despair.

'There are a good many other points of detail which will, no doubt, come to light in good time. But you have one quality which is very rare in a German, Mr. Von Bork: you are a sportsman and you will bear me no ill-will when you realise that you, who have outwitted so many other people, have at last been outwitted yourself. After all, you have done your best for your country, and I have done my best for mine, and what could be more natural? Besides,' he added, not unkindly, as he laid his hand upon the shoulder of the prostrate man, 'it is better than to fall before some ignoble foe. These papers are now ready, Watson. If you will help me with our prisoner, I think that we may get started for London at once.'

It was no easy task to move Von Bork, for he was a strong and a desperate man. Finally, holding either arm, the two friends walked him very slowly down the garden walk which he had trod with such proud confidence when he received the congratulations of the famous diplomatist only a few hours before. After a short, final struggle he was hoisted, still bound hand and foot, into the spare seat of the little car. His precious valise was wedged in beside him.

'I trust that you are as comfortable as circumstances permit,' said Holmes when the final arrangements were made. 'Should I be guilty of a liberty if I lit a cigar and placed it between your lips?'

But all amenities were wasted upon the angry German.

'I suppose you realise, Mr. Sherlock Holmes,' said he, 'that if your government bears you out in this treatment it becomes an act of war.'

'What about your government and all this treatment?' said Holmes, tapping the valise.

'You are a private individual. You have no warrant for my arrest. The whole proceeding is absolutely illegal and outrageous.'

'Absolutely,' said Holmes.

'Kidnapping a German subject.'

'And stealing his private papers.'

'Well, you realise your position, you and your accomplice here. If I were to shout for help as we pass through the village –'

'My dear sir, if you did anything so foolish you would probably enlarge the two limited titles of our village inns by giving us "The Dangling Prussian" as a signpost. The Englishman is a patient creature, but at present his temper is a little inflamed, and it would be as well not to try him too far. No, Mr. Von Bork, you will go with us in a quiet, sensible fashion to Scotland Yard, whence you can send for your friend, Baron Von Herling, and see if even now you may not fill that place which he has reserved for you in the ambassadorial suite. As to you, Watson, you are joining us with your old service, as I understand, so London won't be out of your way. Stand with me here upon the terrace, for it may be the last quiet talk that we shall ever have.'

The two friends chatted in intimate converse for a few minutes, recalling once again the days of the past, while their prisoner vainly wriggled to undo the bonds that held him. As they turned to the car Holmes pointed back to the moonlit sea and shook a thoughtful head.

'There's an east wind coming, Watson.'

'I think not, Holmes. It is very warm.'

'Good old Watson! You are the one fixed point in a changing age. There's an east wind coming all the same, such a wind as never blew on England yet. It will be cold and bitter, Watson, and a good many of us may wither before its blast. But it's God's own wind none the less, and a cleaner, better, stronger land will lie in the sunshine when the storm has cleared. Start her up, Watson, for it's time that we were on our way. I have a cheque for five hundred pounds which should be cashed early, for the drawer is quite capable of stopping it if he can.'

INTRODUCTION

'A Place on the Piano', Eva Ibbotson
'Swept and Garnished', Rudyard Kipling

Rudyard Kipling was one of the most famous authors of his day, loved for his children's stories and also his depictions of the British Empire. At the outbreak of the First World War, Kipling was a fierce believer that the British must fight, and much of his writing at this time took the form of war propaganda. 'Swept and Garnished' uses the horrible image of children displaced and injured at the hands of the enemy to prompt readers to take up arms and retaliate.

Eva Ibbotson's story deals with another child who has been made orphan and homeless by war. In a grand gesture, a wealthy English family decide to retrieve and adopt the child, but when she is found she has already been saved.

What reactions do you think the authors want people back home to have to these stories?

A PLACE ON THE PIANO

Eva Ibbotson

I always thought the war would end suddenly but it didn't – it sort of dribbled away. Six months after I stood with the other boys in my class outside Buckingham Palace – yelling for the king and queen because we'd defeated Hitler – the barrage balloons still floated like great silver grandfathers over the roofs of London. The park railings were still missing, St Paul's cathedral stood in a sea of rubble and there was nothing to be bought in the shops.

My teacher had explained it to me. 'Wars are expensive, Michael,' he said. 'They have to be paid for.'

Rationing got tighter – you still had to have coupons for clothes and fuel. Worst of all was the food. You could hardly see the meat ration with the naked eye, and some very weird things were issued by the government for us to eat. Tinned snoek, for example. Snoek is a South African fish and when Cook opened the tin it turned out to be a bluish animal with terrifying spikes, swimming in a sea of gelatinous goo – and the smell was unspeakable.

'This time they've gone too far,' she said, and she tried to give it to the cat, who sneered and turned away.

I knew quite a lot about rationing because I was a sort of kitchen boy. Not that I worked in the kitchen exactly; I'd just won a scholarship to the grammar school, but I lived below stairs in the basement of a large house belonging to a family called Glossop, where my mother was the housekeeper. We'd lived there, in London, all through the war.

I remember the snoek particularly because we were just wondering what to do with it when the bell went and my mother was called upstairs.

When she came back she looked really happy and excited. 'Little Marianne Gerstenberger has been found. She's alive!'

It was incredible news. Marianne had been thrown out of a cattle train when she was a baby. It was her own mother who had done it. She'd been rounded up with some other Jews and she was on her way to a concentration camp when she found a weak place in one of the boards behind the latrine. She got the others to help her work on it to make a small hole. And then she bundled up the baby, and when the train stopped for a moment she managed to push her out on to the track.

We'd heard a lot about bravery during the last six years of war: soldiers in Burma stumbling on, dying of thirst; parachutists at Arnheim, and of course the Spitfire pilots who had saved us in the Blitz. But the story of Marianne caught us all.

'To do that,' said my mother, 'to push your own baby out on to the track because you knew you were going to your death ...'

At first my mother had tried not to speak of what had happened when Hitler went mad and tried to exterminate the Jews. But my school was the kind where they told you things, and I'd seen the newsreels. I'd seen the bodies piled up when the Allies opened up the camps, and the skeletons which were supposed to be people. Marianne's parents had both perished, but now, as the news came through from the Red Cross in Switzerland, it seemed that the baby had survived. She had been found by a peasant family who had taken her in and was living in East Germany, close to the border with Poland.

'They're going to fetch her,' said my mother. 'They're going to take her in.' And there were tears in her eyes.

'They' were her employers – the Glossops – who lived in the house above us and who she served. The Glossops were not Jewish, but Marianne's mother had been married to the son of their Jewish business partners in Berlin. Glossop and Gerstenberger had been a well-known firm of exporters.

'They're going to adopt her,' my mother went on. She didn't often speak warmly about the Glossops, but I could hear the admiration in her voice.

'She'll live like a little princess,' said Cook. 'Imagine, after being brought up with peasants.'

Everyone agreed with this: the kids in my school, the people in the shops, the tradesmen who came to deliver goods to the basement. Because the Glossops weren't just well off, they were properly rich. Their house was the largest in the square, double-fronted – and furnished as though the war had never been. To go up the service stairs and through the green baize door into the house was like stepping into a different world.

Mrs Glossop and her mother-in-law had spent the war in a hotel in the Lake District to get away from the bombs; and her daughter, Daphne, who was ten years old, had been away at boarding school, but the house had stayed open because Mr Glossop used it when he was in town on business, which meant that the servants had to keep it ready for him whenever he wanted.

So my mother and I went upstairs most days to check the blackout curtains and make sure the shutters were closed and none of the window panes had cracked in the raids – and I knew the house as well as I knew the dark rooms in the basement where we lived, along with the cook and old Tom, the chauffeur-handyman.

I knew the dining room with its heavy button-backed chairs and the carved sideboard where they kept the napkin rings and the cruets which Tom polished every week. I knew the drawing room with its thick Turkish carpet and massive sofas – and I knew old Mrs Glossop's boudoir on the first floor with the gilt mirrors and clawfooted tables – and the piano.

I knew the piano very well. I remember once when I was upstairs helping my mother I heard a V1 rocket cut out above me, which meant I had about half a minute before it came down and exploded – and without thinking I dived under the piano.

It was an enormous piano – a Steinway Concert Grand – but I'd never heard anybody play it. It was a piano for keeping relations on. On the dark red chenille cover which protected it were rows of Glossops in silver frames: old Glossops and young ones, Glossops on their horses and Glossops in their university gowns. There were Glossop children in their school uniforms or holding cricket bats, and there were Glossop women in their presentation dresses ready to go to court. There was even a Glossop who had been knighted, and as I lay there, waiting for the bomb to fall, I wasn't in the least bit scared – I didn't feel anyone would dare to destroy a whole army of Glossops, and I was right. The rocket came down three streets away.

And now Marianne Gerstenberger, who was just seven years old, would have her own place on the piano, and be a Glossop too.

The preparations for Marianne began straightaway, and we all threw ourselves into the work. It may sound silly, but I think it was then that we realized that the war was well and truly over, and that good things were happening in the world.

'We'll put her in the room next to Daphne's,' said Mrs Glossop – and she gave my mother a list of all the things that needed to be done. New curtains of pale blue satin to be sewn, and the bed canopied with the same material. A white fur rug on the floor, the walls repapered with a design of forget-me-nots and rosebuds, and a new dressing table to be lined with a matching pattern. Furniture was difficult to get – you had to have coupons for almost everything – but when you own three department stores the rules don't really apply. The Glossops had always had everything they wanted, and that included food. Parcels from America had come all through the war and they were coming still.

'She can have my dolls – I don't play with them any more,' said Daphne, but Mrs Glossop ordered a whole batch of new dolls and fluffy toys and games from the store.

'Of course she'll be a little savage,' said old Mrs Glossop. 'We must be patient with her.'

She sent my mother out to get one of the napkin rings engraved with Marianne's name and I imagined the little girl sitting in the big solemn dining room with all the Glossop ancestors looking down from the wall, carefully rolling up her damask napkin after every meal.

Actually, I knew exactly the sort of life Marianne was going to lead, because of Daphne.

Daphne didn't speak to me much; she was not the sort of girl who spoke to servants. A year earlier I'd pulled off an Alsatian who was holding her at bay as she played in the gardens of the square, and got quite badly bitten, and while my hands were bandaged she was positively friendly, but it didn't last.

Mostly Daphne was away at boarding school, but when she was at home she led a very busy life. On Saturday morning she put on her jodhpurs and Tom drove her to the park where she went riding – trotting down the sanded paths and greeting other children on well-groomed ponies. On Monday afternoon, she carried her dancing shoes in a velvet bag to Miss Bigelow's Academy and learned ballet, and on Thursdays she did elocution with a lady called Madame Farnari.

Marianne would do all this – but not for long, because as soon as she had her eighth birthday she would be taken to a school outfitter to buy a brown velour hat and a brown gymslip and a hockey stick and go off with Daphne to St Hilda's, where the school motto was 'Play straight and play the game'.

'When you think what that school costs, and the kind of children who go there – all those honourables and what have you – it'll be a wonderful thing for the little thing,' said old Tom, the chauffeur. 'Mind you, she'll have a lot to learn.'

As it turned out, we had several months to get ready for Marianne, because even the Glossops didn't find it easy to get the passports and permits and papers that were needed to bring Marianne to Britain. Things were made more difficult because the village where Marianne now lived was in the part of Germany that was occupied by the Russians and they were very strict about who could come into their zone and who could not.

But at last a permit came through, allowing two people to travel to Orthausen and pick up the little girl. The permit was for a particular week in July and now my mother was sent for again. What's more, she was asked to sit down, which was unusual.

'It's so awkward, such a nuisance,' said Mrs Glossop to my mother. 'But the permit covers the day of the royal garden party and I've been asked to attend. I simply couldn't miss that – and two days later it's Daphne's prize-giving at St Hilda's and of course I must go down for that.'

My mother waited, wondering why she had been summoned.

'My husband would go and fetch the little girl, but he has the annual meeting of the cricket club and then a very important Rotary dinner in Aberdeen at which he's been asked to speak.' She bent forward and fixed my mother with a stern eye. 'So I want you to fetch Marianne. It's so convenient because you speak German.'

This was true. My mother had been studying modern languages at university when my father had married and deserted her, all in three months.

But my mother said she couldn't leave me. This was nonsense, of course, but she said it very firmly. I think she felt that the Glossops should go themselves to fetch their new daughter – or perhaps she was nervous. Since my father betrayed her, she had looked for a quiet life – a life where the two of us would be safe.

'Well, the permit is for two people. I don't see why Michael shouldn't go with you; we don't have to say that he's only twelve years old.'

So it was my mother and I who went to fetch Marianne Gerstenberger, but before we left we were given some very important instructions.

'Marianne has a birthmark on her arm,' said Mrs Glossop. 'Her mother wrote to us about it when she was born. It's on her right arm and it runs from her shoulder to her elbow – and you must make absolutely sure that she does have that mark and in the right place. It's one thing to adopt the daughter of one's husband's partner and another to take in any stray that wants a comfortable home.' And she told us that though Marianne's name had been pinned to her blanket, it was possible that in those frightful times the baby's things had been stolen and given to some other child.

'We will make sure,' promised my mother – and two weeks later we set off.

It was quite a journey. Ordinary people hadn't been allowed to travel all through the war and of course I was excited, crossing the Channel, getting a train to go through the Netherlands and Germany.

Or rather, five trains. Most of the rolling stock had been destroyed in Allied bombing raids. We stopped and started and were pushed out on to the platform and back in again. There was no food to be had on the train, or water, and I couldn't help wondering if it was because she knew how uncomfortable the journey was going to be that Mrs Glossop had decided to send my mother instead. We went through towns that were nothing but heaps of rubble and countryside with burnt and empty fields. It was odd to think that it was we who had caused all this destruction. I'd thought of bombing as something that the Germans did.

We spent the night in a cold and gloomy little hotel on the Belgian border, and the next day we travelled east through Germany.

I asked my mother if this was the route that Marianne's mother would have travelled on her last journey but she didn't know.

We were going through farmland now: fields and copses and little villages. The houses looked poor and small but there were a few animals: cows and sheep. The peasants were struggling to get back to a normal life.

We had to change twice more on to branch lines, travelling on trains so old that we didn't think they would manage to pull their loads. Then in the late afternoon we reached Orthausen.

The village that Marianne lived in was not directly on the railway. The woman who found her must have carried her bundle a long way to her house. My mother and I now walked that road, trudging along the white dust village street with our bags and turning off along a track which ran beside a stream.

Then, late in the afternoon, we crossed a small bridge and came to a wooden house standing by itself in a clearing.

Marianne was sitting on the steps of the porch. She was holding a tortoiseshell kitten on her lap and talking to it – not fussing over it, just telling it to behave. She spoke in German, but I knew exactly what she was saying.

She had thick, fawn, curly hair and brown eyes and she wore a dirndl, and over it a knitted jersey which covered her arms. When she saw us she put down the kitten and then she reached for the bag my mother carried and led us into the house.

The woman who had found Marianne on the railway track was called Mrs Wasilewski. She was very pale with a screwed-down bun of fair hair and a tight mouth. To me she looked like a death's head, so white and forbidding, and I was glad that we were going to take Marianne away from such a cold, stern woman. But Marianne went up to her trustingly and said, here were the visitors from England, and I realized that she did not yet know why we had come.

Mrs Wasilewski offered us some ersatz coffee and slices of dark bread spread with dripping. Her husband was away, working in a sawmill in the north of the country for the summer, to earn some extra money. When we had eaten, Marianne turned to me and took me by the hand, and said, '*Komm*,' and I got up and followed her.

When somebody takes you by the hand and says '*Komm*', it is not difficult to guess what they are saying, but it still seems odd to me that the first moment I understood Marianne so completely, and that she understood me.

The Wasilewskis had a smallholding, but the Germans had commandeered the horse at the beginning of the war and the Russians had taken the cow at the end of it. All the same, the animals that were left seemed to satisfy Marianne. She introduced me to the two goats – a white one, called Bella, and a bad-tempered brown one, called Sidonia, after a disagreeable lady who scowled at everybody in the church. She showed me the five hens and told me their names and the rabbits and the new piglet, honking in the straw.

Actually, it was more than showing – she sort of presented them to me, giving me the animals to hold as if hanging on to a squawking chicken or a lop-eared rabbit must make me the happiest person in the world.

It was far too late to try and make our way back that night – no one knew how the trains would run. Mrs Wasilewski – still unsmiling and gaunt – led us to a loft with two goose-down duvets on a slatted wooden board and we went to bed.

I was sure we'd leave the next morning, but we didn't. My mother helped Mrs Wasilewski with the housework and once again Marianne put out her hand and said, '*Komm*,' and once again I came.

She led me to a part of the stream where the water ran clear over a bed of pebbles. Both of us took off our shoes, but she kept on her jersey, and we walked along the river bed, dredging up bright and glittering stones.

'*Nicht Gold*,' she said, holding out a yellow-veined stone and shaking her head, but she was smiling. She didn't want gold, I could see that. She wanted brightness.

The stream was full of sticklebacks and newts and tiny frogs; all the creatures too small to have been stolen or pillaged in war.

After a while a boy and a girl appeared – a brother and sister – and Marianne introduced me, carefully pronouncing my name in the English way I'd taught her.

We came to a bridge where the current ran quite fast and we each chose a stick and raced it from one side to the other. I hadn't done that since I was at infant school, but you can't go wrong with Pooh sticks, and I found myself wondering if they played it at St Hilda's.

Mrs Wasilewski, still grim and silent, gave us lunch – pieces of salt bacon with beetroot and cabbage from her garden – and afterwards Marianne took me out and showed me the rows of vegetables, and picked a pea pod from the vine and opened it, dropping the shelled peas into my palm.

All that day Marianne stretched out her hand and said, '*Komm*.' She showed me a hedgehog asleep in the potting shed and a place where raspberries grew wild, and I made her a whistle out of a hazel twig. I'd brought my Swiss Army knife, and the whistle was a good one. They don't always work but this one did.

Even the next day my mother said nothing about leaving. We slept on the floor; the work she was helping with was far harder than any that she did in England and Mrs Wasilewski still went round like a zombie, but my mother didn't seem in any hurry to return.

That day Marianne showed me her special tree. It was an ancient oak standing on its own on a small hill and it was the kind of tree that is a whole world in itself. There were hollows in the trunk where squirrels had stored their nuts; beetles sheltered under the bark and a woodpecker tapped in the branches.

Marianne had not *built* a tree-house because the

tree *was* her house. She explained this as we climbed up – and that it was in this house that she kept her treasures. They lived in a tin with a picture of cough lozenges on the lid, and she showed them to me, one by one. There was a tortoiseshell hair slide, a little bent; a bracelet made out of glass beads; a propelling pencil – and her most important possession: a small bear, carved roughly out of wood, which Mr Wasilweski had made on her last birthday. Then she took the whistle I had made for her out of her pocket and laid it carefully in the tin beside the other things, and closed the lid.

But the best thing about the tree was the view. Because it stood on a knoll you could see the surrounding countryside for miles. Marianne pointed to a small farm and told me that the man who had lived there had been killed on the Eastern Front. He'd been a German, of course – maybe a Nazi – but Marianne's face grew sad as she told me about him, which was strange because her mother's people had been so horribly persecuted by men like him.

If she was the child we thought she was …

But in the opposite direction was a low, red-roofed house and she told me that the man who owned it had a litter of sheepdog puppies and he was going to let her have one. There was enough food now to keep a dog, she said joyfully; it was no longer forbidden.

I didn't say anything. She would never be able to bring a dog into England; the quarantine regulations were far too strict, and the Glossops said it wasn't fair to keep animals in town. Even the cat we kept in the basement knew better than to make her way upstairs.

Then on the morning of the third day my mother called me into the kitchen. Mrs Wasilewski was there, more silent and morose than ever. There was a bundle on the table: the blanket Marianne had been wrapped in, I guessed, when she was found on the track, and a few baby clothes. Mrs Wasilweski called Marianne to her side and she came. For the first time, she looked puzzled and anxious.

'Wait,' said my mother. 'We must make sure we have the right child.' And very gently she said, 'Will you take your jersey off, Marianne, and your blouse?'

Marianne looked at Mrs Wasilewski, who nodded. Then she took off her jersey and undid the drawstring of her blouse.

Now she stood before us with both arms bare. From her shoulder to her elbow, her right arm was covered in a dark brown birthmark.

It was exactly what the Glossops had described to us. Without a doubt, the child who stood before us was the child who had been thrown from the train.

My mother and I looked at each other. Mrs Wasilewski stood like a ramrod, her mouth tight shut.

Marianne, still puzzled, reached for her blouse and began to put it on.

The room was very still. Then my mother cleared her throat and looked at me again. She looked at me hard.

'What a pity,' she said clearly to Mrs Wasilewski. 'I'm so sorry. I'm afraid this is the wrong child. We can't take her back with us – her birthmark is on the wrong arm.' And then, softly: 'She will have to stay with you.'

The silence was broken suddenly by a gasp – followed by a kind of juddering sound. Then Mrs Wasilewski went mad. Her head dropped forward on to the table and she began to cry – but you can't call it crying. She erupted in tears, she became completely drenched in them, her hair came down and fell in damp strands across the table. I have never in all my life heard anybody cry like that.

When she lifted her head again she was a totally different woman; she was rosy, she laughed, she hugged my mother and me. And I understood what my mother had understood at once – that this woman who had made Marianne's world with such loving care had been almost destroyed at the thought of losing her.

In the train my mother said, 'I think we'll just say there was no birthmark. We don't want any further fuss about left or right.'

'Yes.' The train chugged on through what had once been enemy territory and was now just the great plain of central Europe. 'I'm going back,' I said. 'Later.' And then: 'Not much later.'

'Yes, I know,' said my mother. 'And I'm going on.'

(And she did too. She gave up her job with the Glossops and went back to finish her degree. We lived in two small rooms and were very happy.)

When we got back we were called up to the boudoir so that the old lady too could hear our story.

'Oh, well,' said Mrs Glossop, when we'd finished. 'It's a pity, when we had so much to offer a child. But it doesn't sound as though she would have fitted in.'

And my mother looked at the piano, with its two dozen important Glossops in silver frames, and said no, she wouldn't have fitted in. She wouldn't have fitted in at all.

SWEPT AND GARNISHED

Rudyard Kipling

When the first waves of feverish cold stole over Frau Ebermann, she very wisely telephoned for the doctor and went to bed. He diagnosed the attack as mild influenza, prescribed the appropriate remedies, and left her to the care of her one servant in her comfortable Berlin flat. Frau Ebermann, beneath the thick coverlet, curled up with what patience she could until the aspirin should begin to act, and Anna should come back from the chemist with the formamint, the ammoniated quinine, the eucalyptus, and the little tin steam-inhaler. Meantime, every bone in her body ached; her head throbbed; her hot, dry hands would not stay the same size for a minute together; and her body, tucked into the smallest possible compass, shrank from the chill of the well-warmed sheets.

Of a sudden she noticed that an imitation-lace cover which should have lain mathematically square with the imitation-marble top of the radiator behind the green plush sofa had slipped away so that one corner hung over the bronze-painted steam pipes. She recalled that she must have rested her poor head against the radiator-top while she was taking off her boots. She tried to get up and set the thing straight, but the radiator at once receded toward the horizon, which, unlike true horizons, slanted diagonally, exactly parallel with the dropped lace edge of the cover. Frau Ebermann groaned through sticky lips and lay still.

'Certainly, I have a temperature,' she said. 'Certainly, I have a grave temperature. I should have been warned by that chill after dinner.'

She resolved to shut her hot-lidded eyes, but opened them in a little while to torture herself with the knowledge of that ungeometrical thing against the far wall. Then she saw a child – an untidy, thin-faced little girl of about ten, who must have strayed in from the adjoining flat. This proved – Frau Ebermann groaned again at the way the world falls to bits when one is sick – proved that Anna had forgotten to shut the outer door of the flat when she went to the chemist. Frau Ebermann had had children of her own, but they were all grown up now, and she had never been a child-lover in any sense. Yet the intruder might be made to serve her scheme of things.

'Make – put,' she muttered thickly, 'that white thing straight on the top of that yellow thing.'

The child paid no attention, but moved about the room, investigating everything that came in her way – the yellow cut-glass handles of the chest of drawers, the stamped bronze hook to hold back the heavy puce curtains, and the mauve enamel, New Art finger-plates on the door. Frau Ebermann watched indignantly.

'Aie! That is bad and rude. Go away!' she cried, though it hurt her to raise her voice. 'Go away by the road you came!' The child passed behind the bed-foot, where she could not see her. 'Shut the door as you go. I will speak to Anna, but – first, put that white thing straight.'

She closed her eyes in misery of body and soul. The outer door clicked, and Anna entered, very penitent that she had stayed so long at the chemist's. But it had been difficult to find the proper type of inhaler, and –

'Where did the child go?' moaned Frau Ebermann – 'the child that was here?'

'There was no child,' said startled Anna. 'How should any child come in when I shut the door behind me after I go out? All the keys of the flats are different.'

'No, no! You forgot this time. But my back is aching, and up my legs also. Besides, who knows what it may have fingered and upset? Look and see.'

'Nothing is fingered, nothing is upset,' Anna replied, as she took the inhaler from its paper box.

'Yes, there is. Now I remember all about it. Put – put that white thing, with the open edge – the lace, I mean – quite straight on that – ' she pointed. Anna, accustomed to her ways, understood and went to it.

'Now, is it quite straight?' Frau Ebermann demanded.

'Perfectly,' said Anna. 'In fact, in the very centre of the radiator.' Anna measured the equal margins with her knuckle, as she had been told to do when she first took service.

'And my tortoise-shell hair brushes?' Frau Ebermann could not command her dressing-table from where she lay.

'Perfectly straight, side by side in the big tray, and the comb laid across them. Your watch also in the coralline watch-holder. Everything' – she moved round the room to make sure – 'everything is as you have it when you are well.' Frau Ebermann sighed with relief. It seemed to her that the room and her head had suddenly grown cooler.

'Good!' said she. 'Now warm my night-gown in the kitchen, so it will be ready when I have perspired. And the towels also. Make the inhaler steam, and put in the eucalyptus; that is good for the larynx. Then sit you in the kitchen, and come when I ring. But, first, my hot-water bottle.'

It was brought and scientifically tucked in.

'What news?' said Frau Ebermann drowsily. She had not been out that day.

'Another victory,' said Anna. 'Many more prisoners and guns.'

Frau Ebermann purred, one might almost say grunted, contentedly.

'That is good too,' she said; and Anna, after lighting the inhaler-lamp, went out.

Frau Ebermann reflected that in an hour or so the aspirin would begin to work, and all would be well. Tomorrow – no, the day after – she would take up life with something to talk over with her friends at coffee. It was rare – everyone knew it – that she should be overcome by any ailment. Yet in all her distresses she had not allowed the minutest deviation from daily routine and ritual. She would tell her friends – she ran over their names one by one – exactly what measures she had taken against the lace cover on the radiator-top and in regard to her two tortoise-shell hair brushes and the comb at right angles. How she had set everything in order – everything in order. She roved further afield as she wriggled her toes luxuriously on the hot-water bottle. If it pleased our dear God to take her to Himself, and she was not so young as she had been – there was that plate of the four lower ones in the blue tooth-glass, for instance – He should find all her belongings fit to meet His eye.

'Swept and garnished' were the words that shaped themselves in her intent brain. 'Swept and garnished for – '

No, it was certainly not for the dear Lord that she had swept; she would have her room swept out tomorrow or the day after, and garnished. Her hands began to swell again into huge pillows of nothingness. Then they shrank, and so did her head, to minute dots. It occurred to her that she was waiting for some event, some tremendously important event, to come to pass. She lay with shut eyes for a long time till her head and hands should return to their proper size.

She opened her eyes with a jerk.

'How stupid of me,' she said aloud, 'to set the room in order for a parcel of dirty little children!'

They were there – five of them, two little boys and three girls – headed by the anxious-eyed ten-year-old whom she had seen before. They must have entered by the outer door, which Anna had neglected to shut behind her when she returned with the inhaler. She counted them backward and forward as one counts scales – one, two, three, four, five.

They took no notice of her, but hung about, first on one foot then on the other, like strayed chickens, the smaller ones holding by the larger. They had the air of utterly wearied passengers in a railway waiting-room, and their clothes were disgracefully dirty.

'Go away!' cried Frau Ebermann at last, after she had struggled, it seemed to her, for years to shape the words.

'You called?' said Anna at the living-room door.

'No,' said her mistress. 'Did you shut the flat door when you came in?'

'Assuredly,' said Anna. 'Besides, it is made to catch shut of itself.'

'Then go away,' said she, very little above a whisper. If Anna pretended not to see the children, she would speak to Anna later on.

'And now,' she said, turning toward them as soon as the door closed. The smallest of the crowd smiled at her, and shook his head before he buried it in his sister's skirts.

'Why – don't – you – go – away?' she whispered earnestly.

Again they took no notice, but, guided by the elder girl, set themselves to climb, boots and all, on to the green plush sofa in front of the radiator. The little boys had to be pushed, as they could not compass the stretch unaided. They settled themselves in a row, with small gasps of relief, and pawed the plush approvingly.

'I ask you – I ask you why do you not go away – why do you not go away?' Frau Ebermann found herself repeating the question twenty times. It seemed to her that everything in the world hung on the answer. 'You know you should not come into houses and rooms unless you are invited. Not houses and bedrooms, you know.'

'No,' a solemn little six-year-old repeated, 'not houses nor bedrooms, nor dining-rooms, nor churches, nor all those places. Shouldn't come in. It's rude.'

'Yes, he said so,' the younger girl put in proudly. 'He said it. He told them only pigs would do that.' The line nodded and dimpled one to another with little explosive giggles, such as children use when they tell deeds of great daring against their elders.

'If you know it is wrong, that makes it much worse,' said Frau Ebermann.

'Oh yes; much worse,' they assented cheerfully, till the smallest boy changed his smile to a baby wail of weariness.

'When will they come for us?' he asked, and the girl at the head of the row hauled him bodily into her square little capable lap.

'He's tired,' she explained. 'He is only four. He only had his first breeches this spring.' They came almost under his armpits, and were held up by broad linen braces, which, his sorrow diverted for the moment, he patted proudly.

'Yes, beautiful, dear,' said both girls.

'Go away!' said Frau Ebermann. 'Go home to your father and mother!'

Their faces grew grave at once.

'H'sh! We *can't*,' whispered the eldest. 'There isn't anything left.'

'All gone,' a boy echoed, and he puffed through pursed lips. 'Like *that*, uncle told me. Both cows too.'

'And my own three ducks,' the boy on the girl's lap said sleepily.

'So, you see, we came here.' The elder girl leaned forward a little, caressing the child she rocked.

'I – I don't understand,' said Frau Ebermann. 'Are you lost, then? You must tell our police.'

'Oh no; we are only waiting.'

'But what are you waiting *for?*'

'We are waiting for our people to come for us. They told us to come here and wait for them. So we are waiting till they come,' the eldest girl replied.

'Yes. We are waiting till our people come for us,' said all the others in chorus.

'But,' said Frau Ebermann very patiently – 'but now tell me, for I tell you that I am not in the least angry, where do you come from? Where do you come from?'

The five gave the names of two villages of which she had read in the papers.

'That is silly,' said Frau Ebermann. 'The people

fired on us, and they were punished. Those places are wiped out, stamped flat.'

'Yes, yes, wiped out, stamped flat. That is why and – I have lost the ribbon off my pigtail,' said the younger girl. She looked behind her over the sofa-back.

'It is not here,' said the elder. 'It was lost before. Don't you remember?'

'Now, if you are lost, you must go and tell our police. They will take care of you and give you food,' said Frau Ebermann. 'Anna will show you the way there.'

'No,' – this was the six-year-old with the smile, – 'we must wait here till our people come for us. Mustn't we, sister?'

'Of course. We wait here till our people come for us. All the world knows that,' said the eldest girl.

'Yes.' The boy in her lap had waked again. 'Little children, too – as little as Henri, and *he* doesn't wear trousers yet. As little as all that.'

'I don't understand,' said Frau Ebermann, shivering. In spite of the heat of the room and the damp breath of the steam-inhaler, the aspirin was not doing its duty.

The girl raised her blue eyes and looked at the woman for an instant.

'You see,' she said, emphasising her statements with her fingers, '*they* told *us* to wait *here* till *our* people came for us. So we came. We wait till our people come for us.'

'That is silly again,' said Frau Ebermann. 'It is no good for you to wait here. Do you know what this place is? You have been to school? It is Berlin, the capital of Germany.'

'Yes, yes,' they all cried; 'Berlin, capital of Germany. We know that. That is why we came.'

'So, you see, it is no good,' she said triumphantly, 'because your people can never come for you here.'

'They told us to come here and wait till our people came for us.' They delivered this as if it were a lesson in school. Then they sat still, their hands orderly folded on their laps, smiling as sweetly as ever.

'Go away! Go away!' Frau Ebermann shrieked.

'You called?' said Anna, entering.

'No. Go away! Go away!'

'Very good, old cat,' said the maid under her breath. 'Next time you *may* call,' and she returned to her friend in the kitchen.

'I ask you – ask you, *please* to go away,' Frau Ebermann pleaded. 'Go to my Anna through that door, and she will give you cakes and sweeties. It is not kind of you to come into my room and behave so badly.'

'Where else shall we go now?' the elder girl demanded, turning to her little company. They fell into discussion. One preferred the broad street with trees, another the railway station; but when she suggested an Emperor's palace, they agreed with her.

'We will go then,' she said, and added half apologetically to Frau Ebermann, 'You see, they are so little they like to meet all the others.'

'What others?' said Frau Ebermann.

'The others – hundreds and hundreds and thousands and thousands of the others.'

'That is a lie. There cannot be a hundred even, much less a thousand,' cried Frau Ebermann.

'So?' said the girl politely.

'Yes. *I* tell you; and I have very good information. I know how it happened. You should have been more careful. You should not have run out to see the horses and guns passing. That is how it is done when our troops pass through. My son has written me so.'

They had clambered down from the sofa, and gathered round the bed with eager, interested eyes.

'Horses and guns going by – how fine!' someone whispered.

'Yes, yes; believe me, *that* is how the accidents to the children happen. You must know yourself that it is true. One runs out to look – '

'But I never saw any at all,' a boy cried sorrowfully. 'Only one noise I heard. That was when Aunt Emmeline's house fell down.'

'But listen to me. *I* am telling you! One runs out to

look, because one is little and cannot see well. So one peeps between the man's legs, and then – you know how close those big horses and guns turn the corners – then one's foot slips and one gets run over. That's how it happens. Several times it had happened, but not many times; certainly not a hundred, perhaps not twenty. So, you see, you *must* be all. Tell me now that you are all that there are, and Anna shall give you the cakes.'

'Thousands,' a boy repeated monotonously. 'Then we all come here to wait till our people come for us.'

'But now we will go away from here. The poor lady is tired,' said the elder girl, plucking his sleeve.

'Oh, you hurt, you hurt!' he cried, and burst into tears.

'What is that for?' said Frau Ebermann. 'To cry in a room where a poor lady is sick is very inconsiderate.'

'Oh, but look, lady!' said the elder girl.

Frau Ebermann looked and saw.

'*Au revoir*, lady.' They made their little smiling bows and curtseys undisturbed by her loud cries. '*Au revoir*, lady. We will wait till our people come for us.'

When Anna at last ran in, she found her mistress on her knees, busily cleaning the floor with the lace cover from the radiator, because, she explained, it was all spotted with the blood of five children – she was perfectly certain there could not be more than five in the whole world – who had gone away for the moment, but were now waiting round the corner, and Anna was to find them and give them cakes to stop the bleeding, while her mistress swept and garnished that Our dear Lord when He came might find everything as it should be.

THE CHARGE OF THE LIGHT BRIGADE

Alfred Lord Tennyson

This poem was written a few weeks after the battle it describes, in which a British brigade of light cavalry was sent to attack some retreating troops during the Crimean War in 1854. However, the order was badly communicated and instead the cavalry found themselves charging at a heavily defended enemy line. While future war poets would focus on the mistakes made by senior officers, this poem focuses on the valour of the soldiers, nobly following orders even though it is obviously a hopeless mission.

THE CHARGE OF THE LIGHT BRIGADE

Alfred Lord Tennyson

I

Half a league, half a league,
Half a league onward,
All in the valley of Death
    Rode the six hundred.
'Forward, the Light Brigade!
Charge for the guns!' he said.
Into the valley of Death
    Rode the six hundred.

II

'Forward, the Light Brigade!'
Was there a man dismayed?
Not though the soldier knew
    Someone had blundered.
Theirs not to make reply,
Theirs not to reason why,

Theirs but to do and die.
Into the valley of Death
  Rode the six hundred.

III

Cannon to right of them,
Cannon to left of them,
Cannon in front of them
  Volleyed and thundered;
Stormed at with shot and shell,
Boldly they rode and well,
Into the jaws of Death,
Into the mouth of hell
  Rode the six hundred.

IV

Flashed all their sabres bare,
Flashed as they turned in air
Sabring the gunners there,
Charging an army, while
  All the world wondered.
Plunged in the battery-smoke
Right through the line they broke;
Cossack and Russian
Reeled from the sabre stroke
  Shattered and sundered.

Then they rode back, but not
    Not the six hundred.

V

Cannon to right of them,
Cannon to left of them,
Cannon behind them
    Volleyed and thundered;
Stormed at with shot and shell,
While horse and hero fell.
They that had fought so well
Came through the jaws of Death,
Back from the mouth of hell,
All that was left of them,
    Left of six hundred.

VI

When can their glory fade?
O the wild charge they made!
    All the world wondered.
Honour the charge they made!
Honour the Light Brigade,
    Noble six hundred!

DULCE ET DECORUM EST

Wilfred Owen

This is possibly the best-known anti-war poem in the English language. Written during the First World War by a young man with personal experience of the horrors of trench warfare, the poem was a bitter response to the attitudes of any who did not fight but encouraged young men to enlist. *Dulce et decorum est pro patria mori* is a Latin quote from the poet Horace that would have been well known at the time as it was often quoted in war propaganda. It translates as *How sweet and right it is to die for one's country.*

DULCE ET DECORUM EST

Wilfred Owen

Bent double, like old beggars under sacks,
Knock-kneed, coughing like hags, we cursed through
   sludge,
Till on the haunting flares we turned our backs
And towards our distant rest began to trudge.
Men marched asleep. Many had lost their boots
But limped on, blood-shod. All went lame; all blind;
Drunk with fatigue; deaf even to the hoots
Of tired, outstripped Five-Nines that dropped
   behind.
Gas! Gas! Quick, boys! – An ecstasy of fumbling,
Fitting the clumsy helmets just in time;
But someone still was yelling out and stumbling,
And flound'ring like a man in fire or lime …
Dim, through the misty panes and thick green light,
As under a green sea, I saw him drowning.
In all my dreams, before my helpless sight,
He plunges at me, guttering, choking, drowning.
If in some smothering dreams you too could pace

Behind the wagon that we flung him in,
And watch the white eyes writhing in his face,
His hanging face, like a devil's sick of sin;
If you could hear, at every jolt, the blood
Come gargling from the froth-corrupted lungs,
Obscene as cancer, bitter as the cud
Of vile, incurable sores on innocent tongues,
My friend, you would not tell with such high zest
To children ardent for some desperate glory,
The old Lie; Dulce et Decorum est
Pro patria mori.

TOMMY

Rudyard Kipling

A Tommy – a redcoat, a British soldier – speaks to us bitterly about the two-faced people back home who give returning soldiers a hard time. Quick to complain about squaddies and their rough behaviour, they are even quicker to cheer them on and hide behind them at the first sign of attack. Rudyard Kipling was a staunch supporter of British soldiers and believed that they were let down by public perception at home, as well as by the incompetence of politicians.

TOMMY

Rudyard Kipling

I went into a public 'ouse to get a pint o' beer,
The publican 'e up an' sez, 'We serve no red-coats
here.'
The girls be'ind the bar they laughed an' giggled fit
to die,
I outs into the street again an' to myself sez I:
O it's Tommy this, an' Tommy that, an' 'Tommy, go
away';
But it's 'Thank you, Mister Atkins', when the band
begins to play
The band begins to play, my boys, the band begins
to play,
O it's 'Thank you, Mister Atkins', when the band
begins to play.

I went into a theatre as sober as could be,
They gave a drunk civilian room, but 'adn't none for
me;
They sent me to the gallery or round the music-'alls,

But when it comes to fightin', Lord! they'll shove me
in the stalls!
For it's Tommy this, an' Tommy that, an' 'Tommy,
wait outside';
But it's 'Special train for Atkins', when the trooper's
on the tide
The troopship's on the tide, my boys, the troopship's
on the tide,
O it's 'Special train for Atkins', when the trooper's on
the tide.

Yes, makin' mock o' uniforms that guard you while
you sleep
Is cheaper than them uniforms, an' they're
starvation cheap.
An' hustlin' drunken soldiers when they're goin'
large a bit
Is five times better business than paradin' in full kit.
Then it's Tommy this, an' Tommy that, an' 'Tommy,
'ow's yer soul?'
But it's 'Thin red line of 'eroes', when the drums
begin to roll
The drums begin to roll, my boys, the drums begin
to roll,
O it's 'Thin red line of 'eroes', when the drums begin
to roll.

We aren't no thin red 'eroes, nor we aren't no
    blackguards too,
But single men in barricks, most remarkable like you;
An' if sometimes our conduck isn't all your fancy
    paints,
Why, single men in barricks don't grow into plaster
    saints;
While it's Tommy this, an' Tommy that, an' 'Tommy,
    fall be'ind',
But it's 'Please to walk in front, sir', when there's
    trouble in the wind
There's trouble in the wind, my boys, there's trouble
    in the wind,
O it's 'Please to walk in front, sir', when there's
    trouble in the wind.

You talk o' better food for us, an' schools, an' fires,
    an' all:
We'll wait for extry rations if you treat us rational.
Don't mess about the cook-room slops, but prove it
    to our face
The Widow's Uniform is not the soldier-man's
    disgrace.
For it's Tommy this, an' Tommy that, an' 'Chuck him
    out, the brute!'
But it's 'Saviour of 'is country', when the guns begin
    to shoot;

An' it's Tommy this, an' Tommy that, an' anything
you please;
An' Tommy ain't a bloomin' fool – you bet that
Tommy sees!

IN TIMES OF PEACE

John Agard

John Agard's poem, written in 2009 as the war in Afghanistan continued on and on, explores the challenge of coming home from war. We are more culturally aware than ever of some of the psychological problems returning soldiers face. 'In Times of Peace' includes imagery of striking contrasts – bubble bath and bodies, boots and butterflies – all designed to help us as readers, who have never been to war, to try to imagine the unimaginable.

IN TIMES OF PEACE

John Agard

That finger – index to be exact –
so used to a trigger's warmth
how will it begin to deal with skin
that threatens only to embrace?

Those feet, so at home in heavy boots
and stepping over bodies –
how will they cope with a bubble bath
when foam is all there is for ambush?

And what of hearts in times of peace?
Will war-worn hearts grow sluggish
like Valentine roses wilting
without the adrenalin of a bullet's blood-rush?

When the dust of peace has settled on a nation,
how will human arms handle the death of weapons?
And what of ears, are ears so tuned to sirens
that the closing of wings causes a tremor?

As for eyes, are eyes ready for the soft dance
of a butterfly's bootless invasion?